Culture and Identity

Politics and Culture

A Theory, Culture & Society series

Politics and Culture analyses the complex relationships between civil society, identities and contemporary states. Individual books will draw on the major theoretical paradigms in politics, international relations, history and philosophy within which citizenship, rights and social justice can be understood. The series will focus attention on the implications of globalization, the information revolution and postmodernism for the study of politics and society. It will relate these advanced theoretical issues to conventional approaches to welfare, participation and democracy.

SERIES EDITOR: Bryan S. Turner, *University of Cambridge*

EDITORIAL BOARD

Jack Barbalet, *University of Leicester*
Mike Featherstone, *Nottingham Trent University*
Engin Isin, *York University*
Stephen Kalberg, *Boston University*
Andrew Linklater, *University of Wales, Aberystwyth*
Carole Pateman, *University of California, Los Angeles*
Tony Woodiwiss, *City University, London*

Also in this series

Virtual Politics
Identity and Community in Cyberspace
edited by David Holmes

Gender and Nation
Nira Yuval-Davis

Feminism and Citizenship
Rian Voet

Citizenship and Identity
Engin F. Isin and Patricia K. Wood

Culture and Citizenship
edited by Nick Stevenson

Interpreting Islam
edited by Hastings Donnan

Culture and Identity
Critical Theories

Ross Abbinnett

SAGE Publications
London • Thousand Oaks • New Delhi

First published 2003

Reprinted 2004

SAGE Publications Ltd
1 Oliver's Yard, 55 City Road
London EC1Y 1SP

SAGE Publications Inc
2455 Teller Road
Thousand Oaks, California 91320

SAGE Publications India Pvt Ltd
B-42 Panchsheel Enclave
Post Box 4109
New Delhi 100 017

British Library Cataloguing in Publication data

A catalogue record for this book is
available from the British Library

ISBN 0 7619 6518 1
ISBN 0 7619 6519 X (pbk)

Library of Congress Control Number available

Typeset by TW Typesetting, Plymouth, Devon
Printed in Great Britain by Selwood Printing Ltd, West Sussex

Contents

Acknowledgements

I would like to extend my thanks to the following people. To Sian, for her willingness to proof read the endless 'draft copies' I produced. To Keith Tester, for his sound advice on the scope of the project. To Chris and Robert Rojek at Sage Publications, for their help in getting the manuscript into production. Thanks are also due to the School of Cultural Studies at Leeds Metropolitan University, whose funding of my recent sabbatical allowed me finally to complete this book.

For my parents

There is change, and departure: but there is also help when least looked for from the strangers of the day, and hiding, out among the accidents of this drifting Humility, never quite to be extinguished, a few small chances for mercy . . .

Thomas Pynchon, *Gravity's Rainbow*

Introduction

I

Why are the ideas of culture and identity important, and why do they demand our attention at the beginning of the twenty-first century? Well, to begin with, they are not simply abstract, philosophical constructions; for the 'self' who participates in everyday social interaction can do so only through its recognition of certain cultural norms, values and ideals. The 'I' who will be the focus of my analysis, therefore, is not the 'existential' being who is permanently embroiled in questions of authenticity: rather, it is the self that emerges through the conflicts and negotiations which define the realm of human culture. In a sense, then, the whole of the discussion that will take place in the book concerns the relationship between the self, conceived as a reflexive agent, the other, who comes as a demand for care and responsibility, and the established structures of social, cultural and economic recognition.

In general, 'post-Enlightenment' philosophy has characterized this relationship in terms of the 'performativity' of the subject: that is, *the degree to which the person who is engaged in the substantive culture of his or her nation state is able to exercise a critical reflection upon its established structures of collective identity*. At one end of the scale, Jürgen Habermas has claimed that the possibility of such judgements arises from the communicative structure of language: for as linguistically competent beings, each of us is able to recognize how the structural organization of social relationships has tended to suppress the free discussion of the ends of modernity. And so for Habermas, the emergence of political groups based around single issues like ecology or animal rights signifies the emergence of an increasingly 'reflexive' public sphere. More conventionally Marxist accounts of the economics of cultural identity, however, have concentrated on the way in which 'the individual' has been reproduced as part of the masses: Benjamin, Adorno and Jameson have all presented compelling accounts of the impact of new image technologies on the reflective autonomy of the subject. Thus, if there is to be a political relationship between 'the masses' and the powers which 'massify' them, this must come through a radical critique of the relationship between culture, technology and economy.

The analysis of culture and ideology that has come out of the Frankfurt School, I will argue, is fundamentally important to a proper understanding of the debates that have arisen from postmodernist theory. For it is only in so far as we have comprehended the massifying power of new media technologies that we can begin to understand the significance of post-modernist ideas like the decentring of the subject, the fracturing of knowledge and the dispersal of the social bond. I will argue that what these ideas contribute to our understanding of the 'place' of the subject within his or her particular culture is an acute sense of the contingency of belonging, and of the necessity of responding to the events of silencing and exclusion through which cultural identity is reproduced. My expositions of Baudrillard, Derrida and Lyotard, then, will concentrate on their accounts of the excessiveness of capital: that is, on the relationship between their respective theories of simulation, *différance* and the sublime, and the possibility of a political response to the infinite amorality of capitalism.

For the moment, however, I need to put the question of culture and identity into a rough theoretical context. Immanuel Kant, in his essay 'What is Enlightenment?', begins his account of political responsibility from the level of moral culture established in bourgeois civil society (Kant, 1991, pp. 54–60).[1] His claim is that once human beings have reached the point at which they are able to exercise their sovereign reason, they are under an obligation to question the traditional forms of religious and political authority which have held power over them. Enlightenment, therefore, is the willingness of an individual to exercise his own judgement in matters of civic responsibility, and to remain faithful to the universal ends of freedom, equality and justice which are proper to human beings as such. A number of important points emerge from this account of Enlightenment. First, the relationship between established forms of cultural identity and the sovereign will of the individual is reflexive; trust, obligation and responsibility are no longer simply habitual relationships. Second, the freedom of the rational will exceeds the immediate demands and satisfactions of the present; the moral stricture is entirely independent of love, friendship and traditional obligations. Third, the nature of this moral stricture is such that it cannot be realized in the 'objective' forms of culture; its demand springs from the idea of a perfect constitution of ends which is always beyond the present organization of law, state and economy. To return to my question about the relationship of the individual to the values of his or her own culture therefore, Kant's essay sets out a discourse of will and reflexive sovereignty which is supposed to exceed every empirical form of work, satisfaction and desire.

It is the possibility of this pure rational necessity of the will which preoccupies Hegel's critique of Kantian morality. In the *Philosophy of Right*, he claims that what is characteristic of the Kantian subject is to be 'inwardly related to itself alone', and that consequently, its judgements about the morality of its actions must remain entirely arbitrary. What Kant presents as the transcendental universality of the moral will, in other words, is a reflection of the amorality of private property relations, for in so far as a person looks into himself for the pure rational necessity of duty, his *actual* motivations – greed, acquisitiveness, self-love – are legitimized by Kant's abstract idea of moral responsibility. For Hegel, then, the establishment of civil society as the sphere of bourgeois property rights demands that we confront the violent individualism that arises from the unfettering of desire from the restrictions of nature (Hegel, 1967b, pp. 127–8). And so if there is to be a civic virtue which is appropriate to civil society, it must spring from a recognition of the 'external' form of universality embodied in the arbitrary play of greed and self-interest. What Kantian morality does, however, is to reinforce this antagonism by presenting the immorally desirous individual, the 'bourgeois', as the figure of progress and Enlightenment.

In Hegel's thought, the relationship between a 'culture' (Hegel uses the term 'ethical life', which refers to the laws, values, ideals and customs of a particular historical epoch) and the individuals who share it, is conceived in terms of the contradiction between 'spirit' and 'history'. Thus, while it is true that the feudal relationship of Lordship and Bondage supports a kind of ethical life – for each knows his place, his duties, his obligations – it remains inadequate to the ideals of universal recognition. The concrete historical form of this culture therefore, can only produce the essentially mutilated identity of the slave (for the product of his worldly activity is always taken away from him), and the arbitrary and violent authority of the master (Hegel, 1967a, pp. 228–40).

The relationship between reflective subjectivity, abstract individualism and state authority that Hegel presents in the *Philosophy of Right* assumes the abstract freedom of the 'I' whose history is traced in the *Phenomenology of Mind*. The fundamental problem which Hegel confronts in his analysis of civil society therefore is how this concrete person 'who is the object of his particular aims', can become reconciled to the obligations which are proper to the concept of ethical life (Hegel, 1967b, p. 122). In itself, Hegel claims, this pure individualism belongs to the realm of understanding; it approaches the world in terms of instrumental goals whose universal significance remains hidden in the play of acquisitiveness and desire. Ultimately, however, the immanence of the universal becomes explicit in the hard necessity of justice and the law: the very possibility of exercising the rights of bourgeois individualism – producing, trading, exchanging – depends upon a basic respect for law, property and rights of ownership. The second part of Hegel's account of civil society, therefore, describes 'the actuality of the universal of freedom' contained in the economy; that is, the system of law and justice which is to impose proper restraint on the excesses of individual self-seeking (*ibid.*, p. 126).

It is in the nation state that the implicit universality of civil society is made concrete; for with their recognition of the law and the institutional organization of justice, self-conscious individuals are formed through the *substantive* universality of ethical life (Hegel, 1967b, p. 155). Put very simply, Hegel's claim is that once the acquisitive individual realizes that his selfhood is possible only within the bounds of the law, his worldly activity is transformed through a reflexive awareness of social responsibility, duty and belonging. This awareness does not take the form of a pure procedural rationality; rather, it leads back to the substantive organization of customs, norms and laws which embody the idea of the state. Ultimately, therefore, the nation state becomes aware of itself – of the structures of recognition, mediation and coercion which belong to its concept – through the self-conscious individuals who live within its substantive culture (*ibid.*, pp. 162–4).

The nature of this relationship has, of course, been the subject of a great deal of theoretical debate: liberals, like Popper and Berlin, have argued that Hegel's philosophy is inherently totalitarian, while other more considered accounts of his work, particularly those of Gillian Rose and Jacques Derrida, have sought to open up his thought to the contradictions and aporias of modernity. What is common to Rose and Derrida's expositions is a concern with the possibility of a Hegelian response to the issues which have come to define our historical present: the primacy of economic relationships; the fetishism of commodities and the infinite extension of human desire; the collapse of the public sphere into a play of 'false needs'; the complicity between scientific knowledge, technological innovation and economic exploitation; and the globalization of capitalism. It is the fate of Hegel's thought therefore to inhabit what Derrida has called a 'Marxist space'; for even if his thought is presented as anticipating the violence of Marx's revolutionary demand (Rose, 1981, pp. 214–20), his notion of ethical life has still been transformed by the urgency and persistence of Marx's critique of capitalism.

As I have said, one of the main concerns of the book will be to look at Marx's transformation of the concept of modernity, and particularly his remarks on the political economy of culture. For Hegel, we have seen that the concept of ethical life, of the substantive culture which supports the existence of the reflective individual, is guaranteed by the inner necessity of spirit. The dialectical logic of implicit unity (Being), separation (Essence) and speculative unity (Spirit), in other words, is enacted in the return of the anarchic individualism of civil society to the substantive mediations of the state (law, justice and right). Marx, however, maintains that it is precisely this return of the acquisitive 'bourgeois' to the necessities of collective life which is impossible. For in so far as the realm of civil society is utterly inimical to the limitation of self-love, exploitation and conflict, it cuts short the logic of recognition through which Hegel reintegrates the acquisitive 'I' with the collective life of the nation state (Marx, 1977d, pp. 26–7). If there is such a reintegration, this can only take place at the level of appearance, for as long as the 'true' conditions of collective life (distributive justice, communal ownership of the means of production) are unrealized, the representations through which we recognize ourselves as autonomous citizens of the nation, remain complicit with the fundamental inequalities of a class society.

This account of the underlying reality (alienation, emiseration, pauper-ization) which is represented in the form of 'ruling ideas' is, of course, the core of Marx's notion of ideology: art, literature, and all of the subdivisions of philosophical thought are conceived as 'nothing more than the ideal expression of the dominant material [economic] relationships grasped as ideas' (Marx, 1977c, p. 64). For Marx, then, the realm of culture is stripped of the spiritual significance which Hegel attributes to it: the ethical, aesthetic and political ideals through which each individual identifies his or her place within the totality of the state, are reduced to simulacra which misrepresent the dehumanizing reality of capitalism. If we are to undertake a serious examination of the relationship between culture, identity and technology therefore we will need to look carefully at this idea of culture as misrepresentation. For it is only in so far as Marx's inheritors (particularly Benjamin, Adorno and Jameson) have sought to conceptual-ize the relationship between the technological reproduction of images, the fetishism of commodities and the exploitative potential of capital, that we can really appreciate what is at stake in postmodernist theories of culture, aesthetics and (performative) subjectivity.

Before proceeding to examine the detail of these theories, however, I need to say a little about the the polemic between a certain rejuvenated form of modernism (specifically, in the work of Jürgen Habermas, David Harvey and Fredric Jameson) and the cultural and political trajectories of postmodernist theory.

II

In his 'Modernity – an unfinished project', Habermas attempts a kind of analytical diagnosis of the 'postmodern' experience of fragmentation and lack of identity. Fundamentally, his contention is that the loss of any shared tradition of moral, ethical and aesthetic norms is a result of the secularizing metaphysics of the Enlightenment. With the demise of a religious world view in which God was the guarantor of harmonious relations between truth, beauty and morality, Enlightenment philosophy set about establishing the a priori rules of moral, cognitive-theoretical and aesthetic judgements (Foster, 1985, p. 9). This determination to separate everyday experience from the disciplinary specialisms of aesthetics, morality and science is, for Habermas, the beginning of an impoverishment of the public sphere that has continued to accompany the development of technological modernity. The hope of a fulfilled Enlightenment, in which the accumulation of expert knowledge would guide the construction of a 'rational social order', has been shattered by the violent domination that expert cultures have assumed over the 'hermeneutics of everyday com-munication' (ibid.). Thus, both the possibility of the effects that have come to define the twentieth century as the end of the Enlightenment project (genocide, Third World poverty, environmental devastation), and the disorientation and irrationalism which has come to pervade the public sphere, should be conceived in terms a structural inequality between expert cultures and the normative potential of linguistically competent citizens.

For Habermas then, the modernist project remains 'incomplete' in the sense that the rationalizing demand of Enlightenment philosophy has been confined to the instrumental organization of social relations. However, unlike Adorno and Horkheimer's account of the failure of the Enlightenment project, Habermas' essay insists that the predominance of techno-scientific control should be conceived in relation to a certain achieved level of moral, aesthetic and political culture: what he calls the lifeworld. *Dialectic of Enlightenment*, as we will see in Part 2, makes a strong case for the collapse of the public sphere into 'the masses' – a collapse which, for Adorno and Horkheimer, abolishes the right of philosophy to present the realm of culture as the accumulation of an essentially human identity. Habermas, however, attempts to show that there is a communicative activity of human subjects which is presupposed by the legal, economic and political relations of 'organized capitalist societies'; and that consequently, the dominance of instrumental reason can never come to the state of completion that Adorno and Horkheimer describe. It is this autonomy of communicative action that Habermas seeks to defend in his account of the 'incompleteness' of modernity. For while it is true that the expert cultures of science, technology, aesthetics and jurisprudence operate with a high degree of independence, it remains the case that their operational demands impact directly on the normative-communicative potential of the lifeworld. What is required of a critical theory of modernity therefore, is 'an illuminating furtherance of the lifeworld processes of achieving self-understanding'; an illumination of the very processes of questioning, assertion, translation and identification which, for Habermas, express the moral culture and practical autonomy of human beings (Habermas, 1995b, p. 17).

The present state of our rationalized modernity then, demands that we attend to the *abstraction* of expert cultures from the communicative activity which has crystallized in the norms, values and traditions of the lifeworld. For even though it is undeniable that the ideology of 'system necessity' has come to dominate the political agenda of modernity, Habermas insists that the fact of this domination demands to be assessed in terms of its impact upon the hermeneutic culture of everyday life. The repudiation of modernity therefore, should in general be conceived as an irrational reaction to the objectifying, moralizing and aestheticizing interventions of expert cultures (Foster, 1983, p. 8). For if it is the case that the aesthetic has descended into the ephemeral enticements of mass culture, and if morality has lost all independence from the demands of techno-science, then this is not because the project of modernity is bankrupt and exhausted, but rather because social theory has yet to articulate the communicative potential inscribed in the lifeworld. Indeed, if we are properly to understand the continued dominance of expert cultures over the communicative infrastructure of everyday life, Habermas claims that we must recognize the complicity of 'postmodernist' (as well as 'premodernist' and 'anti-modernist') thought with estrangement of rational subjectivity from processes of techno-scientific modernization (*ibid.*, pp. 13–14).

Ultimately, Habermas attempts to circumscribe the modern philosophical enterprise as an *interpretive* rather than a *legislative* project. This is important because the distinction which he draws between postmodern thought and his own critical theory, depends upon the possibility of the lifeworld functioning as a sphere of autonomous communicative action. As the 'non-objective whole [of intersubjective experience] which . . . evades the grasp of theoretical objectification', Habermas claims that the lifeworld retains a certain 'ideality' in relation to the expressive powers of individual agents (Habermas, 1995b, p. 50). Thus, any claims which I, as a linguistically competent subject, may make about the infringement of technology upon my personal existence, the absence of reality in modern art, or the destruction and pollution of nature, carry within them a claim to universality that is essentially dialogical. For in so far as such claims are expressed through linguistic and grammatical rules that are intersubjective, they place me in the position of having to justify my case through the deployment of standards of validity that belong to the concept of 'rational will'. This process of justification refers, of course, to Habermas' notion of the ideal speech situation, in which 'no force except that of better argument is exercised; and as a result, all motives except the co-operative search for truth are excluded' (Habermas, 1976, p. 107). Now, while it is certainly true that Habermas intends this configuration of political practice to function as a critical-interpretive ideal (not as a bureaucratic or procedural rationality), his recourse to the universality of language raises serious questions about the disjunction between 'modern' and 'post-modern' temporalities. For example, might not our increasingly virtualized, technological, informatic social relations, mean that communicative action, in Habermas' sense, no longer has time to take place? And further, if the possibility of such dialogical exchange is excluded by the accelerating processes of technological modernization, then on what grounds can it be claimed that consensus, intersubjectivity and deliberation are essential to the 'project of modernity'?

What is important in Habermas' account of communicative action, I would suggest, is the relationship between his attempt to describe the conditions under which the enunciation of particular statements would immediately invoke the dialogical engagement of the other, and his determination to trace the postmodern experience of evanescence, spectrality and lack of identity back to a particular dislocation of the lifeworld. This dislocation, we have seen, begins with the Enlightenment project, and the attempt to determine the a priori rules of moral, aesthetic and cognitive-theoretical judgements. Thus, in so far as the demand for abstract classification establishes the conditions for the dominance of expert cultures, the task of a critical philosophy becomes one of attempting to reinvigorate the dialogical orientation of the public sphere. The ultimate aim of the 'project of modernity', in other words, would be the maximum engagement of expert cultures with the public expression of rational will (the lifeworld); an engagement in which philosophy would function to clarify the social, ethical and political consequences of technocratic organization. Two related issues emerge from this attempt to establish the conditions of rational legitimation. First, there is the relationship that Habermas constructs between historical evolution and the communicative potential of language. His argument is that the guiding thread of every functional, structural or systemic development of human society is the recuperation of the lifeworld as the horizon of rational-dialogical action. Second, there is the claim that postmodernist thought, because of its disregard of the history of modernist project, remains indifferent to the real dilemmas and contradictions of the political. Thus, as long as postmodernist theory refuses to acknowledge the structural deformations of communicative activity that lay at the foundation of the postmodern experience (fragmentation, evanescence), it can do no more than 'remove into the sphere of the far-away and the archaic the spontaneous powers of imagination, self-experience and emotion' (Foster, 1983, p. 14).

The logic of Habermas' arguments about the 'incompleteness' of the modernist project, is significant because it exemplifies a kind of active non-engagement with postmodernist thought. This logic proceeds from the establishment of certain essential characteristics of modernity (characteristics which are validated by an evolutionary theory of history[2]), to the establishment of certain necessary standards of normative and theoretical evaluation. Jameson, in his *Postmodernism*, for example, reproduces this logic when he claims that:

> The constitutive impurity of postmodernism theory ... confirms the insight of a periodization that must be insisted on over and over again, that postmodernism is not the determinant of a wholly new social order, but only the reflex and concomitant of yet another systemic modification of capitalism itself. (Jameson, 1995, p. xii)

Again, the repudiation of 'postmodernism theory' is made on the grounds that there are certain fundamental aspects of modernity – in this case, the inequalities of wealth, power and resources that are intensified by the technological organization of capital – to which every form of social experience must be referred. The postmodernist attempt to theorize the feelings of diversity, limitlessness and evanescence that have decentred the modern subject therefore, is again presented as a kind of wilful determination to have done with the real contradictions of late capitalism. As long as the 'hyperextension' of commodity production is not acknowledged as the socio-economic cause of this form of subjectivity, and as long as postmodernist theory fails to recognize the utility of such labile, transparent, manipulable individuals to the global organization of capital, its pronouncements amount to no more than an ideology of abstract difference and self-serving individualism. I will say more about Jameson's attempt to revive a Marxist critique of postmodern aesthetics in a Chapter 9.

The most consistent application of this periodizing logic appears in David Harvey's *The Condition of Postmodernity*. His claim is that

> strong *a priori* grounds can be adduced for the proposition that there is some kind of necessary relation between the rise of postmodernist cultural forms, the emergence of more flexible modes of capital accumulation, and a new round of 'time-space compression' in the organization of capitalism. (Harvey, 1999, p. vi)

Harvey's argument maintains that postmodernism must be understood in terms of its relationship to the 'compression' of space and time that becomes acute during periods of overaccumulation in capitalist economies. What Harvey is referring to is the rationalization of public, private and geographical space which, drawing its inspiration from the metaphysics of Enlightenment philosophy, has accompanied the rise of modern capitalism. This necessary involvement of a functional space and time in the dynamics of capital accumulation, means that the periodic crises of the world economy are experienced socially and culturally as 'disconcerting and disruptive bouts of space-time compression' (*ibid.*, p. 327). For Harvey, such periods are characterized by a loss of habitus – of those basic securities and affiliations (class, home, nation) that arise from the relative stability of the mode of production, and which function as the basis of everyday forms of legitimacy. In the absence of this spatial and temporal stability, the relationship between science (rational anthropology, functionalism, utilitarianism) and morality becomes increasingly dislocated, and 'the turn to aesthetics (of whatever form) becomes more pronounced' (*ibid.*). Thus, if we are to understand postmodernism properly – that is, in terms of its relationship to 'historical geography of capitalism' – we must recognize that, as a cultural and intellectual movement, it is primarily an attempt to aesthicize the experience of ephemerality and fragmentation (*ibid.*, p. 328).

For Harvey, as for Habermas, this 'postmodernist' assertion of the primacy of the aesthetic, and of the autonomy of cultural practice, is condemned on the grounds of its neglect of the historical conflicts and resolutions that have produced modern culture. Ultimately, postmodern cultural production is far too close to 'sheer profit-seeking' to be considered revolutionary or socially transformative (Harvey, 1999, p. 336). However, we cannot be satisfied with simply presenting postmodernism as an ideological form which feeds directly into the mechanisms of capital accumulation. Rather, the flexibility of postmodern varieties of production, communication and subjectivity should be understood as having arisen out of the old Fordist modernism as an 'opposing tendency'. For in so far as it is the 'internalized rules' of capital that produce both cultural dynamism and economic crises in the mode of production, we must recognize that postmodern flexibility represents one pole of an adaptive process whose variations emerge through the impossibility of resolving the dynamic contradictions of capitalism (*ibid.*, p. 343). Fordist modernity offers stable markets, a 'fixed configuration' of economic influence and political power, well established processes of theoretical legitimation and a secure grounding in techno-scientific rationality. Postmodern flexibility, on the other hand, is characterized by a kind of fantastical virtualization of relations of production: 'fictitious capital, images, ephemerality, chance, and flexibility in production techniques, labour markets and consumption niches' (*ibid.*, p. 339). Harvey's claim is that this opposition between modernist and postmodernist accounts of the relationship between politics, economics and normative legitimacy must be understood in terms of their relative advantages at any give time. In the end, there is little point in pursing debates about whether or not there has been a transition from modernity to postmodernity. For a historically grounded (i.e. Marxist) account of the relationship between cultural and economic production, demands that we recognize that the extent to which any particular economy has adopted the ideology of 'Fordism' or 'flexible postmodernism', will 'vary from time to time . . . depending on which configuration is profitable and which is not' (*ibid.*, p. 344). The 'aesthetic turn' of the postmodernists, in other words, remains an adaptive strategy of capital: a cultural form whose transformations of the established structure of economic conformity and political obedience, are riven with acute economic and political contradictions.

This attempt to fit 'postmodernism' into the conventional Marxist dynamic of base and superstructure, however, refuses any specific engagement with the political discourse of postmodern theory. Harvey's contention that under the discipline of his cultural critique, the sharp distinction between modernism and postmodernism disappears (Harvey, 1999, p. 342), masks a general determination to indict postmodernism as an irrational and irresponsible reaction to the fluctuations of capital. His remarks on the political consequences of 'postmodern flexibility', maintain a close relationship between the 'aesthetic turn' of postmodernist art, cinema and architecture, and 'a penchant for charismatic politics, concerns for ontology, and the stable institutions favoured by neo-conservatism' (*ibid.*, p. 339). Thus, if the underlying necessity of capital should be conceived as an adaptive process, this process becomes all the more pernicious and amoral as its dynamics become more flexible, fictive and immaterialized (*ibid.*, p. 343).[3] The general political significance of postmodernist theory and culture, in other words, is established on the grounds that the historical (geo-economic) conditions for the emergence of postmodern culture have been comprehensively described. As such, Harvey's critique of postmodernism refers only to certain generalized themes – ontology, aesthetics, charisma – that have arisen after the 'fact' of the strategic value of flexibility to the dynamical processes of capital accumulation. In the end, this line of argument fails to recognize that the questions of being and aesthetics that are addressed by postmodern theory, as well as having a history which exceeds any immediately 'ideological' or 'functional' determination, arise out of dilemmas that are directly concerned with the spatial and temporal dynamics of a post-Fordist capitalism. The discourse of progress, consensus and enlightenment, in other words, is not simply dismissed by postmodernist theory as untenably idealistic; rather it is re-evaluated in terms of the complex economy of informatic exchange, telematic communications and technocratic control that has transformed the 'internalized rules' of capital accumulation.

My intention in giving this brief survey of Habermas, Jameson and Harvey's contributions to the 'modernity or postmodernity' debate, is to point out the impossibility of making a fair evaluation of postmodern political theory from *within* the established parameters of either Marxist or liberal democratic thought. The concern with the origins of legitimacy, the return to the transfigurative potential of the sublime, and the extension of the critique of culture to include the impact of new telematic and digital technologies, all demand to be considered in terms of their contribution to our understanding of our own living present. For in so far as postmodernism calls into question the traditional processes through which political legitimacy has been established, transmitted and received, we cannot be satisfied with the reduction of its diverse theoretical claims to the status of a generic form of ideology (Jameson and Harvey), or to the wilful abandonment of the 'established' norms of communicative action (Habermas). Ultimately, my analysis of postmodernism theory will be concerned with the transformation of 'the real'; with the return of metaphysical questions about culture, identity and belonging through the *loss* of our basic certainties about the mode of production, the functional organization of capital and the politics of class affiliation and internationalism. As Derrida put it recently in *Politics of Friendship*:

> We wish only to think that we are on the track of the impossible axiomatic which remains to be thought. Now, if this axiomatic withdraws, from instant to instant, from one ray of the searchlight to another . . . this is because darkness is falling on the value of value, and hence on the very desire for an *axiomatic*, a consistent, granted or presupposed system of values . . . Such a political history [of the object, the mode of production] would deck itself out in 'realism' just in time to fall short of the thing – and to repeat, repeat and repeat again, with neither consciousness nor memory of its compulsive droning. (Derrida, 1997, p. 81)

In the chapters which follow, then, I will pursue the theme of postmodernism as an attempt to trace the ethical, political and aesthetic consequences of this constant transformation of 'the object'. For it is only in so far as the discussion seeks to read postmodernist theory in its own terms, that it will be possible to evaluate its relationship to the accelerated, disjunctive, technological time of the present.

Notes

1. Adam Smith's *The Wealth of Nations* is, of course, concerned with this relationship between the state and the legally free individual. However, Smith's ultimate aim is not to establish the transcendental unity of the moral will and its rights in relation to the sphere of positive law; rather, his intention is to disclose the social utility of self-seeking individualism.

2. See for example, Habermas' 'History and Evolution' (in *Telos*, Spring 1979, 127–43), and Jameson's 'Marxism and Postmodernism' (Jameson, 1998, pp. 33–49).

3. Harvey's objection to Jameson's attempt to evaluate the socio-economic significance of postmodern art and culture is that he comes too close the kind of 'fusion' with the ephemerality of postmodern aesthetics which characterizes Baudrillard's writing on 'simulation' (*ibid.*, pp. 351–2).

Part 1

Postmodernity and Postmodernism

1

Levinas and Bauman: The Ethics of Care

Emmanuel Levinas' writing on the ethical demand of the other has been immensely influential on the work of designating the possibility of a postmodern ethics and politics. We will see in a moment that Levinas' thought continues to occupy Jacques Derrida's reflections on the economics sacrifice (Derrida, 1995), and that it also found a certain resonance in Jean-François Lyotard's later work on the nature of obligation (Lyotard, 1988, pp. 110–15). I will look at the issues which arise from these readings in the sections which follow. My present concern, however, is to examine the relationship between Levinas' writing on the nature of care, obligation and suffering, and Zygmunt Bauman's account of the moral indifference which, for him, marks the transition from modernity to postmodernity. I need therefore, to make a few introductory remarks about nature of Levinasian ethics.

Reading Levinas is a difficult undertaking. His work is characterized by subtle redefinitions of the terms which have come to define the boundaries of ethical responsibility within the Western philosophical tradition (love, friendship, obligation, autonomy). We can, however, begin to make sense of Levinas by examining what is the key relationship in his writing: the relationship between 'the infinite' and the expressive morphology of the human face. The most concise expositions of this relationship are given in the section entitled 'Ethics and the face' in *Totality and Infinity* (Levinas, 1994, pp. 194–219), and in the essay 'Substitution' (Levinas, 1993b, pp. 88–125), which became the central chapter of *Otherwise Than Being*. 'Ethics and the face' begins with a categorical statement of the relationship between the face (conceived as an infinite demand), and the logical determinations of social ontology (totality):

> The relation between the Other and me, which draws forth in his expression, issues neither in number nor in concept. The Other remains infinitely transcendent, infinitely foreign; his face in which his epiphany is produced and which appeals to me breaks with the world that can be common to us, whose virtualities are inscribed in our nature and developed by our existence. Speech proceeds from absolute difference. Or more exactly, an absolute difference is not produced in a process of specification descending from genus to species, in which the order of logical relations runs up against the given, which is not reducible to relations. The difference thus encountered remains bound up with the logical hierarchy it contrasts with, and appears against the ground of the common genus. (Levinas, 1994, p. 194)

The essence of Levinas' claim is that the face, as that which immediately manifests the suffering of the other as 'my' responsibility, is the source of a demand which precedes every moral, legal-contractual or economic organization of duty. The very possibility of 'inter-human relationships' therefore, depends upon this openness of my selfhood (what Levinas calls 'ipseity') to the demand of the other as it is given through the expressiveness of his/her face. For Levinas then, this inscription of suffering is the very form of infinity: it cannot be contained in any systematic articulation of identity (Levinas' complaint against Heidegger is that he reduces human relationships to partial and imperfect revelations of 'Being'); it cannot be evaded or limited (when one is 'called' by the Other, one cannot set any legal, financial or moral restriction on the extent of one's obligation); and it is infinitely particularized (every duty of care belongs immediately and uniquely to a particular soul – there is no 'substitute' who could fulfil its obligation).

Ultimately, it is the unconditional nature of the ethical demand that is implicated in the relationship between ethics and ontology. The law, contractual obligation, economic necessity – indeed, all of the historically and philosophically established categories of 'the social' – are forms that seek to impose justifiable limits upon the ethical relation. Yet we have seen that for Levinas, the ethical demand is by definition illimitable; a transcendent command whose call exceeds every established organization of responsibility. It is the relationship between the logic of totality and the infinite demand of the other, therefore, that is the organizing theme of Levinas writing (Levinas, 1984, p. 289). His primary concern is to show that while the possibility of law, contract and economy arise out of the ethical relationship of the face-to-face, these forms acquire a certain social, historical and philosophical independence from the particularized, unconditional demand of the other. It is this independence that Levinas calls totality: the gathering of moral, legal, political and economic responsibilities into an ordered whole that acquires the legitimacy of 'being'. In a radical sense then, the ethical relation comes *before* the logical hierarchies of social ontology.[1] The very possibility of meaning is born out of the significatory presence of the other as face; for it is his/her expression of need, suffering or distress, that moves me to speak in response to his/her abjection (*ibid.*, p. 207). The sociality of human beings, then, cannot be reduced to the categories of an 'impersonal legality'; for such abstract, contractual relations presuppose the ethical relation of 'being-for'. Totality, in other words, presupposes the ethical-theological transcendence of the face.

This transcendental demand, however, is not just my setting aside the 'objective and common world', and the putting into question of my freedom; it is also 'sermon, exhortation, prophetic word' (Levinas, 1984, p. 213). My speaking in response to the other responds both to his or her particular suffering and to the whole of humanity:

The third party looks at me in the eyes of the Other – language is justice. It is not that there first would be the face, and then the being it manifests or expresses would concern itself with justice; the epiphany of the face qua face opens humanity. (*ibid.*, p. 213)

We have seen that for Levinas, participation in this 'community of infinites' cannot be reduced to the established mediations of ontology: the cognitively integrated 'subject', the economically rational actor, the contractually obligated citizen. The initiation of language comes through the original bond of separation between discrete ipseities; and so it is through the dispersed and 'prophetic' utterings of responsibility for the other that the ethical relation returns as a transcendent, illimitable demand. It is in this sense that the obligation sustained through the proximity of the other is 'anarchic': a relationship 'without the mediation of any principle, any ideality' (*ibid.*, p. 93). The violence perpetrated through the categories of social ontology, therefore, is not a pure negativity that simply destroys the 'inter-human perspective' of the self: it is rather a demand for the enunciation of justice which constantly re-emerges from the reduction of infinite difference to the generic relationships of totality.

The ethical commandment, for Levinas, subsists in the uncoerced redemptions of meaning that only 'I', as the self who is uniquely summoned by the face of the sufferer, can give to his or her suffering. My obligation includes my own mortality; for I am responsible to the point of having my own death become that which can allow the other to die with dignity and significance. Indeed, for Levinas, Heidegger's discussion of *Dasein*'s 'being towards death' is a fundamental misconception of human authenticity. His claim, according to Levina's argument, is that death belongs to *Dasein* as an originary structure of its experience, and that as such, the authenticity of its 'being in the world' excludes the ethical moment of sacrifice for the sake of the other. It is certainly true that we, as human beings, can decide to give our lives in a particular act of heroism. Yet such sacrifices can never alter the fact of the other's mortality, its being towards death (Heidegger, 1983, p. 284). The opening of *Dasein* to the transcendence of Being therefore, depends upon the experience of mortality as radical individuation, as a falling away of the preconstituted responsibilities of everyday existence (*ibid.*, p. 308). For Levinas, however, this relationship of human beings to what Heidegger calls the 'they-self', fails to recognize the phenomenological horizon of the face-to-face. The individuation which marks the ethical relationship, in other words, must not be referred to the impersonal, transhistorical unfolding of Being. For it is in its very essence and possibility a response to the mortality of the other (Levinas, 1994, pp. 232–6).

The fact that each of us is the other's redeemer, means that politics must be conceived as the constant reorganization of justice within the formal-institutional structures of the public sphere (Levinas, 1994, pp. 212–16). This theme of the gaze of the third party is developed more fully in

Otherwise Than Being. Levinas argues that while the demand of the face-to-face must be considered as illimitable and particularized, this does not mean that it simply transcends the moral, legal, economic and political obligations which constitute the being of the social. Rather, the ethical commandment refers each of us to the secular bonds of our communal existence, and so to the more limited, yet necessary, organization of justice in the law. Thus, while we may never *realize* the transcendent demand inscribed in the face of the other, we must constantly return to it in order to redeem the violence of the state (Levinas, 1981, p. 159).

This notion of redemptive history raises important questions about the nature of postmodernity. As we will see, Levinas' thought has provoked a response in French philosophy that has centred around the problem of transcendence. Both Lyotard and Derrida have questioned the possibility of an ethical relation that transcends the general economics of totality, and which refers the difference of the other to the presence of God in the moment of obligation (Derrida, 1990b and Lyotard, 1988). For Bauman, however, Levinas' account of the primacy of ethics has succeeded in establishing the conditions of a radical critique of modernity. For in so far as the possibility of acknowledging the demand of the other is disrupted by the very forces which have defined modernity (technological and bureaucratic efficiency, state governmentality, economic expansion), the drift into the moral ambivalence of postmodernity has to be addressed in terms of the loss of the common resources of ethical obligation (face, incarnation, suffering, love).

Bauman's description of moral space as a spontaneous opening onto the alterity of the other 'which ignores the precepts of cognitive space (or rather proceeds as *if* it has ignored them)' (Bauman, 1993, p. 166), is taken more or less unmodified from Levinas' thought. The 'metaphysical desire' provoked by the face (the desire from which both care and responsibility emerge as the content of the ethical commandment), in other words, constitutes a realm of 'incommunicable' knowledge that is both within and transcendent of the categories of social ontology. Thus, when Bauman deploys the Kantian concept of heteronomy (that which influences the moral will from outside of its pure self-legislation, its pure autonomy), he is referring to those legal, moral and political categories that re-construct the ethical relation within a particular economy of difference and recognition. In the end then, Bauman's account of moral action demands that each of us abandon the 'logos of being' – the logic of rational, recuperable identities and substantive foundations – and respond immediately and without reservation to the expressive alterity of the face. Such an emancipation is not

> contaminated with submission, even if it results in my giving myself up as a hostage of the Others' weal and woe ... I am I as far as I am for the Other. Only, once this ambivalence is papered over or banished from sight, egoism may be set against altruism, self-interest against the common weal, the moral self against the socially endorsed ethical norm. (*ibid.*, pp. 77–8)

As moral beings, in other words, we must respond to the originary desire which designates our moral subjectivity (ipseity) as such: the irrecusable desire to give meaning to the suffering and abjection of the other. This redemptive love can take place only in the total absence of mediation; in the absence of all positive recognition of the reciprocal expectations embodied in the contractual and procedural relationships of the state (totality).

The idea of cognitive space which Bauman presents in his *Postmodern Ethics* proceeds from Levinas' original identification of violence and coercion (heteronomy) with the categories of ontological reason. According to Levinas, it is through these categories that the state is able to present itself as the objective mediation of the ethical relationship: as the comprehensive integration of work, satisfaction and desire into the totality of legal, political, economic and social relations. What Bauman attempts to do with Levinas' specification of ontological reason, is to re-present it as a history of functional-repressive control. Thus, Michel Foucault's genealogy of penal systems is cited as identifying an increasingly 'behaviouristic' imperative in the ordering of social relations: an imperative which, in seeking to regularize and functionalize the disciplinary control which the state exerts over its human resources, also suppresses the unpredictable, dysfunctional expenditure (of care) demanded by the other. Increasingly:

> All social organization, big or small, global-societal or local and functionally specific, consists in subjecting the conduct of its units to either *instrumental* or *procedural* criteria of evaluation. More importantly still, it consists in delegalizing and forcing out all other criteria, and first and foremost such standards as elide the legalizing authority of the totality, and thus render the behaviour of units resilient to socializing pressures. (Bauman, 1993, pp. 123–4)

Bauman identifies three crucial factors in this de-moralization of social space: (1) ensuring that there is distance rather than *proximity* between agent and patient, between the perpetrator of an action and those who suffer its consequences; (2) the exemption of certain 'others' from the class of individuals worthy of moral respect; and (3) the 'dissembling' of human beings into functionally specific traits, each of which has a discrete technical utility that precludes any moral response to the individual as an expressive and vulnerable alterity. It is through these strategies that the state has been able to 'float' moral responsibility: that is, to promote a universal sense that social 'behaviour' ought not to be judged by moral criteria, and that 'my' contribution to the chain of functional or bureaucratic tasks which produce a particular outcome (whatever this outcome might be), should be assessed only in terms of its competence and efficiency. For Bauman then, it is modernity's promotion of the 'moral nullity' of social tasks (what he calls *adiaphorization*), which gave rise to the possibility of the Holocaust. For in so far as technological and bureaucratic systems had become extensive enough to gather their own functional momentum, it became possible for the Nazi party to turn thousands of civil servants, transport workers and party officials into accomplices to genocide (Bauman, 1991).

In *Modernity and the Holocaust* Bauman argues that there is a relationship between the de-moralizing course of modernity and established 'sociological' conceptions of morality. His argument is that such conceptions have, in general, tended to subsume the distinction between good and evil under functionalist accounts of how value systems ensure the fulfilment of 'objective' social needs. This method of analysis is most explicit in the sociologies of Durkheim and Parsons; for both maintain that the individual is ontologically dependent upon the functionally differentiated whole for its moral, psychological and physical integrity. However, it could also be argued that orthodox Marxist constructions of ideology remain equally bewitched by the integrative function of moral codes. For the legislative strictures of ethics remain 'heteronomous' ('other' than the productive self-realization of humanity) only for as long as they continue to justify the re-production of an ungovernable and contradictory simulacrum of 'nature' (bourgeois property relations) within society. What is important here is that this type of theorizing tends to reinforce the belief that the presence of 'evil' within the community of human beings is traceable to the encroachment of 'nature' (anomic passions, unrestrained egoism) upon the unifying structures of the totality. For Bauman, this sociological exclusion of the causes of evil from the structural dynamics of society is directly related to the logic of totality. For as long as the functional integration of social relations is theorized as *the* uniquely moralizing force, the rational administration of human beings is given an implicit, and ultimately disastrous, priority over the demands of care. It is only after we have recognized that evil is socially determined, and that this determination proceeds through the functional-instrumental destruction of moral proximity, that we can begin to unfold the relationship between violence and the historical development of modernity (Bauman, 1989, pp. 169–200).

According to Bauman, however, the onset of modernity does not simply produce an ever increasing weight of functional and disciplinary pressures. It also produces an aesthetic response, whose energy gathers the spontaneity of subjective feeling into volatile and unpredictable occasions of consensus. This aesthetic sociality, which Bauman presents as an 'interruptive' force in the functional trajectory of socialization, however, is quickly distinguished in *Postmodern Ethics* from the originary feelings of care which are prompted by the proximity of the face. The energy of aesthetic sociality is given form in the crowd; in the thrilling and disturbing intensity of those feelings which spring from the massification of the individual. 'Moral proximity', Bauman warns, 'was the nearness of the Face. This one, the aesthetic proximity, is nearness of the crowd; and the meaning of the crowd is facelessness' (Bauman, 1993, p. 130). The cognitive space of postmodern societies therefore is increasingly traversed by 'counter-structural' eruptions of aesthetic sociality – what Bauman calls the collective 'discharging' of energies that are opposed to the work, history and structure of disciplinary socialization. Indeed, the condition of postmodernity, the fragmentation and delegitimation of the social bond and its institutional identity, is presented in *Postmodern Ethics* as a progressive tendency towards the aestheticization of social space.

Unlike Foucault, however, Bauman does not pursue remission from carceral 'normality' in authorial practices (of theatricalization, re-presentation and re-appropriation) which are made possible by existing power relations. Rather, the point of his exposition is to show that the only way of thinking the compossibility of autonomy and responsibility, is through the originary transcendence of the face. Thus, while Foucault's genealogies of sexual, psychological, medical and carceral knowledge do, according to Bauman, present a compelling history of modern disciplinary space, the aesthetic practices which may spring from that space can never erase the traces of functionality. A truly 'transgressive' resistance to the coercive authority of the state, in other words, can spring only from the ethical commandment; that is, from the uniqueness of the invocation I receive from the suffering of the other. This means that, for Bauman, both the legislative rationality of cognitive space and the counter-structural excitation of 'neo-tribal' resistance are ethically null: 'As far as morality is concerned, the two outcomes are much the same. Heteronomy (of rules and crowds) takes the place of the autonomy of the moral self. Neither structure, nor counter-structure, neither socialization of society nor sociality of the crowd, tolerate moral independence' (Bauman, 1993, p. 132). In the end, 'counter-structural' outbursts of aesthetic consensus remain susceptible to the colonizing strategies of the state. For even though they disclose a social space whose dynamics are radically different from those of cognitive spacing, the seductions of the aesthetic – the play of individuals as surfaces, the sensationalism of the spectacle, the egoism of the conspicuous consumption – are always amenable to functional manipulation. The fate of the stranger in the sphere of urban re-presentation (the 'Telecity') therefore, is to remain 'infinitely close' to my monadic egoity, but to be denied any claim upon my moral ipseity. In the state of aesthetic disattention, I notice you only if you amuse or arouse me – and vice versa.

For Bauman, 'the problem of modern society is not how to eliminate strangers, but how to live in their constant company – that is, under the condition of cognitive paucity, indetermination and uncertainty' (Bauman, 1993, p. 159). The role of the state in relation to this condition of universal ambivalence has become increasingly one of 'managing' the disturbing presence of the other: of reinforcing the repressive forms of socialization, of manipulating the seductions of aesthetic space, and of naming and marginalizing those 'selected social targets' who come to symbolise the accursed share of ambivalence (*ibid.*, p. 160). It is within this strategically managed sphere that moral acts must be accomplished. The universal forms of understanding and sensation that come to dominate the life of the individual can offer no guarantees against the exposure of the other to the neglect of aesthetic 'disattention', or to the violence of generic persecutions. Indeed, it is these forms that have intensified the feeling of ambivalence to the point where it seems impossible to act morally within the established relations of social space. The only hope of salvaging moral autonomy from the paralysing shock of postmodern wisdom (and thus from the 'real-world' demands of the culture industry and disciplinary socialization), is the acknowledgement of ambivalence as the signifier of ethical responsibility. The face, as ethical transcendence, always exceeds the rational designation of my responsibility to the other. I cannot limit my response to the suffering alterity that confronts me to a set of logically consistent duties; for the conditions under which those duties have to be enacted must always remain unforeseeable and contingent. So while reason is about making correct decisions (decisions which attempt to eradicate doubt and ambivalence), 'moral responsibility precedes all decisions as it does not, and cannot care about any logic which would allow the approval of an action as correct. Thus morality can be rationalised only at the cost of self-denial and self-attrition' (*ibid.*, p. 248).

This brief account of *Postmodern Ethics* and *Modernity and the Holocaust* is, of course, inadequate to convey the breadth of Bauman's exploration of the ethical dilemmas of postmodernity. Other important issues addressed in his work include the displacement of moral reflection from the lifeworld by scientific rationality, the 'entropetal' tendency of late-capitalist economies, and the difficulty of extending moral sentiments to those who live within the 'grazing fields' of these economies – the so-called 'Third World'. Despite the obvious limitations of my exposition, however, its scope is, I think, sufficient to disclose a tension in Bauman's work: that which exists between the transcendental demand of the other *as face*, and the sociological demand that the ethical relation should have some institutional, or at least procedural, codification. In *Modernity and the Holocaust*, Bauman remarks that what we require after Auschwitz, is:

> [A] new ethics, an ethics of distant consequences, an ethics commensurable with the uncannily extended spatial and ·temporal range of the effects of temporal action. An ethics that would reach over the socially erected obstacles of mediated action and the functional reduction of the human self. (Bauman, 1989, p. 221)

And in *Postmodern Ethics*, he proposes that, 'the moral crisis of the postmodern habitat requires first and foremost that politics ... be an extension and institutionalisation of moral responsibility... long-range ethics makes sense, if at all, only as a political programme' (Bauman, 1993b, p. 246). These remarks are important for our attempt to situate Bauman's account of postmodernity and require some unpacking.

It could legitimately be asked why Levinas' thought requires any further specification. Surely his account of totality (ontology, Being) and infinity (face, alterity) is sufficient to disclose the non-coercive force of the ethical commandment? Indeed, Levinas' response to Derrida's reading of his work suggests that there is a certain futility in the exercise of trying to 'improve' the work of another philosopher; for it is always complete in its own terms (Critchley, 1999, p. 145). Yet Levinas' philosophy remains a provocation; a demand, above all, to specify the fate of the ethical relation within the socio-economic and technological development of modernity. We will see later that Derrida's reading of *Totality and Infinity* attempts to specify a certain kind of respectfulness towards Levinas' account of language, alterity and the ethical demand (Derrida, 1990b). This reading, I will argue, discloses the possibility of an ethical stricture which belongs as a chance, an unforeseen possibility, to the complex structure of the present; to the fact that we who are obligated are obligated only on the basis of the impossibility of our actually becoming 'we'. It is this stricture which distinguishes deconstruction from theology: Levinas' 'community of infinites' has already been summoned by the presence of God in the face of the other, while for Derrida, the relationship between obligation and community always awaits what is unknown, and unknowable, in the future (Derrida, 1995, p. 84). Bauman's attempt to deploy the resources of Levinas' philosophy, on the other hand, is 'respectful' in a very different way. Rather than sustaining the ethical stricture of his thought, both *Modernity and the Holocaust* and *Postmodern Ethics* tend to shift its significance towards a tragic and irrecuperable loss of ethical responsibility.

For Bauman, the ethical dilemma determined by postmodern societies looks like this: how is it possible that the transcendent demand of ethical responsibility could survive the *adiaphorizing* effects of cognitive and aesthetic spacing; and how, given that such a survival is possible, could that responsibility be extended to those whose constitution as 'other' is most extreme? We have seen that, for Levinas, the ethical demand of the face refers us, as human beings, to the formal structures of justice through which society functions as a whole, or totality. Suffering and sacrifice remain intrinsic to this conception of redemptive justice. For in so far as it is the proximity and uniqueness of the other's suffering which opens the possibility of redemptive history, the reconciliation of politics and ethics (of the administrative functions of the state and the demands of the other) is neither a possible nor a desirable end. This, of course, raises questions about the political significance of Bauman's work. For having taken the ethical demand out of the redemptive context of Levinas' philosophy, his thought moves uneasily between the pathos of losing the originary form of 'being for', and the legislative demands of a normative sociology. I will argue later, particularly in the chapters on technology and globalization, that Bauman's approach to the ethical questions of postmodernity is crucially limited by its expulsion of the ghost, or trace, of humanity from the development of technology. For in so far as he returns to the necessity of supplementing the original ethical bonds of humanity (Bauman, 1993b, p. 246), his critique is unable to see beyond the technological attrition of human beings. Thus, if we are to respond to the fate of the other within the 'spectralizing' systems of the postmodern world, we must recognize the complexity of its technical supplementations, and of the unforeseen possibilities of violence and liberation to which these supplementations give rise (Derrida, 1994a, p. 65).

Note

1. This notion of the priority of the ethical relation is phenomenological rather than historical. For Levinas, there was never a primordial community of beautiful souls who would have responded to one another without the constrains of legal, economic and moral responsibility. Rather, the transcendent priority of the other (as face) is disclosed to human beings as the loss of their egoity within the logical organization of totality.

2

Beck and Giddens: Risk and Reflexive Modernity

The most cogent account of the relationship between risk and modernity is set out in Ulrich Beck's *Risk Society* (Beck, 1996a). In general, his contention is that late modernity is marked by the emergence of technologies whose destructive potential is so great that they put at risk the very conditions of organic life. Nuclear power, for Beck, is the paradigm of these technologies. The effects of a serious nuclear accident could not be confined to the immediate environs of the reactor, nor could they be prevented from spreading beyond the geopolitical province of the nation state. The issue of a 'nuclear future' therefore, is immediately one of international responsibility; for beyond the economic disparities that have encouraged the global proliferation of fission reactors, we, as organic beings, share responsibility for the earth's organic systems. This cosmopolitan demand is made all the more urgent by the fact that the effects of radiation would not be limited to a single generation. For we know that the mutations of plant and animal life caused by exposure to radioactive material would be passed on through the genetic processes of reproduction. The risks characteristic of risk society therefore are both cosmopolitical and transgenerational: they affect us at the level of our biological existence, and place all of us in the position of having to take responsibility for the future, not just of humanity, but of organic life in general.

Risk Society therefore, poses a fundamental question: do we go on trusting in the ability of science to solve the problems that arise from the use of technology (problems which threaten absolute catastrophe), or do we begin to question the authority which science, as an expert culture, has exercised over our moral and political judgements? Beck's response to this question is to argue that the public awareness of risk that is characteristic of reflexive modernity, has emerged through the steady technological attrition of organic life. The incidents at Bhopal and Chernobyl, for example, are simply the most visible effects of systemic processes of irradiation, poisoning and contamination. Beck's notion of risk therefore, marks a general intensification of ontological insecurity; a general sense of anxiousness about the technological threat that is posed to the continuation of organic life. We are all exposed to the consequences of living on the 'volcano of civilization'; and we are all potentially subject to the damages produced as 'side effects' of technological systems.

The political responsibilities of civilization risks therefore, can be theorized neither in terms of the sovereignty of particular nation states, nor in terms of the universal benefits of global competition. Rather, we must consider the consequences of living within a technological civilization which, at any time, could bring about its own destruction. It is this profound sense of insecurity which is taken up in Anthony Giddens' sociology of risk. For while he accepts the general account of civilization risks which is given in *Risk Society*, his own work attempts to show how it is possible for the awareness of impending catastrophe to coexist with a sense of social solidarity. For Giddens, the engagement of reflexive individuals with technologically determined risks, is mediated through an implicit sense of trust in the expert systems on which they depend. Indeed, he suggests that it is only within the relative security of the normative expectations that he calls the *Umwelt* that it is possible for social agents to be reflexive about the ethical and political responsibilities of late modernity. I will look more closely at Giddens' understanding of the relationship between risk, security and identity in a moment. For now, however, I need to give a more detailed account of Beck's *Risk Society*.

At the beginning of his book, Beck argues that as the industrial revolution increased the productivity of Western capitalist societies, the relationship between scientific knowledge, technical innovation and economic demand became increasingly close. Under the conditions of 'primary industrialization', in other words, the economy became the principal determinant of scientific research. For unless a particular area of theoretical knowledge was seen to offer the possibility of technical innovation in the production of commodities (that is, to increase the rate at which surplus value could be produced in a particular productive enterprise), it was likely to remain relatively impoverished and undeveloped. This relationship between science and the economy marks the emergence of a transactional logic, in which science, contrary to the universal scepticism of its method, is forced to present its findings as infallible knowledge that awaits conversion into increased productivity, higher profits and a general reduction of material scarcity. What is significant here, according to Beck, is the contradiction that developed between the 'method' and the 'ideology' of science; that, is between the self-critical, self-reflexive procedures through which empirical testing of hypotheses was carried out, and the rhetoric of certainty through which results were presented to the 'consumers' of scientific knowledge (Beck, 1996a, p. 164). For in presenting itself as the true foundation upon which industrial modernity could set about resolving the problems which nature's insufficiency had bequeathed to humankind (poverty, disease, scarcity, war), science entered into a dangerous complicity with the mechanisms of capital accumulation. Civil society, in other words, as the legally sanctioned sphere of individual rights and bourgeois economic activity, assumed an exclusive responsibility for the deployment of scientific knowledge, and for the progress of the human species towards its technological liberation from the constraints of nature. For Beck the danger inherent in this subordination of science is that the political sphere, that is, the state's potential for critical reflection on the consequences of technological innovation, is ultimately reduced to 'rubber stamping' the developments in medicine, agriculture, industry and warfare, which confront it as the accomplished facts of a necessary and legitimate progress (Beck, 1996a, pp. 187–90).

This increasing disempowerment of the political sphere (specifically, the state's progressive exclusion from the decision-making processes through which economic and professional institutions decide how humanity is going to live) is one of Beck's principal concerns in *Risk Society*. For since parliamentarianism has become an irrelevant charade in which parties argue endlessly over whose policies are best attuned to the needs of technological progress, questions about the course which that progress ought to take are excluded from the sphere of legitimate political discussion. This means that throughout the development of primary industrialization, it is economic and professional institutions that have decided which forms of technology are 'objectively' necessary to the continued progress of humanity, what constitutes an 'acceptable risk' in the deployment of such technology, and consequently, who will be most immediately exposed to those risks. Until recently, of course, the logic of primary industrialization has dictated that exposure to risk is something that increases the lower down the class structure one goes. Yet for Beck, this class-based model of risk is no longer adequate to comprehend the catastrophic damages that new technologies are capable of visiting on humanity. And so we need to frame a new conception of risk which emphasizes the 'globality' of the threats posed by nuclear, chemical and medical technologies: threats which, through the closed system of the earth's biosphere, affect the whole (cosmopolitical) body of humanity (Beck, 1996a, pp. 37–8). It is this enclosure of human beings within the fragile economics of nature which is schematized in Beck's account of 'The solidarity of living things', and which is present as an implicit consensualizing power throughout his analysis of the shift from 'industrial' to 'risk' society. I will return to this theme in a moment.

We have seen that, for Beck, a contradiction develops between the method and the ideology of science during the development of primary industrial society. His contention is that science, considered as an instrument of critical inquiry, becomes increasingly sceptical and self-reflexive in its research practices, while at the same time being forced by the general dynamics of the economy to hold on to the ideology of infallibility. What is important here is that, the emergence of technologically produced 'side effects' that can be confined neither to the spatial extent of the nation nor to the present generation who have gambled on the safety of nuclear power and genetechnologies, is what ultimately precipitates the emergence of a 'scientized' politics of risk. As genetically mutable, biologically contaminable beings, we are all susceptible to the effects of radiation and chemical poisoning; and it is this shared vulnerability that, for Beck, becomes the focus of a 'democratic' resistance to the techno-economic powers which have, until now, monopolized the control, development and deployment of technology.

Most of the damage caused by radiation leaks or chemical discharges does not occur through spectacular and highly publicized events like the Chernobyl or Bhopal incidents. Rather, it tends to take the form of an invisible and pernicious accumulation of 'effects' upon nature and the human community. Given the institutional power of those corporations who have invested heavily in a 'nuclear' or 'agrichemical' future for modernity, and allowing for their ability to muster and present the 'infallible' research of science in support of such futures, it is unsurprising that evidence of culpable contamination adduced by affected communities has tended to be dismissed as simply anecdotal and unscientific.

Beck, however, claims that the established relationship between efficient causality (event A is the cause of event B, A→B) and the legal standard of proof of responsibility (a standard which requires a massively comprehensive adduction of evidence concerning specific acts of negligence, definitions of 'acceptable levels' of contamination, and the co-implication of other natural and human conditions in the vicinity of the pollution), can no longer be sustained (Beck, 1996a, pp. 63–4). The kind of damages incurred by human beings through the accelerated development of technology (cellular and genetic mutation, the spread of multiply resistant bacteria, the accumulation of toxins in the body's organic structures) refer, from the beginning, to science for their cognition, definition and evaluation as 'risks'. In primary industrial societies, according to Beck's argument, the colonization of science by those enterprises which control the generation and distribution of capital (industrial corporations, finance capital, the military), determined a general blindness to technological risks that allowed human and environmental damages to be consigned to the category of 'side effects'. Yet with the increasing extent and frequency of such harm, the power of science to enforce its official assignment of particular exposures, contaminations and irradiations to this politically deactivating category, begins to breakdown. Within what Beck conceives as the emergent 'sub-politics' of risk society – a politics of opposition, contestation and mediation which industrial society has precipitated through its pursuit of technological solutions to the side effects of technology – science begins to emerge as the facilitator of a critical dialogue among opposing societal interests (Beck, 1996a, pp. 172–3). Thus, in their function as the only discourses through which technological risks can be properly determined, scientific knowledges begin to shake off their ideological attachments to 'system necessities' and 'objective economic constraints', and to open up newly democratic practices of forensic evaluation, dispute settlement and the cosmopolitical articulation of civilization risks (Beck, 1996a, pp. 231–5).

The concept of 'the political' which runs throughout *Risk Society* is informed by a particular notion of science and its relationship to modernity. Obviously, the idea of a global community of risk – a community whose possibility would depend upon the mobilization of a sense of reflexive anxiety – can retain its ethical force only for as long as the future has not *already* been determined as humanity's technological self-attrition and ultimate self-destruction. Thus, the imperative of determining the extent of the biological, genetic and ecological damage which modern technologies are doing to present and future generations, is presented as a unifying 'interest' inscribed in both the natural and the social sciences – one that begins a critical dialogue between their respective rationality claims. The emergence of this dialogue, which Beck describes as 'a still undeveloped symbiosis' (Beck, 1996a, p. 28), performs two important functions in his account of the politics of risk. First, it opens the possibility of a socio-scientific consciousness of risk; a consciousness whose responsibility to the future is given through the 'present' necessity of bringing the normative-evaluative resources of the social sciences to bear upon the data produced by the natural sciences. Second, it is the activation of this debate about civilization risks, that rejuvenates a political sphere that has been progressively disempowered by the independence of corporate capital and professional organizations from the state. For Beck, the emergence of such a pervasive 'risk consciousness' brings about a crucial change in the orientation of social democracy. The rights that are enshrined in the legal constitution of the state cease to be the abstract guarantees which allow 'non-political' organizations to press on with the labour of technological progress, and become the ethical framework through which citizens are able to recognize the violence to which this labour has subjected nature and humanity (Beck, 1996a, p. 193). The 'implicit ethics' which has begun to haunt the formal autonomy of 'business, the natural sciences and the technical disciplines', in other words, becomes explicit in a 'reflexive' political sphere which would: (1) encourage research in the direction of alternatives to the existing 'system necessities'; (2) protect and expand the highest established levels of social and democratic rights; (3) create institutional spheres in which 'interdisciplinary' evaluations of risk could be subjected to public scrutiny (Beck, 1996a, p. 235).

Anthony Giddens' work shifts the emphasis away from the 'high-consequence, low-probability' risks that are the focus of Beck's writing. Thus, while Beck is concerned primarily with the mobilization of anxiety as political force, Giddens attempts to theorize the relationship between risk awareness and the ontological security of the individual. In *Modernity and Self-Identity* he argues that although risk evaluation has become the dominant form of reflexivity, the fact that this has not reduced social actors to a state of paranoid anxiety testifies to the persistence of a certain level of implicit trust. Technological risks are integrated into our everyday lives as background possibilities, too distant from our immediate concerns to demand serious consideration (Giddens, 1997b, p. 130). Societies that are based on the assessment of risk, in other words, depend upon the filtering out of certain catastrophic possibilities from the realm of practical consciousness. If we are to go on with our everyday lives, we must have a certain degree of trust in those with whom we share social relationships, and in those technological systems and expert knowledges upon which our material security depends. Without this reproduction of ontological security through the filtering structures of practical consciousness – what Giddens, following Goffman, calls the *Umwelt* – there could be no possibility of our continuing to function as reflexive social actors.

As the subject of abstract systems and expert knowledges, Giddens claims that the self has become a 'reflexive achievement': a narrative project that is sustained through the constant reintegration of local involvements, system necessities and global concerns. The threat of a pure technocratic control of the human subject therefore, is always mediated by the practical consciousness that arises from the relationship of the self to its physical embodiment. Giddens argues that under the conditions of high modernity, the body has become an 'outer layer' through which the reflexivity of the self and the demands of technological systems are brought together. One can think of numerous examples of this technical manipulation of the body – contraception, prosthetic supplementation, gene therapy, cloning – all of which give rise, or are about to give rise, to moral and existential questions that the self must confront within the terms of its particular goals and ideals. It is, in other words, impossible to divorce the reality of subjective experience, of expressive selfhood, from the political questions raised by increasing technological specialization and control.

For Giddens, then, the fact that we have all become strategic risk evaluators raises the question of how such a calculative orientation can support a sense of social belonging. For in so far as risk assessment has become the dominant model of subjective reflection, it seems as if the unity between individual consciousness, the integration of society and the experience of ontological security has been crucially disrupted. Giddens' response is to argue that after the traditional sources of collective identity have been displaced by the dynamical processes of modernity, the selfhood of the individual emerges as a 'reflexive project'. The fact that we all live with the uncertainties generated by abstract systems and with the diffusion of expert knowledges throughout the lay population, means that the relationship of the self to the collective life of society has moved beyond the regulative interdependence set out in functionalist sociology (see Durkheim, 1964 and Parsons, 1968). In Giddens' work, the reflexivity produced in modern technological societies is understood as initiating a 'life politics' concerned with questioning, transforming and mediating the 'internally referential systems of modernity' (Giddens, 1997b, p. 223).

This conception of life politics, then, emerges as 'a fully distinctive set of problems and possibilities with the consolidating of high modernity'

(Giddens, 1997b, p. 214). The proliferation of high-risk technologies, the increasing specialization of expert knowledge, the consolidation of the Third and First World economies, and the progressive infringement of abstract systems on the body, all contribute to a reflexive orientation of the self to the conditions of its 'being'. After the disembedding of traditional, locally organized relationships, the self becomes a performative demand: a narrative of authenticity that is immediately linked to the moral and existential dilemmas of the living present. The possibility of Giddens' life politics therefore, depends upon their being a *dialectical* relationship between 'social relations external to the self', and the 'personal decisions' through which particular individuals respond to those relations. The ecological problems generated by the 'the new and accelerating interdependence of global systems', for example, should be understood in terms of their impact upon the life choices of autonomous, reflexive individuals (*ibid.*, p. 221). For it is only in so far as we are prepared to modify our personal activities, to change the acquisitive life styles which perpetuate technocratic domination, that a politics of ecological responsibility is possible. Ultimately, then, this questioning of modernity's technological systems, demands an extension of the state's legal recognition of the self and its reflexive diversity (*ibid.*, p. 226). For it is through the engagement of the self with the consequences of modernization, that it becomes possible to mount a political challenge to the globalized forms of economy, identity and technological integration (*ibid.*, p. 230).

I will develop these introductory remarks in Chapter 11. For the moment, however, I need to give a brief indication of the relationship between Beck and Giddens' work and the political claims of postmodernism.

Clearly there are some basic issues which are common to Beck and Giddens' work on risk, and to the general concept of the postmodern. In particular, the transformation of the spatial and temporal dimensions of the social, the impact of technology on the self and the body, and the reconfiguration of democratic institutions, are themes which bring the politics of risk directly into contact with postmodernism theory. As might be expected, this contact is essentially a repetition of the dynamics set out in the Introduction. Giddens, for example, claims that 'post-modernism is an *aesthetic reflection* upon the nature of modernity', and that, as such, it cannot explain the structural and institutional changes which define our historical present (Giddens, 1997a, p. 47). His argument is that by surrendering the concepts of truth, historical progress and moral necessity to the play of the aesthetic (styles, forms, locutions, desires), postmodernism fails to recognize the dialectical relationship between institutional and subjective reflexivity (Giddens, 1997b, p. 224). In Beck's work, on the other hand, the implication is that postmodernism is one of a number of discourses through which traditional accounts of the political, the economic and the social are rejuvenated by the word 'post' (Beck, 1996a, p. 9). For in so far as postmodernism theory claims to elaborate the conditions of autonomous reflection (the free play of discourse and textuality, the disturbing transcendence of the sublime), it neglects the life experiences of those exposed to the damaging effects of modern technologies (*ibid.*, p. 5). The political significance of reflexivity, in other words, is obscured by its disengagement from the (essentially threatened) 'solidarity of living things' (*ibid.*, p. 74).

Later I will argue that these criticisms fail to distinguish between the different strands of postmodernist thought, and that Beck and Giddens' constructions of risk fail to recognize the complexity of the relationships between humanity, technology and temporality. However, I will also claim that there is a speculative dimension to Beck and Giddens' work which remains essential to the idea of political responsibility. This dimension is expressed in the demand that the relationship between subjective reflection and the legal and political institutions of the state, is the proper focus of a critical politics of modernity. Thus, while I will argue that the 'disembedding' effects of technology are much more complex than Beck and Giddens suggest (see Chapter 11), I will also claim that their work remains faithful to certain 'right of reflection' that belongs to the idea of democracy (Derrida, 1994b).

Much of the recent literature on Beck and Giddens' work has criticized their respective accounts of reflexive subjectivity. The claims they have made for the emergence of new forms of democratic practice and political participation have been questioned on a number of different grounds: that their descriptions of the human subject are too disembodied and rationalistic; that they ignore the hermeneutic culture of everyday life; and that they are largely blind to the influence of gender and sexuality (Lupton, 1999). In general, then, the suggestion is that if we are properly to understand the politics of risk, we must shift our attention to the libidinal, hermeneutic and gender dynamics of the subject. Instead of attempting to specify how subjective reflexivity could transform the legal and political institutions of the state, we should focus on how that reflexivity is mediated, channelled and distributed through non-reflexive modes of experience.

Scott Lash, for example, argues that there is a fundamental difference between the kinds of experience which give rise to 'aesthetic reflexivity', and those which produce the moral and cognitive judgements described in Beck and Giddens' work. According to Lash, aesthetic reflexivity 'is rooted not in self-monitoring but in self-*interpretation*' (Lash, 1993, p. 8); and as such, belongs to a basic level of social experience that cannot be cognitively organized. The self-interpretive subject that Lash depicts in his essay, is guided by the precognitive dimensions of human sociality: the habituation of the faculties of sense and intuition (taste), the signs and symbols which form the collective unconscious. Modernity in its legislative sense therefore, is the imposition of a strict cognitive order upon this hermeneutic sphere: the determination to make the social world conform to the dictates of calculation and reflexivity. What is important here, is that for Lash, the very possibility of organizing the lifeworld through the cognitive demands of risk, presupposes a realm of aesthetic self-interpretation which can only be violently overcome by the demands of risk politics. In the end, Beck and Giddens' work perpetuates a certain Kantianism, in which the categories of legislation and cognition are presented as having rightful primacy over the aesthetic apprehension of self and other. This, for Lash, is inherently authoritarian. For in so far as cognitive reflexivity is extended to every aspect of the lifeworld, the capacity of the subject not to *judge*, but rather to respond *interpretively* to the other, is progressively reduced. The ultimate demand of modernity then, is for a rejuvenation of those aesthetic dispositions that give us a practical/interpretive sense of moral responsibility to others (*ibid.*, p. 18).

This account of 'aesthetic reflexivity', in common with much of the recent criticism of Beck and Giddens, overplays the hermeneutic dimension of social relations. The aesthetic self-interpretation that Lash presents as the other of reflexive self-monitoring, supposedly derives from a 'practical sense' of community that is prior to abstract cognition. This priority is identified as the source of an *interpretative* capacity, which is defined in terms of its responsibility to others. The increasing importance of risk assessment in the self-consciousness of social actors therefore, marks a fatal intrusion of instrumental reflexivity into the hermeneutic resources of the social. For in so far as risk assessment demands a calculative rather than an interpretative relationship to the lifeworld, it remains complicit with the forces of technocratic domination. This argument, however, gives rise to a specific set of issues concerning the relationship of self-consciousness to the technological conditions of its agency. One of the major themes of Derrida's work is the impossibility of disintricating the originary form of 'the human' from the economics of social, cultural and technological supplementation. From *Of Grammatology* onwards, he has maintained that there can be no determinate break between 'civilization' and 'techno-civilization', precisely because there is no possibility of presenting the conditions under which human consciousness would have affected itself as a pure, non-technicized spontaneity. Prosthesis, in other words, belongs to human consciousness even in its most primitive differentiations from nature (Beardsworth, 1998, p. 79). I will examine these arguments more carefully in Chapter 11. However, it is already possible to discern something of the political significance of Derrida's claims about the 'originary technicity' of consciousness. For if it is the case that there is no 'practical sense' of community that is *prior* to technological supplementation, and if the evolution of our technicized consciousness is co-present with the 'hermeneutic' resources of identity, then our responsibilities to the other cannot be referred to what Lash understands as the originary conditions of sociality. The ethical and political reflexivity of human consciousness, in other words, must struggle with the risks of technology from within its own technological intensification, dispersal and spectralization.

Beck and Gidden's work has, in different ways, attempted to theorize the impact of modernity on the ethical resources of human beings, and to situate questions of political responsibility within the techno-scientific constitution of the present. In Beck's work, critical science and the politics of risk are organized around a speculative idea of nature, in which the fate of organic life becomes the planetary concern of human consciousness (Beck, 1996a, p. 74). For Giddens, on the other hand, the increasingly complex interlacing of trust, care and responsibility which results from the spread of expert systems, revitalizes existential questions of being and authenticity: of 'how existence itself should be grasped and lived' (Giddens, 1997b, p. 224). The question that emerges from their respective projects then, concerns the relationship between normative sociology and the resources of philosophical reason. For in so far as Beck and Giddens both present the consequences of risk in terms of a phenomenology of human self-consciousness, we are returned to the fundamental questions raised by modernity and modernization: what remains of the regulative power of nature? what will replace the securities of tradition? how is the private, individuated subject related to the collective demands of my social existence?

Postmodernist thought sets a number of challenges to Beck and Giddens' work on reflexive modernization. Baudrillard's account of simulation, for example, bears directly upon Beck's assumption of the representative powers of the media (Baudrillard, 1996, pp. 207–19), and Bauman's account of the limits of reflexivity maintains that both Beck and Giddens do no more than modify the demands of technocratic control (Bauman, 1993, pp. 199–209). I will argue, however, that although there are difficulties with their respective theories of risk, Beck and Giddens do at least attempt to specify the relationship between self-reflection and the uncertainty that has become characteristic of our historical present. We will see in a moment that deconstruction demands careful attention to this uncertainty, and to the cultural and ideological resources through which it is mediated. For Derrida, the most pressing effects of our technological development (the simulation of the real in the media, the globalization of communications systems, the genetic manipulation of human beings) refer both to philosophical ideals of friendship, responsibility and cosmopolitanism, and to the Marxist dynamics of inequality, exclusion and exploitation. In so far as we must judge these effects from within the disjointed economy of the present, therefore, we are faced with the stricture of having to respond to ecological risks as they repeat, intensify or perhaps exceed the old Marxist dynamics of world capitalism. It is this complexity, I will argue, that escapes the logic of both Beck and Giddens' accounts of risk. For in so far as it is impossible to schematize the disjuncture of our historical present through the unfolding of techno-scientific necessity, we, as human beings, are responsible to a future whose dispersal and reintegration of 'the human' remain disturbingly unforeseeable (Derrida, 1994, p. xix). I will return to this in Chapters 11 and 12.

3

Baudrillard: Media and Simulation

In the Introduction I attempted to specify the terms through which modernist critical theory has engaged with the claims of postmodernism. I argued that it is possible to discern a number of common features in Jürgen Habermas, David Harvey and Frederic Jameson's accounts of the emergence and development of postmodernist thought: namely, the aesthetcization of social and economic relations; the loss of any structural, epistemic or ontological determination of truth; the collapse of moral and ethical criteria into an undecidable play relativity; and the reduction of the political to a mere simulation of collective responsibility. I also claimed that this representation is characterized by a dismissiveness which is both instructive and theoretically unsatisfactory – avoiding, as it does, any detailed engagement with the different strands of the postmodernist 'genre'. There is, however, a sense in which Baudrillard's account of simulation is a determined and consistent attempt to think through the consequences of exactly these effects. His remarks on the media, on the masses and on the 'hyperreality' of social relations, demand that theory abandon any pretence of disclosing authentic or legitimate processes of social integration. For in so far as the digitization of communications systems and the technological reproduction of images has deprived 'the social' of its established system of referents (the essential wants, needs and responsibilities of human beings), it is no longer reasonable to assume *any* relationship between the enactment of the political and the sovereignty of the human will – no matter how this is conceived.

Before proceeding to examine the consequences that Baudrillard draws from this collapse of truth and meaning, however, I need to make a few introductory remarks about his concept of simulation. The collection of essays published in 1999 as *Simulacra and Simulation*, marks the point at which Baudrillard begins to address the consequences of telematic and informatic technologies. The most extended discussion of the fate of the image under the conditions of postmodernity is given in the initial essay, 'The procession of simulacra'. The essay is, I think, best understood as a kind of anti-genealogy, in which the relationship of the image (the signifier) to what is represented (the signified, or referent) is conceived purely in terms of its technological reproduction. At the beginning of the essay, Baudrillard specifies the stages through which the image passes from referentiality into simulation (Baudrillard, 1999, p. 6):

it is a reflection of a profound reality;
it masks and denatures a profound reality;
it masks the absence of a profound reality;
it has no relation to any reality whatsoever: it is its own pure simulacrum.

The original designation of the relationship between the image and reality is given through religious iconography. God, as the universal Being, is the agent who gives truth and authenticity to the production of devotional art. Yet even this theological designation of the sign has its own particular technology. The 'visible machinery of icons' through which the reality of God is expressed, initiates a self-referentiality of signs which exceeds every transcendental determination of His being (Baudrillard, 1999, p. 4). Immediately the image comes to stand in for the word, the law and the being of God, then His transcendence is lost to the infinite refraction of images. Iconography therefore, gives rise to a fundamental questioning of the status of the image and its relationship to the real. This questioning, according to Baudrillard, takes the form of a negative critique of the image – a critique which attempts to set out the resources and techniques through which representation 'masks and denatures' reality. Obviously the most consistent and influential account of the re-presentational power of image is set out in Marx's critique of ideology. For in so far as the 'truth' of capital – its alienation, emiseration and deskilling of productive humanity – is concealed in the legitimizing functions of art, the reproduction of culture becomes an immediate concern of revolutionary politics. I will return to this relationship in Chapter 7.

What is of particular importance here, is that for Baudrillard, the history of the social must be understood as an 'operationalization' of signs which progressively threatens the reality of the referent. Marxism, as we will see later, has continued to theorize the relationship between the technological production of images and the constitution of mass culture, in terms of a 'denaturing' misrecognition of identity and domination. Yet for Baudrillard, this undertaking fails to theorize adequately the effects of telematic and communications technologies on the status of the real. For in so far as the Marxist critique of culture remains tied to the logic of 'second order simulation' (expounding the relationship between the structural conditions of exploitation and their collective misrecognition), it is unable to register the dynamics of simulation that arise from these technologies. Thus Baudrillard's account of a 'transeconomic' capitalism, in which exploitation and expenditure have exceeded all ethical limitations, will attempt to specify the end of the dialectic between alienated humanity and 'objective' historical necessity (Baudrillard, 1995a, pp. 26–35).

Baudrillard specifies two further stages in the transformation of the image: its masking of 'the absence of a profound reality', and finally the total loss of reference to the real in which the image becomes 'its own pure simulacrum' (Baudrillard, 1999, p. 6). In the first instance, simulation arises as a response to the increasing spectralization of social, economic and political reality. The two examples of this 'third order' simulation which

Baudrillard offers are the Watergate affair and Disneyland. His account of Watergate contends that the scandal staged by the media was actually an attempt to keep the collapse of the political within a 'conventional field of perspective' (*ibid.*, p. 16). By campaigning for Richard Nixon's impeachment, in other words, the media did no more than rejuvenate the myth of a state politics whose purposes are independent of the amorality of capitalism. Similarly, the childishness and infantilism of Disneyland functions as a huge 'deterrence machine', designed to place the increasing childishness and infantilism of American culture into some kind of relief. As Baudrillard puts it:

> Disneyland is presented as imaginary in order to make us believe that the rest is real, whereas all of Los Angeles and the America that surrounds it are no longer real, but belong to the hyperreal order and to the order of simulation. (*ibid.*, p. 12)

Both Watergate and Disneyland function as third-order simulacra, whose purpose is to conceal the collapse of the real (truth, meaning, value) into a monstrously self-perpetuating play of simulations. It is no longer simply a question of false representation and misrecognition (ideology), but rather of 'saving the reality principle' (*ibid.*, p. 13).

For Baudrillard, then, the very necessity of the deterrence functions performed by third-order simulacra, signifies the collapse of the real into pure simulation. Telematic and informatic technologies have reached a level of development in which 'the real' (the contingent, the unpredictable, the Other) has been entirely displaced by its simulacra. Sex, for example, has ceased to be about the Freudian dynamics of sexual difference (the pain, anxiety and *jouissance* of the ontogenetic schism which underlies the rational life of humanity), and is forced to conform to the universal standards of communicative performance. It becomes 'a sort of total promiscuity', in which desire is conducted along thoroughly functional, operational and capitalized channels of communication (Baudrillard, 1995a, p. 66). Thus it is that the real becomes hyperreal. For in so far as the reality of sex or class or race has been taken up into the total refraction of signs, it has ceased to exist independently of its technological reproduction. What this means is that the social system has shifted into a kind of hyperfunctionality, whose momentum is sustained by the complete exchangeability of its effects. Work and sex (the masculine and the feminine, the bourgeois and the proletarian, the mother and the citizen) have ceased to be possible elements of an ethical sociality. (See, for example, Hegel's account of the transition from the 'natural' sexual differentiation of the family, to the abstract economic relations of civil society (Hegel, 1967b, p. 121).) Each is made to function in terms of a universal transparency, in which the delimitations of public and private which marked their political differentiation have been erased.

What is important here, is that for Baudrillard, the 'ecstatic' communication of signs has become a total principle: nothing contingent, antagonistic or transcendent can intervene in the universal exchangeability through which sex, capital, politics and culture are hyperrealized. This then, is what Rex Butler has referred to as the paradox of the sign: for 'in so far as the copy completely resembles the original, it is no longer a copy but another original' (Butler, 1999, p. 14). Simulation, in other words, produces its fatal effects through the *hyperrealization* of the social: for once the significatory codes of class, gender, sexuality and ethnicity have become independent of their referents (that is, perfected copies of an irrecoverable reality), all that remains is the circulation of exchangeable models of interpretation, the 'weightlessness' of the hyperreal (Baudrillard, 1999, p. 6).

The concept of simulation therefore, appears to offer substantial evidence of a nihilistic tendency in Baudrillard's work. Indeed, it seems as if we would be hard pressed to defend him against the accusations that Habermas, Harvey and Jameson have levelled against postmodernist thought in general. Yet while I do have reservations about his arguments, especially his account of the end of history and the fate of the political (see Chapter 10), there does remain an obligation to read Baudrillard 'in his own terms' (Butler, 1999, pp. 1–22). For while it may turn out be the case that he overplays the virtualizing effects of the sign, such a judgement requires that we engage with the economy of simulation – that is, with its reconfiguration of the ethical and political space of modernity.

In his essay 'The masses: the implosion of the social in the media', Baudrillard sets out the political consequences of total simulation. He argues that new media technologies do not revitalize the dialogical potential of the public sphere; for once they reach a certain level of saturation, the reflective citizen is overtaken by a constant flow of heterogeneous, escalatory and reversible simulacra. The major consequence of this simulation of reality has, according to Baudrillard, been to abolish any reflexive relationship between the citizen, considered as the addressee of social and political norms, and the representative institutions of liberal democracy (Baudrillard, 1996, p. 214). For in so far as the masses are constantly solicited by the simulacra of sex, beauty, love, morality and suffering, they have become the condition *and the failure* of the social: they both conduct and short-circuit the economy of pure, frictionless simulation through which the social has been hyperrealized. Thus:

> There is and there always will be major difficulties in analysing the media and the whole sphere of information through the traditional categories of the philosophy of the subject: will, representation, choice, liberty, deliberation, knowledge, and desire. For it is quite obvious that they are absolutely contradicted by the media: that the subject is absolutely alienated in its sovereignty. (Baudrillard, 1996, p. 214)

The masses, in other words, are both engaged by the simulacra of communication and disbelieving of them; they both conduct and short-circuit the operational modalities that precipitate the hyperreality of the system.

Baudrillard's critique of the media is extensive and raises important questions about the fate of the public sphere in the epoch of telematic communication. His contention is that the media have absorbed every point of contradiction between opposites (the bourgeois and the proletarian, the masculine and the feminine, the erotic and the obscene, the ugly and the beautiful), and that consequently the reproduction of the social has become a 'precession' of reversible, recyclable simulations. In *Fatal Strategies*, he cites the collapse of the aesthetic into fashion as the prima facie example of how simulation effaces the dialectical logic of the social. For where the rhythm of innovation becomes so rapid that there can be no reflexive communication between the poles of 'beauty' and 'ugliness', both are absorbed into a play of simulacra where the relationship between aesthetics and moral recognition is completely unhinged (Baudrillard, 1996, p. 192). The operational codes inscribed in the hyperreality of fashion, consumerism, promiscuity and pornography, in other words, are entirely virtual; and so the political significance of the 'the masses' is always limited by their technological reproduction. Thus, Baudrillard's understanding of Marshall McLuhan's argument that in telematic media the message becomes confused with its technological mode of organization (McLuhan, 1964, pp. 3–23), should be read against the background of this relationship between the masses and the media. For as the system becomes increasingly evacuated of meaning, so the media redouble their production of the signs of political engagement – the 'third order' simulations of morality and responsibility through which the masses are constantly solicited.

Much of Baudrillard's later writing is concerned with remarking the unforeseen consequences that arise from the operational programming of the social: the 'hyperconformity' of the masses, the rise of terrorism and the proliferation of 'extreme phenomena' (AIDS, cancer, drugs). His abandonment of traditional forms of ethical and political recognition is informed by a pursuit of those simulacra that arise *without will or deliberation* from the collapse of social meaning. This concern with the historical evolution of the masses is certainly not an attempt to designate a symbolic community or a body of active resistance. Rather, as 'the shadow cast by power' (Baudrillard, 1983, p. 48), they are conceived as a kind of negative energy that accompanies every production of meaning. And so when Baudrillard claims that '[t]he masses are a stronger medium than the media' (*ibid.*, p. 44), his intention is to mark their existence as an 'internal limit' to the hyperreality of the system. This structural position of the masses is important. We have seen that for Baudrillard the media have reduced the political to a play of refracted appearances and ephemeral attachments, and that it is consequently unreasonable to appeal to the reflexive or deliberative powers of 'the public'. *In the Shadow of the Silent Majorities*, for example, cites the relationship which has grown up between the masses and public heath provision. What emerges from this relationship is not a reflexive awareness of the self/body as an object of care and responsibility (see Giddens, 1997b, pp. 217–20), but rather an insatiable demand for more treatment, more doctors and more drugs. The masses, in other words, respond to their medicalization with a kind of 'hyperconformity' to the operational reproduction of health. This, of course, is not a moment of deliberated political resistance. Yet the fact that it is produced as a 'reversion' of the system means that it is an unavoidable challenge to the logic of simulation (Baudrillard, 1983, p. 46). If there is a morality which is appropriate to the virtualization of the social, this consists in the stricture of following the play of simulation and hyper-simulation through which the system expands itself. Indeed, Baudrillard's discussion of 'prophylaxis and virulence' in *The Transparency of Evil*, goes so far as to risk invoking extreme phenomena like AIDS, cancer, computer viruses and crack addiction as effects which ultimately save us from the catastrophe of total functionality (Baudrillard, 1995a, p. 67).

Clearly, then, the economics of simulation are far more complex than a cursory examination of Baudrillard's work might suggest. When he claims that simulation has become 'a programmatic, metastable, perfectly de-scriptive machine that offers all the signs of the real and short-circuits all its vicissitudes' (Baudrillard, 1999, p. 2), he is not arguing simply that reality has disappeared into its simulacra. Rather, his claim is that we must understand the production and refraction of those simulacra as a process which has become the *condition of the appearance of the real*. Baudrillard makes it clear that the development of the simulacrum begins with the 'truth' of iconography, its infinite deferral of the reality of God. The ancient 'machinery of icons', in other words, had already instituted a certain economy of simulation – one in which the truth of the referent (the being of God) depended upon the truth of its simulacra (the unutterable truth that there is only refraction, deferral, circulation). What proceeds from this economy, we have seen, is a development of re-presentation in which the image becomes increasingly free from the constraints of referentiality. The transition from iconography to ideology is marked by the dissimulation of the real, and the *absence of reality* inscribed in the relationship between third and fourth order simulacra, marks the 'perfec-tion' of the real through its operational encoding. Sex, work, beauty, love, all become hyperreal; participating in the expansion of the system through their endless reversibility and exchangeability. In the end, history itself is taken up into this precession of simulacra. The events which have informed our understanding of political reality – the October Revolution, the rise of Nazism, Vietnam, Paris '68 – return as ciphers of a scandalous but infinitely redeemable past. For whatever happens now, within our hyperfunctional present, lays claim to the *finality* of violence, revolution or progress (Baudrillard, 1995b, p. 13). The acts of terrorism, for example, that Baudrillard conceives as the counterpart of an increasingly 'total' logic of simulation, are presented in the media as *the* most reprehensible violence; reprehensible because it seems to resist all attempts to bring it into the realm of sense and meaning. The fall of the Berlin Wall and the lifting of the Iron Curtain, on the other hand, appear as the 'true' popular revolution and the triumph of social democracy.

If we are to understand Baudrillard as a moralist, and perhaps to understand the limits of his moralism, we will need to look in more detail at his later writing (from *Simulacra and Simulation* to the present). *In the Shadow of the Silent Majorities* presents a thorough reconfiguration of Adorno Horkheimer's culture industry thesis, in which Baudrillard specifies the difference between the ideological 'denaturing' of the real and its collapse into pure simulation. According to his argument, the relationship between the masses and the production of mass culture is no longer organized in terms of reification of social relations. If the masses do have a political significance, this would lie not in their recognition of the sources of their deception (the axis of kitsch culture, mass media and corporate capital), but rather in their hyperconformity and their resistance to enlightenment. The evaluation of science, technology and risk in Chapter 11, also raises questions about the political functions of the media. Both Ulrich Beck and Anthony Giddens, in different ways, present the dynamics of 'reflexive modernity' as producing a newly communicative public sphere. Beck's account of risk society, for example, assumes that the media will participate more and more fully in the monitoring of risks, and that consequently the public sphere will become the site of an active contestation between technological progress and ecological responsibility. This, however, assumes that the technological organization of communication is essentially *communicative* – an assumption that, for Baudrillard, is extremely dubious.

Chapter 13 raises two issues that are treated in some detail in Baudrillard's later writing: the end of history and the relationship of Western to non-Western cultures. His approach to these issues, as we will see, demands that we understand their dynamics in terms of the effects of global communications technologies. Western culture, according to Baudrillard, has precipitated its ideals of truth, beauty and community into a play of exchangeable representations or simulacra; and so the Western experience has become one of weightlessness and lack of reality rather than progress and moral enlightenment. As this loss of the real becomes ever more acute, the west begins to look to other cultures, and to its own history, to make good its deficits of meaning. In the second instance, there emerges a pernicious fascination with the past, or more specifically with those events in which Western culture has demonstrated its capacity to 'act', to determine itself. And so, for example, our present fascination with representing the Holocaust, takes the form of a nostalgia for a time when events were more real and ethically clear cut (Baudrillard, 1995a, pp. 89–99). The relationships through which the west performs its moral obligations to other cultures, however, are no more redemptive. For Baudrillard, the wars, famines and plagues that are endlessly repeated in the 'developing world', become part of the general economy of simulation; for in so far as the media present them as temporary demands on our attention, they provide an opportunity for us to 'feel guilty', and to discharge our guilt in the 'moving spectacle' of charitable donations and media events (Baudrillard, 1995b, p. 67).

There is, of course, an ironic edge to Baudrillard's remarks upon the fate of modernity. Indeed, he demands that his theory of simulation be understood as a provocation; as an ironic posture which seeks decisive responses from every 'legitimate' simulacra of the real. As he put it in an interview with Sylvere Lotringer:

> All theory can do is be rigorous enough to cut itself off from any system of reference, so that it will at least be current on the scale of what it wishes to describe. (Baudrillard, 1993, p. 125)

The morality of this approach would consist in forcing the advocates of any given system of reference (genetic technologies, for example) to stipulate the ultimate grounds of their legitimacy. For even though the logic of simulation has, according to Baudrillard, become total, the art of provoking its most catastrophic possibilities remains possible (*ibid.*, p. 127). In the end, however, I think it is necessary to go beyond the limits of 'reading Baudrillard in his own terms' (Butler, 1999, pp. 1–22). For while I would agree that much of the criticism of his work has been almost wilfully misguided, I also want to claim that the economics of simulation tends to overplay the 'massifying' effects of media technologies, and to neglect the rights and obligations of reflection that arise from those effects. Following the logic of Derrida's political writings, I will argue that if we are to salvage a meaningful conception of politics from the virtualizing powers of informatic technologies, we need to pay careful attention to his deconstruction of the relations between culture, humanity and technicity. I will examine Derrida's arguments in Chapter 5.

4

Lyotard and Jameson: Postmodernism and the Aesthetic

Clearly there is a close relationship between what has become known as 'postmodernism' and the aesthetic dimension of experience. Indeed, much of the criticism of postmodernist theory has focused on what seems to be a determination to elevate the playful, the ludic and the poetic above the ethical and political necessities of late modernity. Habermas, we have seen, claims that this splitting-off of aesthetic experience from the norms of communicative action established in the lifeworld, contributes to a general state of political disaffection and disempowerment. The ascendancy of an avant-gardist art which bears little relation to everyday experience is seen as alienating the aesthetic from the contradictions (between instrumental and communicative rationality, subjective autonomy and system necessity) in which it originates, and which it ought to reflect. Such an art, according to Habermas, is complicit with a French neo-conservative strand of postmodernist thought, in which the anti-modern forces of Being and the Will to Power are opposed to the communicative potential of the public sphere. Thus Bataille, Foucault and Derrida are all accused of 'remove[ing] into the sphere of the far-away and the archaic the spontaneous powers of imagination, self-experience and emotion' (Foster, 1985, p. 14).

David Harvey, in *The Condition of Postmodernity*, presents another version of the de-moralizing, de-politicizing effects of postmodernist aestheticism. His argument is that the turn to aesthetic spontaneity that is apparent in postmodern critiques of structural and economic necessity, should be conceived as a modification of the dynamical processes of capital. Thus, where 'Fordist modernity' offers stable markets, a fixed configuration of economic and political power and a secure techno-scientific rationality, 'postmodern flexibility' is characterized by its virtualization of relations of production: 'fictitious capital, images, ephemerality, chance, and flexibility in production techniques, labour markets and consumption niches' (Harvey, 1999, p. 339). Harvey's claim is that the opposition between modernist and postmodernist accounts of politics, economics and normative legitimacy, should be conceived in terms of their relative advantages and disadvantages at any given time. In the end, there is little point in pursuing debates about whether or not there has been a transition from modernity to postmodernity. For a historically grounded (i.e. Marxist) account of the relationship between cultural and economic production, demands that we recognize that the extent to which a particular economy has adopted the ideology of Fordism or flexible postmodernism 'will vary from time to time ... depending on which configuration is profitable and which is not' (*ibid.*, p. 344). The aesthetic turn of the postmodernists therefore, remains an adaptive strategy of the mode of production: a cultural form whose transformations of economic conformity and political obedience belong to the spatial and temporal condensations produced by the mode of production.

In the Introduction I claimed that Habermas and Harvey's accounts of postmodern aestheticism follow a similar logic. Basically, this logic proceeds from the establishment of certain essential characteristics of modernity (the communicative pragmatics of the public sphere, the cultural and economic mutability of capital), to the establishment of essential standards of normative and theoretical evaluation. I also claimed that Fredric Jameson's account of the relationship between postmodern culture and late capitalism, exemplifies this evaluative logic. His critique of postmodern art, literature, architecture and film is concerned to show that despite their reflection of fundamental changes in the mode of production (the end of 'organized' capitalism, the globalization of the labour market), they remain ideological forms, whose true significance lies in their misrepresentation of the relationship between 'capital' and new 'aestheticized' forms of work, satisfaction and desire. In the end, the promise of postmodern culture to 'get rid of whatever you find confining, unsatisfying or boring about the modern' (Jameson, 1995, p. xiv), is implicated in the production of 'new people' who are capable of functioning after the demise of traditional forms of national and class solidarity. These people, according to Jameson, are adaptable to rapidly changing patterns of employment, have little attachment to any particular occupation or occupational group, and are highly attuned to the aesthetic-ization of public and private space. The distracted subjectivity that emerges as the counterpart of postmodern culture therefore, demands a careful socio-historical analysis. For Jameson, the social and economic changes that mark the emergence of late capitalism, do not absolve us from the responsibilities of a materialist critique of culture. The fact that the media produce an increasingly 'virtual' experience, and that traditional forms of class and national identity seem to have become little more than simulacra, should refer us to the relationship between the play of appearances and the development of the mode of production:

> Historical reconstruction ... the abstraction from the 'blooming, buzzing confusion' of immediacy, was always a radical intervention in the promise of resistance to its blind fatalities. (Jameson, 1998, p. 35)

Ultimately, the postmodernist attempt to valorize the feelings of diversity, limitlessness and evanescence that accompany the disembedding of human subjects from their established forms of community and recognition, is understood as a determination to have done with the political antagonisms of the mode of production. For Jameson, as long as postmodernism theory refuses to recognize the relationship between the massification of culture, the hyperextension of aesthetic sensibility, and the global organization of capital, it remains an ideology of abstract difference and self-serving individualism.

I will argue later, particularly in Chapter 6, that one of the major difficulties with Jameson's *Postmodernism* is a tendency to neglect the detail of what he calls 'postmodernism theory'. This is particularly apparent in his summation of Lyotard's writing as the 'embattled endorsement of the supreme value of aesthetic innovation' (Jameson, 1995, p. 61). For in so far as he shows little interest in the reading of Kant's *Critique of Aesthetic Judgement* which informs much of Lyotard's later work, he avoids engaging with the ethical and political ideas he has developed since the publication of *Just Gaming* (*Au Just*) and *The Differend*. Before turning to Lyotard's later writings, however, I want to take a more general look at what is at stake in Kant's account of aesthetic judgement.

In terms of the development of Kant's philosophy, the *Critique of Aesthetic Judgement* comes after his establishment of the principles of theoretical knowledge and moral autonomy (Kant, 1982a and 1993). It is divided into two parts: 'The analytic of the beautiful' and 'The analytic of the sublime'. In the first of these, Kant attempts to set out the a priori conditions of the judgement of taste – the estimation of an object or work of art as beautiful. For Kant, this particular judgement is 'independent of all interest' (Kant, 1982b, p. 42), presents itself as a demand for the assent of all men (*ibid.*, p. 50), and follows not from the theoretical cognition of the object, but from a certain harmony of the faculties of understanding and intuition (*ibid.*, p. 72). The feeling of delight which arises from the contemplation of a beautiful object, in other words, immediately refers my judgement to the intelligibility of nature, and to a 'common sense' of the aesthetic possessed by all rational beings. Thus, in so far as I am moved to apply the *concept* of the beautiful to those objects which produce in me the feeling of pure delight, I can be said to be responding to a finality in nature which exceeds the mere excitation of my sensory interest. Both my disinterested pleasure in the beautiful and the pure desire I experience in the moral law therefore, are related to what is literally unrepresentable: the 'supersensible' conditions of unity and finality which cannot be schematized by the understanding. According to Kant, however, the capacity for a reflective estimation of beauty remains a distinctive kind of apprehension. Unlike the moral law, the feelings of pleasure that result from aesthetic judgement give pleasure independently of *all* interest, and arise only after *reflection* upon their object. They also arise from the *subjective* configuration of the cognitive faculties (the feeling of harmony between intuition and understanding, the reflection involved in judging an object to be an expression of the beautiful as such), rather than from an *objective* necessity of the kind determined by the categorical imperative (*ibid.*, p. 224). In the end, Kant insists that our 'common sense' of taste – as a feeling of delight that is independent of all sensuous interest – 'makes the transition from the charm of sense to habitual moral interest possible without too violent a leap' (*ibid.*, p. 225). For in so far as the faculty of taste allows us to recognize that the realm of sense is not arranged simply for our gratification, we come to recognize beauty as the 'symbol' of the moral law.

The second part of the *Critique of Aesthetic Judgement*, 'The analytic of the sublime', is again concerned with nature as finality – although this time, the feelings provoked are disturbing rather than pleasurable, and are beyond the regulative organization of taste. For Kant, the subject's encounter with the awesome magnitudes – the 'absolutely great' – through which nature signifies its totality, produces a sense of 'terror' at the loss of the serial time which is the imagination's a priori principle. The immediate (or 'reproductive') synthesis of magnitudes which reason demands of imagination in the presence of the sublime, does violence to the successive ('compositional') time that is the condition of particular intuitions. Yet for Kant, this feeling of terror is not unmixed; for it is simultaneous with a sense of 'exultation' in reason's capacity to conceive of nature as an intelligible, self-determining totality. Imagination, in other words, experiences terror at its loss of reproductive intuition, for serial time – the transcendental principle attributed to imagination in the first *Critique* – is threatened by the sublime simultaneity of compositional magnitudes. Reason, on the other hand, feels a certain exultation in the presence of the finality of nature – an exultation which, for Kant, again refers the autonomy of rational beings beyond mere sensory interest.

The 'negative pleasure' described in 'the analytic of the sublime' then, is produced through the simultaneous necessity and impossibility of representing ideas of reason in the faculty of the imagination. This unrepresentability presupposes the separation of reason and imagination which Kant attempted to validate in the first and second *Critiques*. According to the former, imagination is the condition of mathematical and geometrical truths; of propositions about quantity, relation and proportion that remain true independently of empirical experience. The faculty of reason, whose legislative necessity Kant expounds in the *Critique of Practical Reason*, on the other hand, is concerned with the concept of autonomy as pure, unrestricted self-determination. As such, Kant's moral will is bound to the self-consistency of the categorical imperative, and must respect the idea of humanity which is inscribed in each particular obligation. In 'The analytic of the sublime', this separation of reason and imagination produces a feeling of 'pleasure-displeasure' (a simultaneous 'pleasure' in possessing a faculty of ideas and displeasure at not being able to represent them) which is a result of the imagination's inability to find an analogue for the idea of totality (Kant, 1982b, p. 119). For Kant, however, this subjective disordering of the faculties – the straining of the imagination after the idea of finality – functions as a 'representation of the object as subjectively final' (*ibid.*, p. 121). The fact that we are disturbed by the power or immensity of nature, in other words, means that we can legitimately regard the feeling of 'pleasure-displeasure' experienced in the presence of the sublime, as schematizing the concept of finality.

> In this capacity, it [imagination] is a might enabling us to assert our independence as against the influence of nature, to degrade what is great in the respect of the latter to the level of what is little, and thus to locate the absolutely great in the proper estate of the subject. (*ibid.*)

The ultimate purpose, or finality, of our cognitive faculties therefore, is disclosed through the dynamic of the sublime. For in so far as the discordant-accord of reason and imagination is not simply assumed but *engendered* in the subject, we must recognize that judgements of sublimity refer to a spontaneously produced independence from the merely sensible. Thus for Kant, the 'common sense' of the sublime possessed by all human beings, is inseparable from their historical destiny: the achievement of a culture in which the moral law is experienced in its pure practical necessity. The sublime, in other words, prepares 'us ourselves for the advent of the moral law' (Deleuze, 1985, p. 52).

In his *Kant's Critical Philosophy*, Gilles Deleuze provides a precise account of the importance of judgement to the architectonic of Kant's system. As examples of reflective evaluation, he argues that the analytics of the beautiful and the sublime disclose the 'art', or 'skill', of judgement as necessary to every transcendental faculty. In the light of the dynamical relations between understanding, imagination and reason set out in the *Critique of Aesthetic Judgement*, we are able to see that even determining judgements of the kind 'this is a house', require some level of deliberation. Kant's account of the 'Schematism of principles' makes it clear that to have a concept of something is not the same as being able to apply it; and that consequently, a deliberative activity of the mind is required for such an application (Kant, 1982a, pp. 181–7). The same is true of the moral law. For in order to conform one's action to its demands, one must first have reference to the categorical imperative. In the case of aesthetic judgements this deliberative activity is no longer hidden: the faculty of judgement 'expresses *a free and indeterminate accord* between all the faculties' (Deleuze, 1995, p. 60). The art of judgement, as it is expressed in proceeding from the manifold of sense to the concept of nature, in other words, manifests the ultimately moral configuration of the faculties. For in so far as aesthetic judgements transcend the causal-phenomenal modalities of being, they register the autonomy of the subject from serial-rational organization of space, time and community, and continue to enlarge the concept of nature beyond the bounds of determinate cognition (*ibid.*).

In his essay 'Judiciousness in dispute, or Kant after Marx', Lyotard claims that:

> What forbids any 'return' on our part to Kant is capital, or the power of indifference. Marx himself is still a name around which many *differends* have arisen, and which still provokes material for litigation and vengeance. (Lyotard, 1991a, p. 352)

In the lengthy discussion which precedes this remark, Lyotard sets out what he understands as the regulative teleology governing Kant's three *Critiques*. For Kant, we have seen that the moral finality of rational intelligence is marked by an immanent accord of the faculties of reason, understanding and imagination. Thus, in the *Critique of Aesthetic Judgement*, the harmony of imagination and understanding produced in the judgement of the beautiful, allows a symbolic figuration of the moral law. For on reflection, the feelings of pleasure and respect occasioned by both moral and aesthetic apprehension exhibit the same formal characteristics: immediacy, disinterestedness, freedom and universality. Even the judgement of the sublime, which proceeds from the radical heterogeneity of reason (whose concepts are, 'in a literal sense', unrepresentable) and imagination, presupposes a logic of exchangeability between faculties. For in so far as the feelings of agitation experienced by the subject are conceived as schematizing the concept of nature, it remains the case that those feelings have already been subordinated to the immanent unity of the laws of nature and the laws of freedom (*ibid.*, p. 238). Now, for Lyotard, what remains interesting about Kant's presentation of the sublime is the fact that the sense of agitation experienced through the power and magnitude of nature, comes very close to transgressing the moral finality of his philosophy. The subject, as he or she is confronted with the spectacle of nature, must judge its sublimity on the basis of feelings of disconcertion and disorientation. These feelings, we have seen, register a *disparate accord* of reason and imagination, in which the latter, through its overextension, comes to schematize the concept of an intelligible nature. Yet for Lyotard, the spontaneity (freedom) which Kant attributes to the relationship between reason and imagination, is crucially limited by an implicit demand that ' [t]he passage from one to the other must be possible ... with injury to none' (*ibid.*). The feelings of loss and bereavement experienced in the sublime, in other words, are always able to return to the finality which reason has discerned in nature – and thereby discharge the *heterogeneity* of thinking and feeling which threatens the moral finality of human beings.

For Lyotard, the difference between the rules governing the operations of reason and imagination is such that they must be conceived as radically incommensurable. The faculty of reason is concerned with speculative ideas (freedom, nature, humanity); the imagination is concerned with the spatial configuration of phenomenal experience. Each has its own particular standards of truth, validity and necessity. Thus, the powerful sensations that Kant describes in the 'Analytic of the sublime', immediately provoke a questioning of the rules through which imagination is made subject to reason's 'speculative' concept of nature. As Lyotard puts it:

> If we do away with this overly consoling Idea [of nature], we are left with the naked convulsions of *differends*. (Lyotard, 1991a, p. 341)

The sensations associated with the Kantian sublime, in other words, arise from the impossibility of reconciling the generic demands of reason and imagination. And so what is experienced by the critical subject is originally a sense of privation – of not being able to apply the principles of reason without immediately doing violence to the integrity of sense.

The transaction between sense and reason described in the 'Analytic of the sublime', Lyotard has argued, discloses a general economy of feeling, spontaneity and judgement which goes beyond the jurisdiction of the Kantian Idea. We cannot, in other words, refer the feeling of being 'disarmed' by particular events – the sense of *is it happening, is it possible* – to the unifying finality of nature. Now, we have seen that 'Judiciousness in dispute' claims that 'what forbids any 'return' on our part to Kant is capital, or the power of indifference'. For Lyotard, the relationship between capital and techno-scientific control should be understood as having accelerated the production of reality to the point where its lack of presence has become the defining characteristic of modernity. The processes of shattering and innovation that are implicit in the very idea of the modern, in other words, constantly increase the generic discourses through which the real is circulated and contested (Lyotard, 1991b, p. 77). Yet it must be understood that this multiplication of difference is the counterpart of the *indifference* of capital – its subordination of heterogeneous rules of formation, presentation and success to the temporal economy of exchange (Lyotard, 1988, p. 173). Avant-gardist art for example, whose stakes ought to be the registration of what is silenced in the economic genre, tends to be drawn into a kind of collusion with capital. For instead of attempting to frame a visual, plastic, literary or kinesthetic language for what goes unphrased in the instantaneity of exchange (the indigenous, the non-white, the non-rational, the non-human), it lapses into formulaic reproduction shock effects (Lyotard, 1991a, p. 210).

At the conclusion of *The Differend* however, Lyotard remarks that:

> The only insurmountable obstacle that the hegemony of the economic genre comes up against is the heterogeneity of phrase regimens and genres of discourse. This is because there is not 'language' and 'Being', but occurrences. (Lyotard, 1988, p. 181)

The 'closure' of the system described in Lyotard's account of economic necessity, in other words, is precisely what gives rise to *differends* – moments of conflict which lack any 'rule of judgement applicable to [heterogeneous] arguments' (*ibid.*, p. xi).[1] Simply by imposing the logic of temporal economy, capital precipitates conflicts and disputes that it can settle only in its own terms (financial compensation, welfare, cultural and educational initiatives). Each particular case therefore gives rise to a victim, or victims, who are denied a language in which to express the wrong (*tort*) which is done to them. For even where the legal and political institutions of social democracy *do* recognize the damage (*dommage*) incurred by the plaintiff, this recognition is always made under the chairmanship of legal-rational authority (in much the same way as Kant's judgement of the sublime remained under the chairmanship of the Idea). Thus, the *differends* that arise from the expansion of the economic genre, await expressions which are beyond the juridical categories of equity and recompense inscribed in the legal system. Their demand is always that of an *event* which cannot be included in any established doctrine of categories, and which places 'us' (mobile, dispersed, situated human beings) under an obligation to phrase what is without language.

It is this obligation to the *differend*, and to the feelings of agitation and disquiet that are its sign, which brings me to Lyotard's remarks on the aesthetic. Avant-gardist art ought to be a kind of transfiguring spontaneity; an expression of the heterogeneous moments which 'disarm' the mechanisms of universal progress. There is then, an irresolvable conflict, or *differend*, between the technical procedures through which art is able to recycle the imagery of the avant-garde, and the avant-gardist phrasing which seeks to reconfigure the sublime. Thus, even after artistic production has become largely formulaic, its complicity with the development of technological means, the massification of public taste and the demands of the economic genre, remains a silencing of its obligation to the unpresentable (Lyotard, 1991a, p. 210). It is this fragile, aesthetic trace of ethical responsibility which, for Lyotard, cannot be erased or operationally discharged. Even the ecstatic transformations of fashion, which Baudrillard presents as the collapse of the aesthetic into the mutability of capital, cannot bring about the complete self-referentiality of the system. For where artistic production is increasingly drawn into the temporal economy of capital, this also sharpens the antagonism between the economic genre and the avant-garde. The very litigations through which capital reduces particular wrongs to silence, are what constantly demand that the avant-garde revolutionize its phrasing of the unpresentable.

Hopefully, this brief exposition has given some sense of the complexity of the relationship between capital and the Lyotardian aesthetic. Yet for Jameson, the value which Lyotard attributes to aesthetic innovation, is compromised from the outset by his insistence upon the prescience of Kant's remarks on the sublime. In the essay 'Transformations of the image in postmodernity' (Jameson, 1998), he argues that, in general, the return to the 'classic texts' of ethics, aesthetics and political philosophy, mark the emergence of a distinctively postmodern sphere of ideology – one whose socio-cultural function is to re-present 'the political' as a realm independent of the development of the mode of production. This return to the great texts of philosophical aesthetics is particularly significant, according to Jameson, given the fate of the image under the conditions of late capitalism. In an analysis that draws upon Sartre's account of the objectifying power of the look, he argues that the panoptical discipline elaborated by Foucault has been displaced by a total acculturation of the social. The division of social space into regularized and predictable domains of power, has been superseded by the utterly free play of the image; a 'play' whose technological media have made the personal, the private and the traditional into objects of a distracted fascination. Thus, where the edifice of social relations has become completely self-transparent, aesthetic experience is reduced to a mere reflex of the operational necessities of the mode of production (*ibid.*, p. 111). For Jameson, the postmodernist return to classical aesthetics is an attempt to justify this infinite extension of aesthetic experience. For in pursuing traditional conceptions of beauty (the decorative, the ornamental) through an ecstatic multiplication of images, postmodernism fails to recognize the stricture of the modernist sublime: artistic registration of whatever exceeds the established unity of culture with the tasteful and the pleasant (*ibid.*, p. 123).

In the final section of his essay, Jameson presents an account of the distracted, historicizing tendency of postmodern cinema. His exposition proceeds through the 'art-house' aesthetics of Jarman's *Caravaggio* (which he accuses of fetishizing the beautiful and ignoring all social historical context), to populist 'nostalgia films' which substitute 'breathtaking images' for the narrative demands of past events. In the end, this 'postmodern' complicity between the commodification of the image, the aesthetics of the beautiful, and the historicization of the present, marks the decline of a certain utopian poesis (Benjamin and Adorno) and the rise of 'decorative space filling' (film, advertising, MTV) (Jameson, 1998, p. 131).

A few concluding points suggest themselves. First, there is the obvious parallel between Jameson's and Baudrillard's arguments concerning the fate of the aesthetic. Both claim that the technological play of images has crucially undermined their aesthetic value; and that consequently, it is pointless to expect any innovation in the art of the beautiful which would redeem their transformative power. (We should note, however, that the operational logic to which Jameson refers the technological reproduction of images is much closer to Adorno's conception of reification than to Baudrillard's account of hyperreality.) Secondly, Jameson's identification of postmodern aesthetics with a kind of ahistorical pursuit of the beautiful, completely ignores Lyotard's concern with the sublime. Far from neglecting the latest transformations in the mode of production, I would suggest that Lyotard's account of the temporal economy of capital presents the effects of informatic and technological control at their most extreme. For even though the *reproduction* of the sublime is constantly solicited through the incentives of capital, its originary spontaneity (the feelings of agitation, suspension) arises out of the the very 'indifference' of the commodity form. As far back as *Libidinal Economy*, Lyotard has maintained that capitalism, considered as a flow of intensities, has no internal or external limits – although the logic of equivalence through which this flow is rationalized is what immediately demands attention (Lyotard, 1993, pp. 138–42). Thirdly, and finally, there is the question of the political itself, or rather of the political significance of art and the aesthetic. Jameson's remarks in 'Transformations of the image' make it clear that the fate of the aesthetic is determined by the mode of production; and that if it is pointless to hope for a politically transformative 'art', this is because the technological resources of capital have already exceeded the graphical intensity of the sublime. Lyotard's later writing on the aesthetic, on the other hand, argues that the feelings and events that mark the sublime, arise from the processes of rationalization through which capital expands its temporal economy. Thus, if the artistic response has lost its poesis – its 'revolutionary conduction of affects' – this is because the monstrous indifference of capital demands a kind of sublime inhumanity (Williams, 2000, p. 136). There is, then, no hope for a politics of poetic-aesthetic reconciliation; for there remains only the trauma of 'bearing witness' and the labile and unpredictable responses that such enactments can provoke. The postponement of disaster.

I will return to the detail of Lyotard's and Jameson's arguments about the relationships between art, capitalism and the political in Chapter 8.

Note

1. Lyotard's idea of judgement as that which proceeds immediately from the occurrence of *differrends* (events of pure heterogeneity), is what marks the difference of his political thought from the messianic demands of deconstruction. In the chapter which follows, I will attempt to show that Derrida's reading of Heidegger demands that we understand the question of Being, its dispersal into of the 'living present', as a political obligation; a responsibility that is sensitive both to its complicity with the conditions of its enunciation ('saying'), and to the unforeseeable horizon of the future.

5

Derrida: Deconstruction and Identity

Derrida's writing creates a certain anxiety around the idea of the postmodern, and consequently around the idea of a postmodern politics. This anxiety can, I think, be traced to three sources: (1) his complication of the problem of defining postmodernism; (2) his questioning, both implicit and explicit, of the resources deployed in postmodernist theory; and (3) his return to a certain politics of enlightenment and reflection. Thus, in so far as my account of postmodernism and its political implications will follow a deconstructive line, I need to make some introductory remarks concerning the significance of each of these issues.

As we have seen, the general structure of the arguments set out by Jameson, Harvey and Habermas is to propose that there is a set of universal characteristics that define postmodernist thought (aestheticism, abstraction, nominalism, ahistoricism), and that these characteristics are complicit with the increasingly autonomous dynamics of system necessity (abstract systems of knowledge, expert cultures, global exploitation, media saturation). The problem which deconstruction poses for both Marxist and liberal democratic theory therefore, is one of classification – of trying to specify its complicity with the moral and political weightlessness of postmodernism. This, of course, raises serious questions about the legitimacy of categorizing postmodernist theory as a generic form of ideology. For the moment, however, I will have to suspend such questions. My immediate concern must be to examine the ways in which deconstruction has been subsumed under Marxist and liberal democratic definitions of postmodernism.

I have argued that there is a certain homogeneity in Habermas, Jameson and Harvey's accounts of the generic nature of postmodernism. All of them have claimed that postmodernist theory is an ideology that has emerged out of the reorganization of the mode of production, and that as such, it should be understood in terms of its consequences for the infringement of techno-economic necessity upon democratic practice. In Harvey's work, the relationship between capital and postmodernism is clear. He argues that the postmodernist pursuit of the aesthetic dimension of experience encourages a certain flexibility in the established rationality of production. Late capitalism, in other words, should be understood in terms of a dialectic between postmodern flexibility and Fordist standardization – the question of predominance always being settled in terms of which is most profitable at any given time. Jameson's argument is rather more sophisticated, in that it attempts to show how the postmodern aesthetic (the absence of historical narrative in popular film, the primacy of the decorative and the ornamental in mass culture) has contributed to the production of 'new people' capable of living and working within the accelerated temporality of the global market. His claim is that it is through the engagement of the popular imagination with the sheer immediacy of the present (in video games, MTV, virtual reality), that the social and political conflicts produced by the globalization of capital have been managed. As a good Adornian, therefore, Jameson gives short shrift to deconstruction: Derrida's dispersion of the legislative powers of the text is presented as 'one of the transformations of everyday life and of the psychic subject designated by the term postmodern' (Jameson, 1995, p. 339). What Derrida has done, in other words, is simply to *assume* the conditions that define postmodernity (the loss of structural integration, subjective identity and universal recognition); and so his work forgoes any possibility of a historical critique of the present (*ibid.*).

In *The Philosophical Discourse of Modernity*, Habermas argues that Derrida's transcription of the Heideggerian question of Being can do no more than encourage the primacy of myth and irrationalism in the sphere of politics:

> Derrida develops the history of Being – which is encoded in writing – in another variation from Heidegger. He too degrades politics and contemporary history to the status of the ontic and the foreground, so as to romp all the more freely, and with a greater wealth of associations in the sphere of the ontological and archewriting. (Habermas, 1994, p. 181)

This statement requires some unpacking. First, there is the question of Habermas' reading of Heidegger. Put simply, this reading suggests that Heidegger's attempt to characterize the Western philosophical project as the distribution of Being into increasingly abstract categories of epistemology, morality and aesthetics (Heidegger, 1987, pp. 187–9), is ultimately a denial of the discursive potential of language. By conceiving Enlightenment ideals of truth and rational autonomy as the displacement of an originary (Greek, pre-Socratic) proximity of Man (*Dasein*) to the question of Being, Habermas contends that Heidegger obscures the dialogical unfolding of language that is co-present with the project of modernity. The strange indeterminacy of Being which, for Heidegger, plays around every organization of the right, the good and the beautiful is, for Habermas, an occultation of politics; the subsumption of communicative reason under the demands of an utterly indefinite authority. Second, there is the question of Habermas' reading of Derrida's reading of Heidegger. Clearly what is being claimed in the statement above is that Derrida's transcription of Heideggerian thought is an intensification of the indeterminacy of Being, and of its potential for violent interjections into the mediating practices of the lifeworld. The resources of Derrida's critique of metaphysics, in other words, are presented as forcing the basic structures of language (intersubjectivity, universality, performativity) beyond their inherently *communicative* rationality. For in so far as trace, supplement and *différance* continue to follow the dispersal of Being, they overdetermine every possible enunciation of consensus and agreement. Thus for Habermas, the very thing that has come to define philosophy as philosophy – the search for solutions to 'palpable social pathologies' – is called into question by deconstruction (Habermas, 1994, p. 181). Every conceivable issue (technocratic control of the body, environmental devastation, globalization) spirals off into a multiplicity of esoteric 'readings', none of which has any interest in reconfiguring the terms of communicative democracy. In the end, deconstruction, through its neglect of the difference between literary criticism and philosophy, is unable to avoid falling back into the free play of the aesthetic (*ibid.*, p. 210); a free play which, for Habermas, opens the way to the end of philosophy and to the political mythologies of Being (racism, fascism, nationalism, religious fundamentalism).

In order to meet these objections I need to look in more detail at Derrida's relationship to Heidegger.

In his *An Introduction to Metaphysics* Heidegger proposes that language 'can only have arisen from the overpowering, the strange and the terrible, from man's departure into being' (Heidegger, 1987, p. 171). The tropes and modulations through which language came to be, were ultimately poetic expressions of *Dasein*'s confrontation with the overpowering presence of Being. Living within the demands of this poetic language therefore, must be understood as living within a resource that constantly reopens the question of Being, moving beyond its appearing and dissimulation within the 'governing order' (*ibid.*, p. 170). What is important here, is Heidegger's claim that language initiates a clash of true (authentic) apprehensions of Being, and that it is the necessity of this conflict that founds the historical essence of *Dasein* (*ibid.*, p. 152). For in so far as this essence unfolds through the epochal questions which designate the history of humanity – the predominance of the 'ready to hand' over the question of Being, the loss of the spiritual destiny of Europe, the massification of humanity – it is impossible to confine the questioning of Being within a logic of consensus, communication and intersubjectivity. Now for Derrida, this Heideggerian insistence upon the 'strangeness' of the language in which Being reveals itself, remains tied to the heroic destiny of *Dasein* – its struggle with the spiritual emptiness of technological modernity. The concepts of trace, supplementarity and *différance* that inform his transcription of Heidegger therefore, specify a complex reconfiguration of the economy of 'living in' the established order of Being. We know that for Derrida 'there is nothing outside of the text'; and that, consequently, the Heideggerian pursuit of Being should be understood as the circulation of 'presence' through the legislative resources of metaphysics. And so the strange excessiveness of language that Heidegger identified as part of the historical-existential destiny of *Dasein*, becomes in Derrida's writing the interruptive necessity of speech. What is 'said' in the text, in other words, is legislative in the sense that it seeks to suppress the residue and excess (of otherness) that is produced through the necessity of the 'saying' (enunciation). Speech, therefore, occurs both as the necessary consequence of living within the resources of the text, and as the *chance* of ethical and political enunciations that remark the logic of supplementarity at work in every form of legislation.

For Derrida, speaking and writing against the legislator always runs the risk of falling back into the legislative necessity of the text that is 'remarked' (Bennington and Derrida, 1993, pp. 308–9). Thus, the stricture under which deconstructive writing ought to operate, is that of seeking to register those events that interrupt the veracity of the said. Such a registration, of course, brings us back to Derrida's 'quasi-transcendental' ideas (trace, supplementarity, iterability and *différance*). For in so far as these are incommensurable remarks upon the text and its dispersal of effects, they demand that the writer attend both to her naming of the interruption and to its independence from the legislative force of the said. Julia Kristeva's essay 'Women's time', for example, is careful to point out the dangers of feminist critique becoming complicit with the demands of male 'obsessive' time. The first wave of feminism demanded a place within the structures of social, economic and technological progress; the second wave attempted to determine a uniquely feminine time, characterized by the separateness of natality from the violence of patriarchal history. In the first case, the danger of complicity with the demands of an obsessive progress is clear. For in so far as winning a place in the order of history is given priority over the difference of the feminine, the first wave leaves the basic assumptions of male-obsessional time untouched. Yet for Kristeva, the second wave, in attempting to determine the essence of women's 'cyclical' time (the time of natality, nurturing, motherhood), gives rise to questions about the critical provocation of the feminine. As an 'essence' opposed to the violence of masculine identity, the feminine refuses all accommodation with the law and civil society. Such a refusal, in the name of the *nature* of the feminine, however, is no longer engaged with the text as a dispersal of contingent effects. Its ultimate recourse is to the violence which it originally attributed to the nature of the masculine (Kristeva, 1992, p. 203). Thus, the final gesture of 'Women's time', is to suggest that the possibility of an ethics of sexual difference will depend increasingly upon a certain 'aesthetic' recognition of 'the multiplication of every person's possible identifications . . . – *the relativity of his/her symbolic [and] biological existence*' (*ibid.*, p. 210, original emphasis).

This complex stricture, in which the author must both acknowledge and seek to avoid the complicity of her writing with the legislative text, cannot, as Habermas has argued, be reduced to a ludic and irresponsible multiplication of 'readings'. (Nor can it be thought of simply as a re-presentation of postmodern ideology, as Jameson has claimed.) In deconstruction, the possibility of ethics depends upon the degree to which we remain responsible to the events of *différance* which arise out of the legislative resources of the text. This responsibility is always discharged within an 'economy of violence': the clash of those necessarily contingent enunciations that arise from the text, and which disperse, reconfigure, undermine or reiterate its authority (Derrida, 1990b, p. 148). Thus, 'the saying', as the enunciation of what is unforeseen in the unity of 'the said', can arise only out of the *impossibility* of unifying the ethical demand in any set of deductive rules or categories. As Derrida puts it in *The Other Heading*:

> I will even venture to say that ethics, politics and responsibility, *if there are any*, will only ever have begun with the experience and experiment of aporia . . . the condition of possibility of this thing called responsibility is a certain experience and experiment of the possibility of the impossible: the testing aporia from which one may invent the only *possible invention, the impossible invention*. (Derrida, 1992, p. 41, original emphasis)

The responsibility that arises out of this deconstructive 'testing' therefore, is not only to the violence inscribed in the textual resources of culture, identity, politics and technology, it is also to the force of its own enunciation. It is only in so far as we remain prepared to remark the violence of our own remarking, that we can remain open to the idea of peace as the 'transcendental horizon' of the economy of violence (Derrida, 1990, p. 148).

Destruction then, is not simply nihilistic assault on metaphysics; for it is clear that Derrida's thought demands a particular attention to the economics of gathering (presence) through which then necessity of the law is organized. Thus, even if we have been satisfied that that there is a postmodernist 'genre' (at least in the sense proposed by Habermas, Harvey and Jameson), I would suggest that the critical resources deployed in Derrida's thought, announce a general economy that continues to operate within such 'postmodernist' reconfigurations of politics, culture, subjectivity and identity. (See, for example, the encounter between Lyotard and Derrida over the political and philosophical significance of Heidegger's association with Nazism (Derrida, 1990a and Lyotard, 1990).) Deconstruction then, raises fundamental questions about the concept of postmodernism. For in so far as it is a working through of the resources of the logos – that is, of the resources of Western philosophical reason – it configures an ethical responsibility that would operate between events of unmediated alterity, and the metaphysics of presence. The old aporias of violence, autonomy and the law continue to recur, yet their demand for resolution is now a question of tracing the effects of universal identity, and of transforming its formal structures. This means that the possibility of recognizing the other (the immigrant, the woman, the Jew) as a practical political demand, requires a type of judgement that would be satisfied neither with the search for pure particularity and difference, nor with the established logics and technologies of totality. Such a judgement would arise from the aporetic structure of 'dual responsibility'. For in its difference from the dominant structures of political integration, the other is both an untranslatable alterity (a form whose ethical imperative lies in its very difference from the powers of totality), and the demand that this alterity should be 'organized' within formal-legislative structures of recognition (Derrida, 1992, p. 41).

This then, brings me to my second point: Derrida's questioning of the resources deployed in postmodernist theory. My purpose in adopting the concept of dual responsibility as the guiding thread of my exposition, is not to show that the theorists I have chosen as exemplifying certain crucial elements of postmodernism are simply wrong or misguided. Rather, I want to suggest that within each theorization of the postmodern, there is a disposition, either towards difference or totality, which organizes its political enunciations. We need, then, to give some examples of how this disposition operates.

We have seen that in Bauman's work, Levinas' narration of the ethical commandment marks the possibility of a radical form of social critique: one in which our understanding of the institutions of ethical life is no longer guided by the assumptions of functional necessity or structural integration, but is rather a kind of sensitivity to the distantiating and depersonalizing tendencies of modernity. Bauman's pursuit of the ethical temper of postmodernity therefore, traces the legal, technological and disciplinary determinations of social space. In *Modernity and the Holocaust*, his exposition is focused on the ways in which the 'enchainment' of bureaucratic and technological functions (the organization of trains for deportation, the 'sanitized' killing accomplished by gas chambers and crematoria) was able to overcome the basic moral responses of human beings. In *Postmodern Ethics*, the emphasis shifts to the distracted relationships of postmodern space; to the 'proximity' of bystanders who are fascinated by, yet ethically disengaged from, the events of terrorism, famine and war that characterize our historical present. The question that arises from Bauman's critique of modernity therefore, is that of redemption: for while the 'infinity' of Levinas' ethical commandment is played out in the events of a tragic history (the law can never peacefully subsume the other), Bauman's writing seems to approach, and to withdraw from, a regulative organization of global space. His work, in other words, is haunted by the possibility that there might be a form of universal phrasing which, having moved beyond Levinas' economy of time and redemption, could designate a non-coercive, cosmopolitan politics.

If Bauman's relationship to Levinas is one that seeks to extend the ethical commandment into the realm of consensual legislation, then Derrida's is one that attempts to place Levinas' thought in a 'provocative' relation to the metaphysics of social identity. Derrida's 'first reading' of Levinas in 'Violence and metaphysics', takes the form of a closely argued defence of Heidegger against Levinas' claim that he simply 'neutralizes the existent in order to comprehend or grasp it' (Levinas, 1994, p. 46). For Derrida, the importance of Heidegger's axiom that Being cannot be reduced to the being of particular existents, is that it excludes the possibility of simply 'adding' his thought to the list of philosophical ontologies. Being, in Heidegger's usage, is what is differentiated from particular existents; it is that which opens and exceeds the relationship of *Dasein* to ethical, aesthetic and political determinations of its world 'as world'. Thus, the thought of Being, as Derrida remarks in 'Violence and metaphysics', 'can have no human design ... it is doubtless the only thought which no anthropology, no ethics, and above all, no ethico-anthropological psychoanalysis will ever enclose' (Derrida, 1990b, p. 137). What Derrida is insisting upon here, is Heidegger's thought of an unrepresentable, precognitive origin that is both determined and dis-simulated in every particular ontology. And so the tropes through which Levinas deploys the ethical relation (ipseity, the anarchic principle, substitution), would belong to the Heideggarian economy of 'letting be' that determines the historical disclosure of Being.

Levinas, we have seen, defines metaphysics as the pure, non-violent discourse that responds to the alterity of the face. Reading from Heidegger's text, however, this ethico-ontology could not escape the logos of letting-be: it could not extricate itself from the categories which deploy and redeploy the essence of humanity, and which do so without reflection upon how that essence is related to the precomprehension of Being. For Derrida therefore, the metaphorical relationship of the face to the supremely substantive existent (God) which is expounded in *Totality and Infinity*, is an evasion of the Heideggarian question of Being. For although the possibility of Levinas' ethics is opened by the preconceptual unity of 'enjoyment', the phenomenology that it institutes (an ethics of 'resemblance' that avoids the Hegelian categories of absolute subjectivity, universal mediation and so on) evades the basic Heideggarian question: 'in what manner [does] the existence of man belong to the truth of Being' (Derrida, 1990b, p. 142).

The contingent privilege that Derrida gives to Heidegger's notion of Being in 'Violence and metaphysics', is intended to expose the impossibility of determining the ethical relation as something which originates beyond and before the textual resources of philosophical reason (the logos). We have seen that, for Heidegger, Being is always dissimulated by the categories of ontology, and that consequently language begins not with the pure phraseless invocation of the other, but with with the predicative necessity of speech ('determination', 'offering', 'possibility'). For Derrida, Levinas' 'language without a phrase' – the articulation of unconditional care, of pure non-violence – could offer nothing to the other: it would give him or her no chance of working within the economy of presence, or of exercising the autonomy that the legislative strictures of the law make possible. 'A master who forbids himself the phrase would give nothing. He would have no disciples, only slaves' (Derrida, 1990b, p. 157). Yet

Derrida's questioning of Levinas' deployment of absolute transcendence (the face in its relationship to the language, Being and autonomy of the other), does not undertake simply to re-establish the primacy of Heidegger's notion of Being. Rather, Levinas' claim to present a 'non-philosophy' – the absence of speech, supplementarity and power from the relationship of 'being for' – is, for Derrida, an active solicitation of philosophical discourse. The attempt to exclude the resources of the logos from the origin of philosophical thought ultimately demands a profound reflection upon the relationship of philosophy to its non-rational origins. And so Levinas' description of a transcendent difference (the face) that occurs 'beyond philosophy', demands to be thought of as an 'awakening of the logos to its origin ... [to] its other (*ibid.*, p. 149); as a stricture which, while it is determined within the necessity of presence, always exceeds any moral, political or forensic 'knowledge' we may have accumulated.

Where then, does this leave Derrida's account of political responsibility? We have seen that Levinas' writing is presented in 'Violence and metaphysics' as a powerful provocation to think the relationship between ethics and ontology. What emerges from this provocation, according to Derrida, is the immediacy and impossibility of the ethical demand: the 'experience and experiment of aporia' that arises from the alterity of the other. In the end, however, Levinas' ethical commandment is abstracted from the economy of presence; it refers to a 'community of infinites' (Beings with faces which resemble the face of God), all of whom are sources of an unconditional demand. Thus, my obligation to the suffering of the other is an obligation that is without limit, without language and without violence. Two important points emerge from this designation of the ethical relation. First, there is the question of the religious authorization that is inscribed in Levinas' thought. In *The Gift of Death*, Derrida argues that it is the revelation of God through the human face that founds Levinas' ethical commandment, and that consequently, 'he is no longer able to distinguish between the infinite alterity of God and that of every human' (Derrida, 1995, p. 84). The ethical relation, in other words, always returns for its authorization to the authority of the divine. Second, there is the question of the text and the economy of violence which it institutes. Again in *The Gift of Death*, Derrida outlines the necessity of entering into this economy, *even and especially through the strictures of ethical obligation.* The story of Abraham discloses the terrible solitude of this demand: the fact that the father (Abraham), who alone hears God's commandment to sacrifice his only son (Isaac), must keep silent about his duty to God and seem as a murderer to his wife, family and the keepers of the law (*ibid.*, p. 62). For Derrida, there is a sense in which all ethical obligations are met in this way. For in so far as responsibility can be assumed only by taking a particular demand to be absolute, such responsibility must always come into conflict with the 'social' obligations under which we live (*ibid.*, pp. 68–9). The ethical, in other words, always demands an awareness of the violence of its own strictures.

Derrida's reading of Levinas then, is focused on his attempt to establish the transcendence of the ethical demand. Such a demand, he argues, relies upon the originary difference of every face; its capacity to express a uniquely designating obligation. The problem with this, according to Derrida, is that it abstracts ethical judgements from the economy of violence which opens their possibility. Thus, the ethical demand which arises from deconstruction is that we attend to the events through which the resources of presence (mediation, integration, consensus, identity) disclose their incompleteness, their *différance*. The inscription of patriarchal authority in the law, for example, is an ethical demand in the sense that what is announced by the law is always a parting from its postulated necessity – a parting whose occurrence is what constantly provokes the enunciation of 'the feminine'. In so far as the difference of the other is both presented and dispersed through the textual resources of the law, we are responsible to what cannot be named within these resources: the alterity that is spoken with every enunciation of identity. For Derrida, then, Levinas' insistence that the transcendence of the face precedes and exceeds every determination of identity, is a legislative enunciation that has taken the *relative* alterity of sexual difference and re-presented it as the absolute alterity of the other. The economy of the same, in other words, includes and conceals a moment of *oppositional difference* – the difference of gender – that is encrypted in Levinas' ethical commandment (Bennington and Derrida, 1993, pp. 212–28). In the end then, the question of sexual difference is made secondary to an obligation (of care for the other) that has already excluded 'the feminine' as an ethical demand (Levinas, 1994, pp. 123–5).

This deconstructive stricture is immediately political. For if it is acknowledged that we can only discharge our responsibility to the other by registering the impossibility of its inscription in the law, culture and morality, then ethical reflection becomes a matter of questioning of the resources of presence/Being. The deficiency of Levinas' thought therefore is that

> the other cannot be absolutely exterior to the same without ceasing to be other; . . . consequently, the same is not a totality absolutely closed in upon itself . . . having only the appearance of totality in what Levinas calls economy, work and history. (Derrida, 1990, p. 126)

The redemptive eschatology which characterizes Levinas' thought remains, for Derrida, a provocation to think the fate of the other *within* the resources of totality. And so when he claims that in Heidegger's philosophy the 'thought of Being is as close as possible to non-violence' (*ibid.*, p. 146), he is claiming that an ethical politics is promised to the idea of peace as a 'transcendental horizon'. Political reflection, in other words, is obligated to the social, economic and technological conditions of the present through the speculative and uncertain lines which they open into the future. The growing sophistication of technology, for example, demands an urgent transformation of the founding oppositions of political thought: the human and the technological, the masculine and the feminine, the bourgeois and the proletarian. For in so far as these oppositions are increasingly difficult to sustain, increasingly 'spectralized', we are placed in the position of having to receive the other as an event (the unforeseen occurrence of a demand which cannot be organized through established categories of justice and legality) for which we have no established criteria of judgement. This demand is ultimately an obligation to judge the difference of the other in its relationship both to the violence of the past and to the unforeseeability of the future: to resist a purely technocratic modalization of time, and to remark those techno-alterities through which the present is put 'out of joint' with itself (Derrida, 1994a, p. 23; Beardsworth, 1998, pp. 81–4).

To return finally to Bauman, one of the characteristics that defines the postmodern in his writing is the intrusion of instrumental reason into the moral and political relationships of the lifeworld, the agora. In general, people will act on the advice of experts rather than follow the duties of care which arise from their proximity to others. The question which arises from this postmodern predicament then, is whether the multiplication of specialist knowledges (and the demise of the legislative role of intellectuals), is something which will produce a new rationality of consensus, or whether the demands of operational necessity will continue to override every attempt to reflect upon the fate of the individual within the system. The very nature of postmodernity, according to Bauman, means that we cannot modalize its historical disjuncture through conventional theories of historical progress (Marxism, functionalism, idealism). And so the outcome of the present demise of philosophical reflection – either increasing technocratic control or the revitalization of philosophy – cannot be determined in advance (Docherty, 1993, pp. 128–40). What is certain, however, is that the ethical commandment will remain vulnerable to the functional integration of society. And so if we are to retain any sense of responsibility, Bauman argues that we must frame 'a new ethics of distant consequences ... [an] ethics that would reach over the socially erected obstacles of mediated action and the functional reduction of the human self' (Bauman, 1989, p. 221).

This demand raises a number of important issues. First, there is the question of his relationship to Levinas. What Bauman appears to be claiming is that it may be possible to organize the ethical commandment into a kind of communicative rationality; a rationality in which the originary demand of the face would be disseminated and intensified. This, I would suggest, is quite at odds with the redemptive-theological significance that Levinas gives the ethical commandment (Abbinnett, 1998b, pp. 112–13). Second, Bauman's demand for an ethics of 'distant consequences' is informed by a particular understanding of technology. Rather than engaging with the relationship between human consciousness and its technological supplements, Bauman assumes the transcendence of the ethical commandment, and takes the technological aspect of modernity to be an *adiaphorizing* power opposed to the assumption of responsibility. This opposition, in other words, assumes an originary relationship of ethical obligation that *precedes* the effects of technology. For Derrida, on the contrary, human consciousness is technological in its very inception. It evolves through supplementations which begin with the simplest hand tools and proceed to the digitization of memory and cognition. Ultimately then, we must recognize the increasingly 'spectral' nature of humanity, and attempt to announce the fate of the other as he or she is dispersed within the technological systems of society. Thus, the demand which emerges from the fact of the Holocaust is not simply that we recognize the morally distantiating effects of technology; it is that we attend to the cultural, economic and political antagonisms through which 'the technological' is presented (and re-presented) in its necessity. Such an attention, as Beardsworth points out, is immediately promised to the future; for it refuses every purely philosophical, techno-scientific or sociological modalization of time (Beardsworth, 1996, p. 157).

How then, does this demand that we should judge the fate of the other from within the aporetic temporality of presence, relate to the political claims made by Baudrillard and Lyotard?

We have seen that for Baudrillard, the 'ecstatic' communication of signs has become a total principle: nothing contingent, antagonistic or transcendent can intervene in the universal exchangeability through which sex, capital, politics and culture are hyperrealized. Simulation, then, produces its fatal effects through the *hyperrealization* of the social. For once the sign has become completely independent of the referent, there is only the circulation of different models of interpretation, the 'weightlessness' of the hyperreal (Baudrillard, 1999, p. 6).

Now for Baudrillard, this total liberation of the sign from the referent reduces the political to an infinitely circular relationship between the masses and the media. We can summarize. The masses have no determinate existence; they are simply the product of the constant solicitations of the media to be sexually liberated, fashionable, virile, healthy and responsible consumers. Such solicitations have, through the very technological processes of their reproduction, ceased to refer to anything beyond the simulation of 'the social'. Sexual liberation, for example, passes out of the dynamics of patriarchal domination and becomes a constant, pornographic staging of the body and sexuality. These simulacra, according to Baudrillard, are characterized by their hyperfunctionality – the fact that they have turned every contingent and unpredictable appearance of 'the real', into an operational component of the system. Everything, in other words, takes on a kind of monstrous transparency, from which the messianic demand of the future is progressively expelled. The masses, then, are precisely what is produced by the constant solicitations of the media. They are nothing 'in-themselves', and we would be wrong to expect any kind of political agency or deliberation from them. Their structural position vis-à-vis the media, however, means that they do retain a kind of short-circuiting potential. For in so far as they are created (and re-created) by the media, they produce unforeseen effects of 'hyperconformity' – effects that can reduce the logic of the system to absurdity. In the end, all that is left to political theory is to enter into a kind of complicity with the system; to force the 'precession of simulacra' beyond their appearance of legitimacy and to precipitate (unforeseen) events of 'dysfunction'.

What is a stake in this account of simulation, I would suggest, is the 'post' of postmodernity. For Baudrillard, the branching of Enlightenment thought into the political prescriptions of Marxism, psychoanalysis, and feminism has reached a point where the social contradictions upon which their logic depends have dissolved into simulation. The vocabulary of socialism, for example, still retains certain political potency, but only in so far as it has become a *simulacrum* of class allegiances which no longer designate the 'reality' of the social. Postmodernity therefore, is the hyperrealization of modernity: the transformation of its ideological projects into functionalized solicitations of the masses.

This raises some distinctively Derridian questions (and brings me to Derrida's reconfiguration of Enlightenment politics). First, there is the question of presence. We have seen that for Derrida Western philosophy is in general characterized by the writing of origins: the pursuit of what is absolutely independent of the resources of the text. Thus, the 'quasi-transcendental' structures that Derrida deploys in his transcriptions of Rousseau, Marx and Heidegger, are designations of discrete economies in which the presence of the referent (nature, productive humanity, *Dasein*), is constantly supplemented by its 'others' (writing, capital, technology). This then, is what Derrida means by *différance*: the constant deferral of the presence of the referent through the resources of the text. The logic of *différance*, as Derrida applies it to the history of philosophy, marks a temporal dis-organization of systems in which the establishment and rearticulation of concepts becomes problematic. For in so far as the ethical and political force of the origin can emerge only through the unfolding of its future, the stability of every foundational concept depends upon its lack of presence (Being) at the 'beginning' of the text (see Bennington and Derrida, 1993, pp. 70–3). *Différance* therefore, designates the 'gathering' through which any particular system maintains its inner differentiation; a gathering that is simultaneously the dispersal of the origin into an economy of supplementations and traces that exceeds the possibility of totalization.

This deconstructive understanding of the economy of the text, is important because it demands that we question the logic of closure which is implicit in Baudrillard's account of simulation. In their jointly written book, Bennington and Derrida agreed that Bennington's 'systematic' exposition of Derrida's thought ('Derridabase'), should be accompanied by a response written by Derrida himself ('Circumfession'). The point of the exercise was to show that, no matter how comprehensive Bennington's exposition was, it could not effect a closure of Derrida's thought; and that in fact the real interest of the project lay in the 'surprise' of Derrida's response to the systematic presentation of his own philosophy (Bennington and Derrida, 1993, p. 1). Now, the logic of simulation that Baudrillard presents in his later writing, maintains that fourth-order simulacra, whose technological reproduction has taken the image beyond any reference to the real, precipitate society towards the hyperfuctionality of all its systems. The simulacra of sex, politics, morality and desire produce a totally capitalized, totally amoral solicitation of the masses. If there is anything surprising to come from this technological systematicity, therefore, it has already been determined that this should take place as the hyperconformity of the masses to the solicitations of the media (more medicine, more pornography). The question arises, then, as to whether this circular relationship between the masses and the media is anything more than the reproduction of technological determinism. Baudrillard is quite clear that we cannot expect political reflection from the masses, and that we would be wrong to treat their hyperconformity as an expression of collective will or intention (Baudrillard, 1996, p. 214). Thus, in so far as the only expression of contingency within the system is limited to a subjectless conductivity of effects, we might legitimately ask whether such effects simply precipitate the operational necessity of the system. If there is to be a politics of massification, in other words, it can only arise from the events of exclusion and violence that accompany the technological organization of the social. I will return to this in a moment.

Lyotard's thought presents a rather different problematic. We have seen that in his later writing politics arises from the heterogeneity of different genres of discourse. For as beings situated within a universe of competing claims, we have to judge the *differends* that arise from specific events of conflict in the absence of any universal rules of mediation. In general therefore, Lyotard maintains that any genre which seeks to establish itself as hegemonic (the universal form of settlement and mediation), will always engender events of silencing and exclusion which demand to be given expression, to be 'phrased' (Lyotard, 1988, p. 181). It is this dispersed and heterogeneous demand that constantly reactivates the political, even in the most organized systems (the temporal economy of capital, for example). Indeed, it is what underlies Lyotard's account of the political significance of the aesthetic in the essays on avant-gardist art (Lyotard, 1991a, pp. 181–95 and 196–211).

Lyotard's account of the end of metanarratives has frequently been criticized on the grounds that it is self-referential. In general, the claim is that the contextualism of his later writing (from *The Postmodern Condition* onward), depends upon the validity of his description of the relationship between language, being and judgement. Thus, *The Differend*'s recourse to such nominalist configurations as 'the phrase regime', 'the sentence' and 'the archipelagos', gives rise to philosophical questions about the relationship between humanity (those who are summoned to judge *differends*), and the unfolding of being (the transcendent, dissimulated condition of history). Conventional responses to Lyotard's theory of judgement have tended to concentrate on the aestheticism of his ethical and political demands; or to argue that justice is impossible on the basis of the pure heterogeneity of phase regimen and genres of discourse (Jameson, 1995, pp. 55–66; Habermas, 1995b, pp. 114–46). A more disturbing response to his negotiation of the question of being, however, is given in Jean-Luc Nancy's essay 'Lapsus Judicii', which demands to know the grounds upon which it is possible to claim that judgement *as such*, is judgement without a rule or concept (Benjamin, A., 1992, pp. 162–5). For in so far as the only justification which Lyotard can offer is his own designation of the 'critical post', his theory of responsibility to particular *differends* appears to begin with an arbitrary event of self-legislation. (See Lyotard's own account of political authorization in *The Differend*, 1988, pp. 145–7.) It could of course be argued that the devices which Lyotard deploys are intended merely as *analogical* configurations of the relationship between judgement and the absence of determinate concepts (Bennington, 1988, p. 176). Nancy, however, maintains that such configurations imply that Lyotard has been unable to dissolve the Heideggarian question of Being into sentences – precisely because his theory of judgement prejudges its own necessity.

The core of Nancy's argument therefore, is that the moment of prejudgment which haunts Lyotard's account of justice and responsibility, refers us to the question of Being. In order for their to be political judgements, it is necessary that the transcendence of the origin is recognized as an irreducible structure of the present.[1] (Derrida's notion of *différance* entails a similar argument: that the origin is both 'present' and 'dispersed' within the temporal economy of the text.) In a brief reply to Nancy, Lyotard has claimed that to return to the question of Being is ultimately to return to questions about the origin of truth – questions which, by their very nature, threaten the political significance of philosophy (Benjamin, A., 1992, p. 163). Thus, if what defines the philosophical enterprise is the search for rules by which to judge particular events (a constant 'unpreparedness' before the demands of the other), then 'Auschwitz', as emblematic of the politics of Being, would name the point at which this search is abandoned and the destruction of the other is taken up (Lyotard, 1988, pp. 97–106). Yet the claim that Nancy's argument does little more than reinvigorate the search for the true foundations of political authority is problematic. Lyotard's appeal to the historical consequences of the politics of truth (National Socialism, Stalinism) fails to answer Nancy's specific objection: that his thought precipitates the occurrence of *differends* (and the spontaneity of judgement) only by refusing to recognize the primacy of the question of Being in the reproduction of identity, community and belonging. Bennington, in his article 'Ces petits *differends*: Lyotard and Horace', argues that the question which Lyotard's writing leaves open, is that of the possibility of judging Being (the irreducible, the dissimulated), without having already absorbed its appearing into religious, mythological or metatheoretical configurations (in Benjamin, A., 1992, p. 163). Such a judgement is, I will argue, the demand of Derrida's 'dual responsibility': the stricture of referring unforeseen events (difference, alterity) to the reinscriptions of the origin (nature, *Dasein*, spirit) which structure the presence of 'the social'.

It is the tension between universal recognition (spirit, identity, gathering), technocratic control (capitalization, reproduction) and the radical heterogeneity of knowledge (agonism, untranslatability, spectralization) therefore, that is the condition of ethical and political judgement. For Derrida, we have seen that the possibility of responding ethically to this disjunctive present, cannot be schematized through any pre-established set of rules; and that such a response is marked by an 'experimental' openness to events of alterity which arise from the organization of presence. For example, the development of new medical-prosthetic technologies has precipitated a crisis in established biological and philosophical definitions of the human; a crisis in which we are immediately confronted with questions about the technological management of reproduction, the invention of transsexuality and the uncoupling of human identity from the regulative construction of nature. Judging the consequences of this intervention therefore, is both necessary and impossible. For even though the resources of conventional moral recognition are threatened by techno-scientific innovation, the moment of being called to decide one's responsibility to the other (the clone, the transsexual, the cyborg) cannot be evaded or covered over by scientific rationality. One's unique obligation to the other is political in the sense that it is always a questioning of the legitimacy of law, both in terms of its textual/philosophical inscription, and of its application to the social, cultural, economic and technological reproduction of identity.

If there is a duty to defend the right of human beings to philosophical reflection therefore, this arises from the relationship between system necessity, technological supplementation and the radically democratic intention of Enlightenment thought. Such a disjunctive economy is, for Derrida, the promise of a democracy to come: a clash of irreconcilable necessities that is always the revival of the ethical and the postponement of its political fulfilment. In his essay 'Call it a day for democracy', he makes clear that it is no longer credible to theorize political reflection as an incremental process of public enlightenment (Kant or Habermas, for example). For in so far as the 'techno-economic mutation of the media' is about the simulation of democracy, our obligation to the present is turned over to the immediate time of newspapers and telematic communications (Derrida, 1992, pp. 96–7). However, Derrida's admission that the public sphere can no longer be conceived in terms of 'a logic of simple "consciousness" . . . and of a juridical concept of responsibility' (*ibid.*, p. 107) does not signify the end of reflection as a political demand. His writing requires that we analyse the simulacra of the political not just in terms of their own temporality (as Baudrillard does in his account of the retreat of political ideologies into pure simulation), but also as raising questions about who is addressed by the media, who has the right of response to them and how this response is related to the demands of democracy *to come*. Such questions cannot be conceived in terms of a 'scientific or philosophical objectification' of the masses. For in so far as they arise in dispersed and incalculable moments which defy the statistical reproduction of the average (the incalculable response of a minority of readers to new and original acts of literature, for example), their demand for a right of response exceeds the logic of mass solicitation (*ibid.*, p. 105). Thus, the promise of democracy, in its linkage to the undecidability of the future, is given as a weak messianic demand with every operational simulation of the political (*ibid.*, p. 109). Such weakness, however, should not be confused with impending erasure.

Note

1. The general significance of Jean-Luc Nancy and Philippe Lacoue-Labarthe's recourse to the question of Being is a Heideggarian concern with the technological organization of society. Both are in broad agreement with the thesis expounded in Heidegger's essay 'The question concerning technology': namely that Western metaphysics, having determined the conditions under which truth becomes a matter of correctness and being the abstract identity of things, allows the transformation of world into the 'ready to hand' (Heidegger, 1996, p. 322). With the loss of Being as the transcendent demand around which the polis is maintained, politics is reduced to the circulation of modernist ideologies of progress, accumulation and efficiency – all of which presuppose the functional reduction of *Dasein*. Thus for Heidegger, modernity is characterized by the total administration of the social: a pure instrumentality which has ruptured the relationship between the question of Being and the question of politics. Nancy and Lacoue-Labarthe, in their original response to Heidegger (given in 1980 as an introduction to the Cerisy colloquium on 'The ends of man'), attempted to take his thesis beyond the spiritual and aesthetic gestures of his later writings (the concept of community expounded in 'The origin of the work of art', for example (Heidegger, 1996, pp. 139–212)). Their paper was concerned to 'retrace' the political (*le politique*) in the light of Heideggger's disclosure of the complicity of politics (*la politique*) with the functional organization of totality. In the end, they argue that the only option is to withdraw from the politics of opinion and dispute (*doxa*) in order to contemplate the originary conditions upon which such conflicts are founded (the question of Being). Simon Critchley, in his *Ethics of Deconstruction*, argues that such a withdrawal is ultimately a politics of waiting, a kind of quietism which can only watch for the signature of Being within the historical-metaphysical violence of totality (Critchley, 1999, p. 215). As such, Nancy and Lacoue-Labarthe's analysis of the totalitarian trajectory of *la politique* (they are clear that this generic term includes liberal democracy) remains insensitive to the *distribution* of violence within different political forms. Critchley goes on to argue that this insensitivity marks the impossibility of a Heideggerian politics. For in so far as *le politique* is withdrawn from the human consequences of ideological organization (consequences which Critchley argues demands to be understood in terms of Levinas' ethical commandment), there can be no possibility of 'interrupting' the

politics of totalization. Critchley also claims that deconstruction falls into the same Heideggarian trap of infinite withdrawal, and that consequently it requires a Levinasian supplement in order to become a genuinely political project (*ibid.*, p. 236). I will argue that this is to ignore the 'messianic' significance of Derrida's reading of Heidegger.

Part 2

Media, Culture and Identity

6

Technology, Ideology and the Culture Industry

Introduction

I want to begin this section by looking at Marx's notion of ideology as the imaginary resolution of real conflicts. Famously, Marx implicates the entire edifice of 'bourgeois culture' (art, literature, philosophy) in the production of a 'false consciousness' of the violence of capitalist relations of production. In the chapter which follows, I will examine the way in which three of Marx's twentieth-century inheritors, Walter Benjamin, Theodor Adorno and Fredric Jameson, have developed his ideology thesis in relation to the media-technological transformation of capitalism. In particular, I will address the following:

- Marx's original designation of 'ruling ideas' in *The German Ideology*;
- Horkheimer and Adorno's account of the rationalization of social relationships, the technological reproduction of popular culture (film, TV, radio) and the creation of 'the masses' (*Dialectic of Enlightenment*);
- Benjamin's understanding of the relationship between art, culture and the technological reproducibility of the image ('The work of art in the age of mechanical reproduction');
- the relationship between capitalism, history and redemption as it is sustained in Adorno's *Negative Dialectics* and Benjamin's 'Theses on the philosophy of history';
- Jameson's account of the postmodern culture as a 'reflex' of the increasingly mobile, increasingly globalized organization of capitalism.

Marx: Culture as Ideology

There is a sense in which Marx's early writings on ideology are an attempt to determine how the spontaneity of subjective judgement is related to the social and economic conditions of cultural production. In *The German Ideology*, for example, he remarks that:

> Consciousness can never be anything else than conscious existence, and the existence of men is their actual life-process. If in all ideology men and their circumstances appear upside-down as in *camera obscura*, this phenomenon arises just as much from their historical life-process as the inversion of objects on the retina does from the their physical life-process. (Marx, 1977c, p. 47)

The 'inversion' to which Marx refers in this passage is the transformation of the ideas, concepts, categories, thoughts and representations which emerge from the 'material' processes of social reproduction, into an independent domain of human self-recognition. The realm of 'culture' (art, metaphysics, morality, ethics, law), in other words, becomes increasingly distinct from the 'real' conditions under which human beings produce their means of subsistence; and as such, it establishes an abstract social and political praxis that serves to reinforce the exploitation and conflict of capitalist relations of production. The ideals of freedom and equality which inform the political thought of Kant and Hegel, for example, remain part of this general determination of 'culture as ideology'. For in so far as neither acknowledged the logic of exploitation that takes place within the sphere of civil society (in both Kant and Hegel, the differentiation which occurs through the division of labour is destined to return to a transcendental concept of humanity), neither was able to move beyond the point of 'merely interpreting' the world of practical human activity (Marx, 1977c, pp. 122–3). These interpretations, even though they represent what for Marx is the highest development of the 'idea' of human freedom, are part of a history of ruling ideas that 'are nothing more than the ideal expression of the dominant material relationships' (*ibid.*, p. 64.). The concepts of autonomy and legality through which Kant and Hegel present the responsibilities of citizenship therefore, are understood by Marx as an ideological politics in which 'the citizen' participates only as an abstract self-identity (Marx, 1977d, p. 56). The real condition of his or her appearance in the 'constitutional' life of society – the fact that he or she must participate in the universal exploitation reproduced by the economy – appears only as the spectre which haunts every reformulation of the rights, duties and obligations of citizenship. For Marx, then, the authority of the state as it is constituted under capitalism is dependent upon its ability to re-present 'factual' differences of class, property and wealth as necessary forms of individuation, rational autonomy and moral responsibility. This ideological power, of course, begs the whole question of the relationship between culture and politics. For in so far as the modern state must deploy the ideals of citizenship into the practical life of civil society (the realm of coercion, exploitation and the fetishism of commodities), Marxism demands that we attend both to the logic of representation (distortion, false identity) which determines cultural reproduction, and to the development of the technologies through which this reproduction is carried out.

Marx's understanding of the relationship between culture and political authority has been immensely influential in the development of modern social and political theory. Antonio Gramsci, Louis Althusser, Walter Benjamin and Theodor Adorno have all attempted to develop the original terms of Marx's critique of ideology, and to trace the fate of culture in late modernity. Before examining the political consequences of this development, however, we need to be clear about what Marx is saying about the production of culture in capitalist societies. Most obviously, he is claiming that the realm of culture is a reflection of the material/economic inequalities between classes; and that, in general, culture re-presents those inequalities as natural, inevitable and legitimate. This much is confirmed in the synopsis of the 'base-superstructure' relation which Marx set out in his Preface to *A Contribution to the Critique of Political Economy*:

> The mode of production of material life conditions the social, political, and intellectual life-process in general. It is not the consciousness of men that determines their being, but on the contrary, it is their social being that determines their consciousness. (Marx, 1977d, p. 389)

Yet Marx's concept of ideology does not simply designate a realm of abstract re-presentations of 'social being'. Rather, the forms of ascetic individualism, romantic love, sexual conformity and moral acquisitiveness that have appeared in bourgeois society, are understood as 'false satisfactions' which reproduce the general self-alienation of humanity. The truly social needs that are constituted in the mode of production, in other words, remain unrecognized as long as the state is able to reproduce a certain conformity – of opinion, desire, satisfaction, achievement – among those who continue to be 'dehumanized' by the expropriation of surplus value. The categories through which social humanity recognizes itself as free, autonomous and responsible therefore, *presuppose* the abstract individualism of civil society. For in so far as bourgeois conceptions of the citizen, the consumer, the entrepreneur and the artist proceed from the unquestioned legitimacy of private property, their ultimate significance must always be sought in the perpetuation of class domination. In the end, the history of human culture is for Marx the history of 'ruling ideas'; ideas which have their foundation in '[t]he class that has the means of material production at its disposal' (Marx, 1977c, p. 64). If there is ever to be an authentically human culture, this can only arise out of a revolutionary transcendence of private property relations.

Adorno and Horkheimer: Culture Industries

Marx's ideology thesis then, carries within it a certain dialectical necessity. For in so far as the realm of culture continues to refine the ideals of liberty, equality and justice, it also sharpens the contradiction between those ideals and the exploitative reality of the mode of production. The cultural praxis which is determined by capital, in other words, is conceived as part of the historical necessity through which socialized production will replace the inequalities of private property and the class system (Marx, 1977c, pp. 48–52). For Marx then, the economic and technological development of capitalism has the effect of increasing both the *objective necessity* of exploitation and the *awareness* of that exploitation among the exploited. For Adorno and Horkheimer, however, the evolution of capitalism, far from transforming the proletariat into a 'class for itself', has all but destroyed the possibility of revolutionary politics.

Dialectic of Enlightenment begins with an exposition of the relationship between Enlightenment philosophy and the rationality of control which has come to dominate the mode of production. The 'spirit' of Enlightenment, according to Adorno and Horkheimer, is born out of humanity's subjection to the blind forces of necessity. This necessity is originally experienced as the overwhelming power of nature; the power that is deified and appeased in the mimetic ceremonies of primitive societies (Adorno and Horkheimer, 1986, pp. 3–17). In classical antiquity, this power is expressed as 'fate', or the inescapable destiny which each individual brings with them into the world, and which he or she is powerless to evade. In Sophocles' tragedy *Oedipus Rex*, for example, the drama unfolds around the inevitability with which events bring Oedipus to knowledge of his patricide and his incestuous marriage to his mother. In the end, he has no recourse to justice; he must accept his fate, and become the blind admonitory figure who attests to the divine necessity of the law. For Adorno and Horkheimer, this relationship of human will to the forces which determine our fate as *fate*, is precisely what is at stake in the Enlightenment project. And so when Kant claimed that 'Enlightenment is man's emergence from self-incurred immaturity', he was demanding that we, as beings capable of *rational self-determination*, should not simply surrender to the forces of blind necessity (Kant, 1991, p. 54). The possession of a rational will, immediately places us under an obligation to control the 'inclinations' which bind us to nature, and to criticize those political institutions which stand upon nothing more than the authority of tradition. The notion of free will which Kant places at the core of his philosophy therefore, is essentially *legislative*; its rationality stands opposed to every manifestation of nature (affection, passion, love) in the individual, and to every social tie which has not been subjected to the formal demands of reason.

For Adorno and Horkheimer, the a priori categories through which Kant determined the realms freedom and necessity situate the moral subject within a universe of rigorously formal demands (Kant, 1985, p. 39). And so it is only in so far as we repress the inclinations which originate in our physical being (violent acquisitiveness, sexual rapacity) that we can participate in the moral order of civil society. The bourgeois individual therefore, is formed through the demands of pure rational necessity; he is the embodiment of a heroic abstinence which constantly asserts itself against the chaotic, instinctual life of nature (*ibid.*, p. 43–80). Hegel's objection to this account of moral autonomy, we have seen, is that it remains institutionally disembodied; that the pure disinterestedness of the Kantian subject is without ethical content. In order to overcome this abstraction of the ego therefore, we must attend to the universality that is implicit in the separation and difference of civil society. With Hegel then, the demands of reason pass over into the objective structures of social, economic and political life, and every sphere of human existence becomes subject to the power of the ordering universal. What Horkhiemer and

Adorno detect in this Hegelian ontology, is the beginning of a process of rationalization through which the original ideals of Enlightenment philosophy (freedom, equality and self-determination) are lost to the functional-systemic necessities of capital (*ibid.*, p. 25).

In general, these necessities are understood in *Dialectic of Enlightenment* as arising from the evolution of capitalism. The creation of surplus value, as Marx predicted in *Capital*, has become increasingly dependent on the utilization of technologies which increase the efficiency of productive enterprise. What Marx could not foresee, however, was the degree to which new media technologies would be able to determine the relationship between production and consumption. Film, television and radio are conceived by Adorno and Horkheimer as media which complete the integration of the masses into the economy of corporate desire. The notion of a proletarian culture is lost; for the possibility of such a culture depends upon a collective experience of suffering that would exceed the established economics of production, consumption and exchange. What has actually happened, however, is that 'culture' has become an object of technological reproduction, and as such has lost everything of the transformative potential which Marx attributed to it:

> Nothing remains of the old; everything has to run incessantly, to keep moving. For only the universal triumph of the rhythm of mechanical production and reproduction promises that nothing changes and nothing unsuitable will appear. Any additions to the well-proven culture inventory are too much of a speculation. (Adorno and Horkheimer, 1986, p. 134)

This technologically produced culture is, for Adorno and Horkheimer, the necessary counterpart of corporate capitalism. It is the perpetuation of the stereotypical models of decency, sexuality, attractiveness, femininity, heroism and romance through which the desires of the masses are rendered stable and predictable. Characteristically, then, the culture industry seeks to impose a 'false identity' upon the masses; to make the entirety of their social, psychical and existential being subject to the reifying (objectifying, rationalizing) powers of capital. The films, television and radio programmes, magazines and newspapers which are consumed by the masses, tend to represent the economic necessity of the system as universally desirable. They intervene between individual consumers and the arbitrariness of corporate power, so that there is nothing left for the individual to synthesize or criticize (Adorno and Horkheimer, 1986, p. 124). Popular culture simply reproduces the unity between mass taste and the satisfaction it already receives in the consumption of commodities. Indeed, for Adorno and Horkheimer, an absolute distinction must be made between 'art' and the 'technological production' of the culture industry. Film technologies, for example, cannot reproduce the complex textuality of great literature; for the medium itself is only sufficient to present the grossest outlines of plot, character, mood and emotion. In the end, the productions of the culture industry expect '[n]o independent thinking from the audience' (*ibid.*, p. 137): they simply reproduce consumers who are incapable of reflecting upon the barbarism of their fate.

For Adorno and Horkheimer, then, there is an inherently totalitarian tendency in Enlightenment thought; for what started out as an assertion of the universal rights of humanity has degenerated into an uncontrollable and disordered will to power. This expansion of the power of instrumental reason, however, is not simply the historical outcome of the Enlightenment: it must also be conceived as an essential part of the development of the mode of production. Indeed, the very concept of 'late capitalism', as it is expounded in *Dialectic of Enlightenment*, is designated through the total integration of economy and society. What the culture industry does therefore, is to extend the operational necessities of technology (standardization, predictability, replicability) from the realm of commodity production into the realm of social integration. For Adorno, the 'human element' of culture arises out of the existential differentiation of the individual, its *Existenz* (Adorno, 1990, pp. 173–4). And so the ties of family, friendship, love and affection which constitute the 'natural' origin of society, emerge as a kind of collective response to the isolation in which each of us confronts our own mortality. The technologies of mass communication which Adorno and Horkheimer discuss therefore, function to breakdown these human ties; each of us becomes an entirely transparent, predictable and replaceable unit within an undifferentiated mass of identical units. The political significance of *Dialectic of Enlightenment* then, lies in the demand that we no longer think in terms of public 'space' (and its associated ideas of reflection, deliberation and subjectivity), but rather, in terms of the reification of every sphere of work, satisfaction and desire.

What Adorno and Horkheimer describe is the destruction of all the natural ties which have supported human society, and the loss of the literary, artistic and political forms through which this violence might have been registered. Great art, whose defining characteristic had always been to disclose its complicity with conventions of style and taste, is no longer possible; for the means of technological reproduction have replaced its reflective demands with the constant repetition of the banal and the expected (Adorno and Horkheimer, 1986, pp. 130–1). Ultimately, then, the secret tendency of culture to mask its complicity with the legal and political violence of its epoch is made manifest in the culture industry's reproduction of 'kitsch': those representations of the 'eternal' forms of romance, heroism and sacrifice which draw us away from the barbarism of the present. As Adorno put it in *Minima Moralia*:

> Today, when the consciousness of rulers is beginning to coincide with the overall tendency of society, the tension between culture and kitsch is breaking down . . . In administering the whole of mankind, it [kitsch] administers the breach between man and culture. (Adorno, 1996, p. 147)

This collapse of culture into kitsch is, for Adorno, all the more culpable 'after Auschwitz'. For in so far as the Nazi genocide attests to the fact that there is no inherent purpose to existence, and that the achievements of Enlightenment culture could provide no guarantee against the 'scatological' enticement of the masses, to go on writing lyric poetry or producing art which seeks the eternal in nature is wilfully to ignore the crises of our age (Adorno, 1990, pp. 165–8). The hopeless idealism of kitsch is not simply without artistic merit; it constantly reinvigorates exhausted ideals of unity and harmony in the masses.

The crucial question raised by Adornian Marxism is that of redemption: how we, as beings whose humanity has been lost to the artifice of the culture industry, are to redeem the violence of our age. Adorno's answer to this question refers us back to fate of the individual within the system; or more specifically to the processes of individuation through which capital reproduces its political economy. We know that, for Adorno, there is something unique about each particular existent, and that its subsumption under the demands of universal identity always determines a certain violence. With the establishment of the culture industry, this process of subsumption becomes pervasive: every individual, in every sphere of its existence, is made subject to the demands of economic necessity. This process of reification, however, cannot be accomplished through sheer technological efficiency. Each advance in the integration of the system redetermines the conflict between universal and particular; a conflict which, for Adorno, is suffered in the bodily existence of the individual (Adorno, 1990, pp. 361–5). The redemptive quality of Adorno's Marxism then, is expressed in his registration of the fragility of particular existents. The idea of 'micrology' which he presents at the end of *Negative Dialectics*, is an attempt to acknowledge the dispersed and indivisible sufferings of those who inhabit the reified totality of monopoly capitalism (*ibid.*, p. 407). And so the moral and aesthetic temper of his critique is deeply melancholic; for it remains responsible to the damaged life which the particular must lead after its 'day of creation'.

Modernity therefore, has determined a particular fate for artistic representation. On the one hand, the fact of Auschwitz has robbed existence of its essential purposiveness, while on the other the culture industry is constantly seeking to make good this loss through the mass production of kitsch culture. It is under these conditions that art must determine its relationship to its concept: for it must seek to disclose, in its limited independence, the violence of the system which makes it both possible and necessity (Adorno, 1999, p. 194). Such disclosures are, by definition, disturbing pieces of micrology; they reject the traditions of taste and symmetry, and force us to to question the smooth, technological integration of society. One might think here of art works like Damien Hirst's comment on the relationship between nature and technology, *Mother and Child Divided*. This, however, raises a problem. For if the culture industry continues to expand through increasingly powerful communications technologies, and if those technologies are, as Adorno and Horkheimer claimed, repetitive and trivializing, then where will such art works produce their effects? Who, in other words, will be there to receive them?

Benjamin: Culture and Techological Reproducibility

One possible way out of this dilemma, would be to argue that the technological production of images determines a transformative potential which is unique to the modern epoch. Film and photography, in other words, would open the *possibility* of a mass political imagination that would arise out of the re-presentation and intensification of everyday experience. This is the position explored by Walter Benjamin in 'The work of art in the age of mechanical reproduction'. We should, however, be careful not to present Benjamin's work simply as a 'solution' to the dilemmas posed by the culture industry thesis. His sketch of the transition from auratic to post-auratic art is marked by an acute awareness of the reactionary potential of mass communications technology. The epilogue to 'The work of art', for example, points to the uniquely massifying power of film: its ability to represent the 'eternal' characteristics of a people (*Volk*) to itself, and to dramatize their historical destiny. Yet beyond this massifying artifice there lies a critical potential: the possibility of pulling into focus the social political and ethical dilemmas that arise from the technological constitution of our 'living present'. There is a sense, I will argue in which this transformative potential is what remains at stake in postmodernist accounts of the aesthetic. Baudrillard's work, as we will see, develops the logic of technological reproduction to the point where the reflective distinction between art and fashion has utterly collapsed. Lyotard's account of the sublime and the avant garde, on the other hand, attempts to salvage the politically transformative power of art from the capitalization of high culture. Before examining their respective positions, however, we need to look more closely at Benjamin's understanding of the historical and political significance of the aesthetic.

Like Adorno, Benjamin's relationship to Marx is complex and difficult to specify. There is certainly a sense in which his writing seeks to respond to what he understands as the essence of historical materialism – the 'weak messianic power' of every generation to redeem something of the suffering of its forebears (Benjamin, W., 1992, p. 246). Also, the analysis of culture that is characteristic of his work, retains the Marxist practice of immanent critique; of subjecting established categories of justice, beauty and morality to the 'profane illumination' of history. Marx and Benjamin, in other words, both sought to understand the mode of production in terms of the developmental tendencies that were propelling it towards its historical future. In Marx's writings, we have seen that this analysis is focused on the critique of bourgeois political economy and the formulation of radically transformative categories like 'surplus value' and the 'rate of exploitation'. 'The work of art', on the other hand, is focused on the 'outmodedness' of bourgeois art; or rather on the conflict which arises from the bourgeois demand for timeless, unique and authentic pieces of art work, and the rise of the technologically reproducible image. For Benjamin, this conflict between the ideological power of bourgeois culture (its representations of morality, good taste, control, forbearance) and the revolutionary potential of film and photography, is crucially important. He develops the idea that the economic 'base' and the ideological 'superstructure' are in fact 'asynchronic'; and that consequently we can be justified in treating the 'image sphere' (the realm in which culture and tradition are re-presented) as an autonomous realm of political action.

According to Benjamin, the evolution of technologically reproducible images (printing, photography, cinema) demands to be recognized as a *possible extension of the apperceptive powers of the masses* – not just as completing the transformative power of ideology. In 'The work of art', he claims that the criteria of essence, authenticity and timelessness through which art has attempted to capture the 'aura' of particular objects, belong to levels of technological development which limit both the graphical and the apperceptive powers of humanity. Auratic art originates in the ancient demands of magic and religiosity. For we may surmise, Benjamin claims, that the sacred images with which Stone Age man decorated his dwelling place were primarily 'cultic' in their significance, and not intended for public display or contemplation. With the emergence of photography, however, 'exhibition value begins to replace cult value all along the line'. The very earliest photographic portraits, with their 'fleeting expression of the human face', mark the last appearance of aura before the medium expands the field of representation beyond the authority of the cult (Benjamin, W., 1992, p. 219). The invention of photography, in other words, is the point at which the religious significance of the icon is displaced by a different economy of representation. For in so far as the technological powers of the medium have exceeded the auratic values of divine inspiration and eternal truth, the image attains exactly the political significance which Benjamin is determined to pursue:

> When the age of mechanical reproduction separated art from its basis in cult, the semblance of its autonomy disappeared forever. The resulting change in the function of art transcended the perspective of the century; for a long time it even escaped that of the twentieth century, which experienced the development of film. (*ibid.*, p. 220)

We can discern, then, a logic of technological anticipation in Benjamin's essay. Woodcut printing was the first artistic form in which the hand of the artist was replaced by a device designed to facilitate the re-production of the image. Photographic technology is the heir to this primitive kind of reproducibility – subjecting, as it does, the object to *entirely* technological processes of manipulation and dissemination. These processes, of course, anticipate the emergence of film technology at the beginning of the twentieth century. For in so far as photography is able to suggest a dynamics of speed, continuity and fluidity, its configuration of images demands the technological means to present the spectacle of movement. Indeed, this demand for a properly kinesthetic medium is what is expressed in the artistic devices of cubism, surrealism and dadaism. Each, in its own distinctive way, attempted to capture the dynamism of technological society; and yet each could do no more than press against the inherent restrictions of literary, graphical and sculptural innovation. The artistic movements which grew out of modernity, in other words, created a demand for the optical register of film (*ibid.*, p. 230).

In his essay on surrealism, which predates 'The work of art' by at least six years,[1] Benjamin remarked that

> metaphysical materialism ... as is attested to by the experience of the surrealists ... cannot lead without rupture to anthropological materialism. There is a residue. The collective is a body too. And the *physis* that is being organized for it in technology can, through all its political and factual reality, only be produced in that image sphere to which profane illumination initiates us. (Benjamin, 1997b, p. 239)

This complex quotation requires some unpacking. The 'anthropological materialism' which gets ruptured by the surrealist response to technological modernity, is the kind of providential history which is the counterpart of Enlightenment metaphysics. Kant's 'Idea for a universal history', for example, maintains that despite the apparent contingency of human events, there are certain peculiarly 'historical' occurrences that disclose the ultimate purpose underlying the existence of the human species. Nature, in other words, is organized so as to produce, 'in the long run', the confederation of states which will ensure the peace and prosperity of humankind (Kant, 1991, pp. 41–53). For Benjamin, however, the impact of technology on human experience, cannot be subsumed under this kind of idealist teleology (Benjamin, W., 1992, pp. 245–58). However, the 'residue' to which he refers in the quotation is the residue of the *physis*, or providential nature, which is the foundation of rational anthropology. Thus, although we can no longer assume that history has an underlying purpose, we must still confront the shocking, distracting and disorientating effects of technology on the physical constitution of humanity. It is these effects, in other words, which supply the body of the collective with a nervous system, giving it a sensory 'innervation' which demands to be represented. To return to the impact of filmic images, then, we can now see that the 'tactility' of these images corresponds to the physical demands exacted by the technological organization of human society. Film, in other words, has a revolutionary-imaginative potential which brings the transformative power of technology into the 'image sphere to which profane illumination initiates us'. Each of us, confronted with the spectacle of our own distracted existence, is forced to reflect upon the necessities – of work, habitation, communication – that have come to rule our lives (*ibid.*, p. 229).

What the essay on surrealism demands, and what 'The work of art' attempts to clarify, therefore, is an 'interpenetration' of technology, body and image, in which 'all revolutionary tension becomes bodily collective innervation' (Benjamin, 1997b, p. 239). Marx's demand for transcendence of the existing reality of collective life becomes a matter of channelling the tensions of that life into the 'profane illumination' of the image. For in so far as films are able to involve the masses in a tactile re-presentation of their bodily experience – through the distortion and decontextualization of familiar objects, for example – they sustain the possibility of a public reaction that is simultaneously distracted, reflexive and moral. The possibility of a redemptive or 'messianic' history therefore, emerges through the interpenetration of technology, body and image which is, by definition, a phenomenon of the masses. It is within the 'image sphere' of the film, in other words, that the physical attrition of the present is brought into relation with the suffering of the past and its *possible* redemption in the future (Benjamin, W., 1992, p. 255).

For Benjamin, what remains significant about the bourgeois art of the late nineteenth and early twentieth centuries, is its attempt to sustain the principles of genius and authenticity against the technological expansion of the image sphere. Initially, photography and film were conceived as inferior to works of fine art in which the moral and religious demands of aura were clearly visible. True art, it was claimed, is executed under the stricture of divine inspiration and seeks the signature of God in every facet of the created world. According to Benjamin, however, the emergence of photography and film initiate a reconfiguration of experience, in which the concepts of 'eternal value' and 'authenticity' are profoundly threatened by the speed with which images can be produced and communicated. For it is only in so far as a work of art can be definitely identified as 'an original' that its presence to the perceiver can maintain its morally enlightening value. This tension between the shocking effects of modernity and the reactionary demand that the timelessness of things should be the subject of art, is a recurrent theme in Benjamin's writing. In his essay 'Some motifs in Baudelaire', for example, he remarks that the melancholic beauty of Baudelaire's poems derives from his awareness that 'the price for which the sensation of the modern age may be had [is] the disintegration of aura and the experience of shock' (Benjamin, W., 1992, p. 190). In 'The work of art', this tension is expressed in terms of the relationship between fascist politics and the persistence of cultic ideals of genius, eternal value and mystery (*ibid.*, 1992, p. 212). For Benjamin, the importance of this persistence lies in the fact that it is prolonged by the very technological media whose development has called the 'metaphorical' basis of bourgeois authority into question. Fascism, in other words, demands an 'auratic processing' of the experience of technological modernity. The ideals of timelessness and eternality are identified as attributes of the masses as they are assembled in political rallies, compete with each other in sports events, and ultimately fight and die in the theatre of industrialized warfare. Such events, as Benjamin points out in his epilogue to 'The work of art', constitute a demand for filmic reproduction; a demand in which the *Volk* is gathered into a spectacle of war and ceremony that discharges the messianic power of its generation (*ibid.*, p. 234–5).

As political responses to the crises of modernity, both fascism and communism disclose fundamentally reactionary possibilities of the aesthetic. Fascism shows that the mass distraction made possible by visual technology has become essential to the political manipulation of social and economic crises. The 'Tour of the German inflation' presented in *One Way Street*, for example, makes it clear that any political resurrection of the German nation state would have to resurrect feelings of Germanic identity from a condition of total economic collapse (Benjamin, 1997b, pp. 54–5). Nazism's historic intervention in the life of Weimar Germany was a response to crises – of unemployment, hyperinflation, social dislocation – whose scale seemed almost sublime, and whose consequences incalculable. The images of the *Volk* massed together in preparation for war therefore, derived their political power from the 'mysterious contact' between the image of the German spirit and the threat of its annihilation. The 'proletarian art' which emerged in Russia after the revolution however, retained a thoroughly bourgeois nostalgia for the past. For although it achieved a certain democratization of culture, the political significance of pieces like *The Conspirator Surprised by the Police* or *The Poor Governess Enters Service in a Rich Merchant's House* remained tied to the 'eternal spirit' of the revolution. In the end, the Bolshevik art which Benjamin found in the galleries of Moscow, depicted the kind of idealized heroism which had characterized the 'reactionary' temper of the bourgeoisie (*ibid.*, p. 182–4). Under fascism, then, cinematic representation provokes the violent anti-modernism of *Führer* cult; under communism, the imaginative power of visual art is limited to a constant remaking of *the* revolutionary moment.

The essential characteristic of nineteenth-century bourgeois art was its attempt to present the moral parameters of bourgeois political life (decency, self-reliance, fidelity). The reproduction of this realm of artistic metaphor, however, was continued against the background of an increasingly technological society; a society whose 'moral' cohesiveness was already being challenged by innovations in manufacturing, architecture, communications and cinematic techniques. This is why so much of Benjamin's writing – particularly the massive *Arcades Project* – is concerned with the social and cultural transformations of nineteenth-century Europe. For it is in this 'original' configuration of the relationship between technology and cultural and artistic conservatism, that Benjamin attempts to trace the political consequences of technological modernity. Fascism and communism, we have seen, are attempts to reinvigorate the power of tradition (being, persistence, substantiality) by means of the very technologies which have made the foundations of bourgeois society so insecure. And so if the transformative power of technology is to be mobilized in a way which does not seek the re-establishment of aura as the foundation of political authority, then our own living present must be conceived as the heir to a nineteenth-century inheritance whose possibilities have as yet gone unfulfilled. This demand that the present should be conceived in terms of its relationship to the unrealized potential of the past, returns us to the 'profane illumination' which ought to inform political practice in the age of technological reproducibility. The failure of the 'revolutionary intelligentsia' to make political contact with the masses is for Benjamin due to the fact that their imagination of proletarian experience – and its transformative potential – is limited by the 'liberal-moral-humanistic ideal of freedom' (*ibid.*, p. 236). What surrealist art and literature began to do, however, was to question the continued validity of the auratic categories which defined the moral parameters of liberal democracy. By attending to the 'outmodedness' of the forms in which new technologies made their impact on the cultural and economic life of nineteenth-century society – 'the first iron constructions, the first factory buildings, the earliest photos, objects that have begun to be extinct' (*ibid.*, p. 229) – surrealist art called into question the ideals unintentionally parodied in bourgeois taste and culture. Technology, in other words, is disclosed as the cause of a shocking and inevitable destitution of things; a destitution which, for Benjamin, is fatally attractive to the authors of cinematic technique and to the historical-revolutionary imagination of the necessities which currently determine our lives (Benjamin, W., 1992, p. 229).

Yet even surrealism's attempt to transform the destitution of past objects into 'revolutionary nihilism' (Benjamin, 1997b, p. 229), is touched with a certain 'mystification' of the forces of technological modernity. Both Breton and Apollinare, for example, end up by claiming that scientific innovation originates in 'surrealistic rather than logical thinking' (*ibid.*, p. 232). According to Benjamin's account of the dynamics of post-auratic art, such 'overheated' debate about the unity of the surrealistic imagination with the technological liberation of humanity, can only serve to disclose the limits of surrealism's representation of modern experience. In 'The work of art', Benjamin remarks that 'one of the foremost tasks of art has always been the creation of a demand which could be fully satisfied only later' (Benjamin, W., 1992, p. 230). And so while futurism, dadaism, cubism and surrealism all make their own attempts to capture the dynamics of modern experience, their media of expression – painting, writing, sculpture, poetry – impose fundamental limitations upon their ability to transform that experience into a political relationship of the masses to the technological body of society. It is clear from Benjamin's literary-philosophical descriptions of Paris, Moscow and Berlin, that the possibility of such a relationship begins with the transformation of urban space made possible by architectural techniques and building technologies. From the nineteenth century onwards, the urban environment evolves as the *physis*, or embodiment, of technological innovation; its buildings, arcades, factories, public spaces, thoroughfares are constantly changing in response to technological innovations. The nature of human perception in this constantly transformed urban space cannot be subsumed under a priori principles of recognition; for every experience of the modern city is characterized by a transience and porosity which defies identification as either public or private, disciplined or spontaneous, sacred or profane. So if, as Benjamin claims, the purpose of art has shifted from the production of contemplative representations of ethical life (the bourgeois family at home with their 'enslaving objects', for example) towards a mediation of the relationship between humanity and technology, then we must acknowledge that artistic production bears directly upon the political exigencies of the present. For in so far as the experience of modernity is characterized by the constant adaptation of human beings to the shocks, dangers and risks that are encountered in the metropolis, technologically produced art must aim at a futural representation of the adaptive spontaneity already in play in 'the masses' (*ibid.*, p. 233).

We have seen that cubism and futurism are both 'deficient attempts of art to accommodate the perversion of reality by the apparatus' (Benjamin, 1992, p. 243). Both try to capture technologically produced distortions of space and time through media which belong essentially to the contemplative tradition of art. And so while futurism and cubism might begin to express the disquieting transience and porosity of urban experience, they are no more than anticipations of the representational effects made possible by film. This new, explicitly technological medium cannot simply re-present the stability of bourgeois moral life. Rather, its power to specify, to enlarge, to slow down or to speed up the already shocking and disorientating nature of modern experience, means that the content of filmic representation always carries within it the possibility of reimagining the technological body of society. Film, in other words, has the power both to expand and intensify the experiences of shock which mark the adaptation of the masses to the scientific, technological and economic forces of modernity. Indeed, Benjamin compares Freud's disclosure of the unconscious motives of everyday speech and action with the power of film to pull into focus the forms of proletarian experience that arise in technological society. As a distinctively modern, distinctively technological sphere of attention therefore, film has a certain transformative potential. It offers the possibility of radical reconfiguration of perception, whose 'unexpectedness' is able to cut across the processes of social, economic and political reification (Benjamin, W., 1992, p. 229)

At the end of the essay on surrealism, Benjamin remarks that the technological body of modern society demands to be represented. This demand, we have seen, can only be satisfied technologically – that is, through the capacity of film to expand and intensify the adaptive powers of human beings within the exigencies of their living present. Allowing then, that the experience of technologically constituted necessity remains essentially proletarian (for Benjamin, technological reorganizations of work, transport, habitation and communication are experienced by the masses as a 'second nature' over which they have little control), universal representation of the social body emerges as the demand of a new revolutionary politics. Such a politics would arise not from the cumulative alienation of the working class as a historical subject, but rather from the physical and psychological adaptability of the masses to the forces of technocratic control. There is, however, no necessity that this transform-ative representation should be recognized by the dominant political authority: Benjamin's account of fascism shows that film can be used to great effect in channelling the mass experience of modernity into the production of a 'timeless' national identity. It is important therefore, to keep in mind that his understanding of the transformative significance of film is essentially speculative. His notions of unconscious optics and distracted attention attempt to disclose the futural-imaginative potential which film brings to the technological organization of society, and to situate that potential within the context of historically established political ideals. Thus, while the representational techniques of film do begin to bring about a transformation of the perceptual powers of the masses, this transformation takes place within the cyclical re-enactment of hegemonic ideals which Benjamin describes in his 'Theses on the philosophy of history' (Benjamin, W., 1992, pp. 252–3). This version of revolutionary politics is ultimately responsible to an imagined/unconscious social future whose possibility is always threatened by the return of 'the eternal', 'the timeless', 'the true' principles of political authority.

The possibility of wresting the present from auratic configurations of truth, community and identity returns in Benjamin's correspondence with Adorno. In a letter to Benjamin concerning his notes towards the *Arcades Project*, Adorno complains that his account of urban experience tends towards an obsessive and undialectical cataloguing of details (Adorno *et al.*, 1977, pp. 110–33). Benjamin's project, in other words, is charged with abandoning the method of speculative materialism; the method which, for Adorno, demands scrupulous attention to the cultural, economic and psychological transformations through which the modern individual has been made. Adorno's accusation that Benjamin's writing had lapsed into an obsessive positivism, however, fails to recognize the historical signifi-cance of his critique of perception. Benjamin's philosophy of experience begins with a questioning of Kant's account of the a priori categories that determine phenomenal experience. Kant's fundamental dictum that the absolute, the 'thing-as-it-is-in-itself', is beyond all possibility of appercep-tion is disputed on the grounds that such a radical separation both presupposes and reinforces the reduction of experience to causal transac-tions between objects. This experience provides the basis of a distinction between knowledge and metaphysics in which the latter is restricted to sketching the legislative domains – of law, ethics, morality – which follow from the certainty of phenomenal cognition. For Benjamin, however, the reduction of experience to the causal transactions of objects which confront the 'knowing subject', itself depends upon the entire metaphysics (and theology) that is implicated in the Enlightenment project. And so if Kant's epistemology depends on this objectifying metaphysics, then, Benjamin argues, it cannot be legitimate to maintain that the conditions of its possibility designate the set of all possible relations between the subject and reality.

Freed from this Kantian restriction, Benjamin claims that metaphysics 'can emerge as essential to every form of human experience' (Benjamin, 1997a, p. 105). For in so far as my present perception of the world and its objects can be separated neither from its generational ideals, nor from the shocks and discontinuities of historical transformation, any 'future metaphysics' must attempt to articulate a continuum between philosophy, experience and imagination (*ibid.*). Thus, if there are no universal categories through which epistemological certainty can be determined, and if we must admit that our experience is always constituted through the 'continuous multiplicity of knowledge', then the task of speculative criticism must be to look at the ways in which dominant forms of perceptual organization have impacted upon the possibility of autonomous imagination of the future (*ibid.*, 1997a, p. 108). Nazism, for example, attempted to transform the German nation state through a technological reproduction of the 'aura' of the *Volk*; a reproduction whose 'futurity' is proclaimed in the centuries of glorifying war and conquest that were to sustain the 'Thousand Year Reich'. The presentation of empirical data in Benjamin's work therefore, is done neither out of an obsessive positivism nor out of a flagrant neglect of the massifying powers of technological modernity. Rather, it constitutes a demand that political theory attend to the continuity of freedom and experience; a continuity which, for Benjamin, can be recognized only in the everyday relations which both open and constrain the futural imagination of the present.

I want to conclude this section by making a distinction. This distinction has to do with historical time – or, more precisely, with the 'lateness' of late capitalism. We have seen that for Adorno, the method of speculative idealism demands attention to the increasingly close relationship between the technological production of culture (reification) and the growth of a monolithic 'bloc' of industrial capital. We have also seen that for Benjamin, Adorno's attempt to extend Marx's ideology thesis to the technological reproduction of images begins with an altogether too deterministic account of new aesthetic media. The evolution of artistic productivity from its contemplative-auratic forms into the 'distracted' spectacle of the film, demands a critique of Marx's notion of art as 're' or 'mis' representation (Benjamin, W., 1992, p. 212). This difference in the historiological structure of Adorno and Benjamin's accounts of culture and technology, is fundamental to understanding the relationship between Marxist and postmodernist theories of culture. I will argue shortly that Fredric Jameson's attempt to account for postmodern art, culture and theory as the 'reflex of another systematic modification of capitalism', reproduces Adorno's logic of increasing reification (Jameson, 1995, p. xi).

The temporality of capital, in other words, is disclosed as an infinite continuum of cultural phenomena, each of which momentarily reinvigorates the mass sensations of freedom, satisfaction and desire without affecting the logic of objectification. Benjamin's attempt to expound the technological transformation of the aesthetic, however, prefigures the messianic temporality which he describes in the 'Theses on the philosophy of history'. For Benjamin, the mechanical reproducibility of the image demands that we approach aesthetic experience in terms of its reconfiguration of the present. The technological arts of film and photography bear witness to the historical tragedy of reification (the 'storm of progress'), while at the same time pointing towards its unrealized possibilities of emancipation (Benjamin, W., 1992, p. 249). This difference between the messianic time of Benjamin's 'Theses on the philosophy of history' and the endless repetition of the culture industry, is essential to a proper understanding of the relationship between Marxism and postmodernism. For it is only in so far as we are prepared to acknowledge that postmodernist theory has specified a certain aesthetics of deferral, repetition, intensification and simulation, that the possibility of salvaging a Marxist critique of culture remains open.

Jameson: the Cultural Logic of Late Capitalism

In the introduction to the book I proposed a classification in which Jameson's work was characterized by a concern with the fate of aesthetic experience under the conditions of late capitalism. I need briefly to reiterate the main points of his argument. In a recent essay, 'Transformations of the image in postmodernity' (Jameson, 1998, pp. 93–135), Jameson proposes that postmodern theory has become increasingly concerned to rehabilitate the classical texts of ethics, political theory, aesthetics and theology. His claim is that this 'return' to the metaphysical questions which occupied philosophy before Marx's disclosure of the ideational powers of the mode of production, marks the emergence of a distinctively postmodern ideology. According to Jameson, the postmodernist reversion to the traditional questions of philosophy, is marked by a neglect of the historical conditions under which those questions became urgent. The importance of the aesthetic in this abstraction of politics from traditionally Marxist concerns, then, lies in its re-emergence as an explicitly metaphysical pursuit of the beautiful. For in so far as the relationship between the development of the forces of production and the evolution of artistic productivity is neglected by postmodernist aesthetic theory, the most important effect of late capitalism is erased from the sphere of political critique: the sheer commodification of the image.

Jameson's essay provides a lengthy discussion of how the field of vision passes beyond the panoptical discipline of Foucault's carceral society and eventually fulfils its technological intensification in the 'enjoyment' of universal visibility (Jameson, 1998, p. 111). What is important here is the saturation of public and private space by a culture which has become dislocated from the strictures of truth and beauty. For where everything becomes 'acculturated', the 'traditional distinctiveness, or "specificity", of the aesthetic (and even culture as such) is necessarily blurred or lost altogether' (*ibid.*). The aestheticization which is charateristic of post-modern culture therefore, should be conceived as the ideological reflex of an increasingly rationalized, increasingly global organization of capital. Film, video and computer technologies determine a visual experience in which the intensity of the image does no more than repeat the commodi-fied wants and desires of late capitalism. For Jameson, this aesthetic instantaneity is inimical to any historical understanding of its relationship to the mode of production. And so the temporal awareness which informs postmodern politics, is ultimately a reflection of the processes through which capital has completed its rationalization of public, private, national and global space.

In an assessment of the fate of culture that is reminiscent of *Dialectic of Enlightenment*, Jameson remarks:

> Here [within the spatial-objective processes of capitalism] homogeneity has become heterogeneity, in a moment complementary to that in which absolute movement changed into absolute stasis, and without the slightest modification of a real history that was thought to be at an end. (Jameson, 1998, p. 72)

The 'play' of cultural heterogeneity that is celebrated in postmodern theories of the aesthetic, in other words, demands to be referred to those material processes which have brought about the total reification of social and cultural life. For both Jameson and Adorno, this reduction of culture to the organizational demands of late capitalism produces a certain violence (what Adorno often refers to as 'barbarism') in which the satisfactions of everyday life become increasingly calculable, predictable, standardized elements in the administration of 'the collective'. Crucially, however, Jameson's account of this process differs from Adorno's in that while the latter describes it as an inevitable consequence of the extension of the Enlightenment's instrumental teleology to the realm of cultural production, Jameson is concerned to show how late capitalism has exceeded the corporate-industrial logic whose history is presented in *Dialectic of Enlightenment*. We need then to specify the factors which, for Jameson, differentiate the postmodern stage of capitalist development from the 'nexus of rationality and social actuality' set out by Adorno and Horkheimer.

In the introduction to his *Postmodernism*, Jameson proposes that postmodernity is characterized by 'the consumption of sheer commodifi-cation as a process', and that consequently his own cultural critique must be understood as a comprehensive modification of Adorno and Hor-kheimer's culture industry thesis (Jameson, 1995, p. x). Empirically, Jameson enumerates the following as causative factors in the emergence of the aestheticized culture he identifies with the postmodern: competition and cooperation of multinational corporations replacing the old 'imperialist' competition of nation states; the emergence of an international division of labour (and the dissolution of 'national' proletarian solidarities); the power of corporate finance (Second and Third world debts and the constitution of a new global hegemony); the development of increasingly sophisticated communications and media technology (and the rise of information as a commodity); computerization and automation; Third World production (and the shift of multinational capital out of traditional 'first world' locations); the crisis of traditional labour (and the decline of 'old style' socialism). This enumeration of the social, economic and technological factors involved in the transition to 'late capitalism', is important because it begins to clarify the regulative structures which inform Jameson's critique of postmodernity. What he is concerned to do throughout the analyses of film, video, architecture and culture which comprise *Postmodernism*, is to argue that postmodernist aestheticism is 'only the reflex and concomitant of yet another systematic modification of capitalism itself' (Jameson, 1998, p. xi). In its promise to get rid of whatever is 'boring or confining' in modernity therefore, postmodern culture should be understood as an aesthetic transformation of the masses; a transformation whose necessity arises with the total commodification of the image (*ibid.*, p. xiv).

If there is an ethical imperative that issues from Adorno's critical theory, it is that we should 'attempt to contemplate all things as they would present themselves from the point of view of redemption' (Adorno, 1996, p. 247). Such a demand is founded upon Adorno's insistence that modern culture should be conceived as a progressive descent into the 'hell' of technologically reproducible images, meanings and reactions; the hell which threatens to complete humanity's 'conversion into appendages of machinery' (*ibid.*, p. 147). As we have seen, Horkheimer and Adorno's theory of late capitalism sets out the dynamics of the mutually reinforcing processes through which humanity is forced into ever more 'abstract' social relations. Their account of the collapse of the Enlightenment project into an ideology of systematic control, makes it clear that the expansion of surplus value depends upon the functionalizing powers of instrumental reason. For without the increasing penetration of social and cultural relationships by the demands of speed, uniformity and replaceability, there could be no possibility of establishing the administered unity of mass production, commodified culture and consumption set out in *Dialectic of Enlightenment*.

This account of the relationship between the commodification of culture and the rationalization of capital returns us to Jameson's attempt to extend Adorno's critique. Clearly, the sense in which we should understand the relationship between commodification and rationalization presented in *Dialectic of Enlightenment*, is instrumental rather than moral: corporate finance administers the desire of the masses in order to ensure that what is produced finds consumers already disposed to the apparent novelty of its products. For Jameson, however, this account of the commodity as a form which faithfully mediates between the rational-administrative powers of corporate finance and the homogeneous desires of the masses, is inadequate to understand the latest phase of capitalism. His claim is that the logic of reification set out by Adorno and Horkheimer has been superseded by the 'consumption of sheer commodification as a process' (Jameson, 1995, p. x). This modification of the relationship between culture and economy cannot, according to Jameson, be conceived in terms of the functional perfection of the object: the total reification of relations between the mass of consumers and corporate capital. The social and political dynamics of commodification have to be reconceptualized, taking into account the structural changes in the mode of production enumerated above. For Jameson, these changes produce a far more anarchic, de-regulated form of commodification than the one presented in *Dialectic of Enlightenment*: a form which demands that social criticism concentrate on the relationship between the techno-scientific development of capitalism and the celebration of difference, evanescence and heterogeneity which he calls 'postmodernism'.

As we have seen, Jameson argues that postmodern culture is no more than the 'reflex' of structural changes that have occurred in the mode of production. This claim, I will argue, proceeds from two assumptions: the first about the possibility of producing a dialectical critique of 'sheer commodification as a process', the second about the political significance that such a critique would have. The critical stance which Jameson develops in his later work, is characterized by its attempts to retain the speculative-materialist significance which Adorno attributed to ideas of nature, humanity and community. His analysis of postmodern culture is concerned to show that postmodernist art, literature and film have extended our ludic-aesthetic experience into a narrative of spectacular events unconnected to the political crises of the present. In the end, this ideological presentation of time as the pure distraction of the 'now', is organized around the production of 'new people' capable of functioning after the demise of traditional forms of class solidarity, the globalization of capital, and the total penetration of human experience by electronically produced images. Such people would be adaptable to rapidly changing patterns of employment, have little attachment to any occupation or occupational group, and be highly attuned to the aestheticization/ commodification of public space. And so for Jameson, the kind of insubstantial subjectivity which emerges as the counterpart of post-modern culture, demands a critical articulation of the conditions which formed it:

Historical reconstruction ... the abstraction from the 'blooming, buzzing confusion' of immediacy, was always a radical intervention in the promise of resistance to its blind fatalities. (Jameson, 1998, p. 35)

Instead of abandoning the methodological strictures of Marxism in an attempt to determine the uniqueness of postmodern culture, in other words, we need to trace the play of technologically produced appearances back to the objectively self-coordinating logic of the mode of production. For Jameson, as for Adorno, the future of radical politics depends upon recognizing the relationship between culture, aesthetics and the techno-economic dimension of desire.

There is, then, a sense in which Jameson's critique of postmodernism can be seen as an extension of Adorno's critique of kitsch culture (Adorno,1996, pp. 225–7). For in so far as he attempts to identify the ludic and distracting strands of postmodern art, culture and theory, his major concern is to expound the relationship between the cultural transformation of subjective identity and the technological evolution of capitalism. This, I think, raises a question about the critical economy of Jameson's writing. For having defined postmodernism as a kind of nominalist aesthetic (the valorization of evanescent and incommensurable events), he then approaches the major strands of postmodernist theory from the perspective of one who is in possession of the truth of their identity (Jameson, 1998, p. 37). Thus, in spite of the originality of his modification of Adorno's critique of culture, Jameson's determination to regard Baudrillard, Lyotard and Derrida's work simply as variations on a general theme, discloses a crucial ambiguity in his writing. For while he is prepared to acknowledge much of what postmodern theory has proposed concerning the technological evolution of the mode of production (the 'spectralizing' power of digital and informatic technologies, the media saturation of society), he remains determined to preserve the negative unity of late capitalism.

At the beginning of *Postmodernism*, Jameson acknowledges that his analysis of the acculturation of the social draws significantly on Baudrillard's ideas of simulation and hyperreality. This borrowing of concepts from the postmodernist genre immediately raises the question of commensurability. The logic of Baudrillard's account of 'transeconomic capitalism', as we will see in a moment, is escalatory. The argument which Baudrillard pursues in *The Transparency of Evil* is that Marx's critique of capital expresses an entirely consistent logic from which the necessity of revolutionary transcendence would indeed follow from the damage incurred by productive humanity (Baudrillard, 1995a, pp. 26–35). If, in other words, the ethical parameters of exploitation could actually be expressed through the concepts of emiseration, deskilling and alienation, then the revolution would already have occurred as a result of capital's total abstraction of human labour. For Baudrillard, however, the logic through which Marx characterized his own historical present could not include the possibility of a 'transeconomical' capitalism, whose powers of exploitation and commodification would exceed any possible return to the dialectics of proletarian solidarity. Marx's account of the imperialist phase of capitalism, for example, maintains that there will eventually come a point at which there are no more cheaply exploitable resources (both human and natural) and that this will lead to an international crisis of economic growth. For Baudrillard, however, the teleological structure of Marx's critique has been exceeded by the logic of transeconomical capitalism. The concept of exploitation through which Marx expounded the revolutionary potential of colonialism and imperialism has to be revised in view of the increasingly post-industrial nature of capitalist economics. Where once it was the production of commodities that was of primary importance in the international turnover of capital, it is now specialist knowledge, techno-scientific innovation and the flow of information that are of paramount importance. Thus, the gap between 'Third' and 'First' world economies is reproduced through the logic of simulation: scientific knowledge constantly redefines what are to count as 'resources' (our expanding conception of biodiversity, for example), technological innovation makes those resources exploitable and, at the same time, Third World nations are maintained through the accumulation of massive 'virtual debts' which constantly extend their exploitability. In the end, the logic of simulation through which capital fulfils its amorality can never give rise to that concatenation of suffering which brings down the edifice. For Baudrillard, capital is deadly repetition ('metonymy'), a functional logic that constantly exceeds the boundaries of its functioning (*ibid.*).

I will argue later that Baudrillard's analysis of hyperlogical capital underplays the ideational conditions through which the exploiter–exploited relationship is historically constructed and transformed. However, there is an important sense in which Baudrillard's account of the relationship between the media, simulation and capital discloses something of the limits of Jameson's Marxism. What Baudrillard's later writing has succeeded in doing is to register the extremity of the powers of telematic and communications technology – especially in relation to the politics of collective will. Thus, in so far as Jameson is determined to trace the power of simulation back to an Adornian dialectics of violence, poesis and critique, his Marxism articulates a significance of objects, nature and human beings which redeems the facticity of mass culture. But what if this facticity, as Baudrillard claims, operates *exclusively* through technological procedures of simulation and solicitation? And what if the practico-redemptive significance of the referent has been utterly lost within the hyperlogical transactions of capital? Baudrillard's remarks on transeconomic capitalism therefore demand that we reflect on the nature of any continued commitment to a Marxist critique of culture – and in particular the attempt to reintegrate 'late-capitalist' forms of exploitation and technological representation into the dialectics of political enlightenment.

Note

1. Howard Caygill's commentary on 'The work of art in the age of mechanical reproduction' makes a number of acute observations on the differences that exist between the three drafts of Benjamin's essay (Caygill, 1998, pp. 97–118). The version from which I have quoted is the final draft, which was completed in 1939 and reprinted in the English collection *Illuminations*.

7

Information, Simulation and the 'Silent Majorities'

Introduction

In this chapter I will look at Jean Baudrillard's account of simulation and its relationship to both Marxist and postmodernist economies of culture, identity and community. In particular, I will examine the 'evil possibility' determined in Baudrillard's writing: namely, that in our media-saturated world, the image (simulacrum) has supplanted the real, and that the ethical, political and aesthetic configurations of experience have exceeded any reference to what is not already included in the economy of simulation. Specifically, then, I will cover the following issues:

- the relationship between the image and the referent presented in Baudrillard's essay 'The precession of simulacra';
- the collapse of 'the real' (sex, love, class conflict, socialism) into the 'weightless' play of images (simulacra) staged by the mass media;
- the relationship between simulation and the 'amorality' of capitalism;
- the creation of 'the masses' as an inert body of consumers who simply absorb every solicitation to act, to deliberate, to choose (*In the Shdow of the Silent Majorities*).

Capitalism and Simulation

Before turning to the detail of Baudrillard's account of simulation, I need briefly to situate his work in relation to the concepts of commodification, technology, representation and ideology which have been set out in the previous chapter.

There is certainly a sense in which it is possible to read Baudrillard's work as announcing postmodernity as the worst possible outcome of the Marxist critique of culture. The concepts of simulation and hyperreality which have informed his work since the publication of *Simulacra and Simulation* (Baudrillard, 1999), seem to take the feeling of catastrophe which pervades Benjamin and Adorno's writing beyond any hope of salvation. We have seen that, for Adorno, the reification of social and cultural relations, the collapse of art into the kitsch triviality of the culture industry, and the reduction of the individual to a passive consumer of images and commodities, has still to be understood from the 'standpoint of redemption'. And so even if it is the case that every aspect of social existence has been invaded by the demands of instrumental reason, such a violent colonization does at least reveal 'micrological' traces of the originary forms of human community (work, love, desire, natality). Benjamin's notion of messianic time, on the other hand, is focused on the constant re-evaluation of the past (as 'having been') that is demanded by the 'living present'. Photography and cinematography are conceived as technological innovations that demand a radical shift in our understanding of the social and ideological functions of art. The state of emergency precipitated by fascism's manipulation of the image, for example, stands as the absolute demand of Benjamin's own historical present; a demand which exceeds auratic representation of the past, and which configures the messianic responsibility that befalls every generation. Thus, even though the disastrousness of the modern epoch appears to mark the end of every sacred form of community and obligation, the very coming of the end refers us to a transcendence (the messianic or the micrological) which restores the ethical significance of politics.

Baudrillard's account of the collapse of social reality into simulation, however, is an explicit denial of the possibility of any such transcendence. Close to the beginning of *Simulacra and Simulation* Baudrillard remarks of simulation that:

> It is no longer a question of imitation, or duplication, nor even parody. It is a question of substituting the signs of the real for the real, that is to say of an operation of deterring every real process via its operational double, a programmatic, metastable, perfectly descriptive machine that offers all the signs of the real and short-circuits all its vicissitudes. (Baudrillard, 1999, p. 2)

This initial definition raises a number of important issues. First, we need to be clear that Baudrillard's use of the term simulation does not simply denote the collapse of social reality into a kind of parodic mimesis; a self-consciously 'aestheticized' re-enactment of the goals and ideals of modernity. Second, we should understand Baudrillard's account of the relationship between the real and its representation as a kind of anti-genealogy of appearances, in which it is the very possibility of the social, the ethical and the political which is at stake. For it is only in so far as 'we' (self-conscious human beings) are able to regard the signs and images through which the real is presented to us as signifiers of a transcendent reality, that we are able to live within the moral, legal and political codes of society. Baudrillard makes it clear that the origin of this transcendental guarantee is religious. God, as the Universal Being, is the agent who infallibly sustains the value of the sign as the bearer of his own truth and goodness. Yet even this theological origination of the sign is afflicted with a certain excess; a disruptive logic of appearances that is always beyond the control of the transcendent reality which deploys it. It is the 'visible machinery of icons', in other words, that initiates the fatal self-referentiality of signs which Baudrillard will call simulation (*ibid.*, p. 4). As soon as the the icon comes to stand in for the word, the law and the being of God, then His transcendence is lost in the infinite refraction of images. In the end, even the devotional splendour of religious iconography is insufficient to deter the thought that 'God himself was never anything but his own simulacrum' (*ibid.*, p. 4).

What is important here – and this brings me to my third point – is that, for Baudrillard, the history of the social must be understood as an 'operationalization' of signs which progressively challenges the reality (the transcendence, the necessity) of the referent. Indeed, he argues that we must understand the idea of social evolution in terms of a logic of presentation, concealment and deterrence which culminates in the total absorption of the real into the play of simulation. Initially, the image is taken to be 'the reflection of a profound reality', the reality of a transcendent God (*ibid.*, p. 6). Yet as we have seen, iconography gives rise to a fundamental religious and philosophical questioning of the status of the image and its relationship to the real. This questioning, according to Baudrillard, takes the form of a negative critique of the image; a critique which attempts to disclose the resources and techniques through which representation 'masks and denatures' reality (*ibid.*). This moment corresponds to the Marxist critique of ideology. For in so far as we have been able to identify a common thread running through the cultural critiques of Benjamin, Adorno and Jameson, it is their respective attempts to reconfigure the relationship between ideological forms of cultural production and the objective reality of the economic base. In the previous chapter, however, we saw that Baudrillard's later writing deploys the concept of a 'transeconomic' capitalism in order to denote the breakdown of any causative or speculative relationship between the 'logic' of capitalist accumulation and the 'alienation' of humanity from its transcendent purposes and ideals (Baudrillard, 1995, pp. 26–35).

So, if the Marxist critique of ideology remains tied to the logic of what Baudrillard calls 'second-order simulation' (that is, to the logic of a transcendental referent which is always 'denatured' by the ideological conditions of its appearance), and if this logic has, as he claims, been fatally undermined by the hyperrealization of capital, then we need urgently to examine the political implications of this slide into total simulation. To continue with the economy of appearances set out in *Simulacra and Simulation*, Baudrillard specifies two further stages in the evolution of the image: its masking of 'the absence of a profound reality', and finally the complete loss of reference to the real in which the image has become 'its own pure simulacrum' (Baudrillard, 1999, p. 6). He maintains that when the system of signs becomes totally self-referential, as it now has, '[it] becomes weightless . . . that is to say never exchanged for the real, but exchanged for itself, in an uninterrupted circuit without reference or circumference' (*ibid.*). What this means is that the system of signs – or, more precisely, the system of moral, legal, economic and political norms through which 'the social' expands its hyperfunctionality – is no longer encumbered by any reference to a reality beyond its autonomous self-generation. The violent contingency of the real which has been variously named 'capital', 'sex', 'gender', 'race' or 'culture' is stabilized within a system of universal equivalence where it can no longer exert any regulative power over its simulacra. Sex, for example, ceases to be about the Freudian dynamics of sexual difference (the pain, anxiety and *jouissance* of the ontogenetic schism which underlies the rational life of humanity), and is forced to conform to the universal standards of communicative perform-ance. It becomes, in other words, 'a sort of total promiscuity', in which desire is conducted along channels of communication which are thorough-ly functional, operational and capitalized (Baudrillard, 1995a, p. 66). In the end then, it is the collapse of the real into simulation which produces the necessity of a 'deterrent function' of the system – one whose simulacra of popular morality (Disneyland and Watergate, for example) are designed to reinject some sense the real into the operational circuit of simulation (Baudrillard, 1999, pp. 12–14).

The account of Watergate presented in *Simulacra and Simulation* suggests that the 'scandal' staged by the media and pursued through the judicial processes of impeachment of the president, is actually an attempt to keep the collapse of 'the political' within a 'conventional field of perspective' (*ibid.*, p. 16). The dramatization of Watergate *as if* its truth could be established through the contestation of left- and right-wing orthodoxies (that democratic government has been dangerously under-mined by agencies like the CIA, that Richard Nixon was simply a morally corrupt individual), in other words, amounts to no more than a 'third-order simulation'; a masking of the fact that politics has long since lost any independence from the amorality of capital. For Baudrillard, the circuit of simulation has become so complete that any attempt to circumscribe the 'truth' of particular events – Watergate, the Gulf War, the famines in the Third World, the stock market crash of 1987 – is always an arbitrary imposition of causes and finalities. Events within the system have become no more than abstract points at which heterogeneous 'models' intersect *without the necessity of dialectical communication*. Simulation, therefore, is the 'implosion of agonistic poles'; the coexistence and exchangeability of every contradictory truth 'in a generalized cycle' (*ibid.*, p. 17). There is never any 'objective' resolution of events into their dialectical-historical reality; only the circulation of different models of interpretation, the 'weightlessness', or 'ecstasy', of the hyperreal.

Our present epoch then, is characterized by the erasure of those dialectical oppositions which have sustained both Marxist and enlighten-ment conceptions of historical progress. Each distinctive category of the ethical life of society (the aesthetic, the economic, the sexual, the political) has passed beyond the regulated self-othering through which it is destined to overcome its complicity with the established order of domination.[1] In *Fatal Strategies*, Baudrillard cites the collapse of the aesthetic into fashion as a prima facie example of how simulation destroys the dialectical logic of the social. For where the rhythm of innovation has become so rapid that there can be no reflexive communication between the poles of 'beauty' and 'ugliness', both are absorbed into a play of simulacra where the relationship of aesthetics to moral recognition becomes completely unhinged (Baudrillard, 1996, p. 192). In *Simulacra and Simulation*, it is work and sex which exemplify this collapse of dialectical mediation into the pure exchangeability of simulation (Baudrillard, 1999, p. 18). For each is made to function in terms of the same operational demands – demands which destroy the boundaries of privacy, seduction and meaning which mark their 'ethical' differentiation. Hegel, for example, is very clear that the family, as 'ethical mind in its natural or immediate phase', is a sphere of activity and recognition which ought not to be made directly subject to the abstract juridical demands of the state (Hegel, 1967b, p. 110). What is significant here is that the 'ecstatic' communication of signs has become a total principle; nothing contingent, antagonistic or transcendent can intervene in the universal exchangeability through which sex, capital, politics and culture are hyperrealized. Everything that appears in the system is, by definition, without objective reference to the real. And so the fate of those institutions (law, state, civil society) whose authority is founded upon the historical contradictions of 'the social', is to become mere simulacra of the old dialectical figures of ethical progress.

I would suggest, therefore, that the basic question which underlies the politics of simulation is this: if it is now impossible to determine the loci of 'real' political power, what are the articles of faith that continue to solicit the participation of 'the people' in the symbolic order of the social? Some Foucauldian answers immediately suggest themselves: (1) that material productivity is an established good; (2) that power is a necessary coercive force which imposes a 'real' order of disciplinarity; and (3) that within this order we are able to make reliable distinctions between truth and illusion, good and evil, the moral and the immoral. For Baudrillard, however, Foucault's discursive model of politics assumes a concrete referentiality of power in which it is still possible to identify 'the self' as a moment of dispersed authorial practice. His claim is that the stakes of the game have crucially changed; that the economic, sexual, medical, aesthetic, and psychiatric strictures set out in Foucault's genealogies, have been fatally undermined by the exponential progress of simulation.[2] Capital, for example, has become a 'monstrous' consumer of every moral, legal or contractual form of obligation (Baudrillard, 1999, p. 15). It is no longer, nor was it ever in reality, the model of technological development and division of labour which, for Foucault, continued to underlie the panoptical regulation of society (Foucault, 1979, p. 221). Sexual desire, which appears in Foucault's writing as an openness of the subject that is constantly re-engendered by the confessional technologies of modernity (Foucault, 1980, p. 70), has, for Baudrillard, lost its transgressive power to the progress of a universal androgyny; the reduction of sexual difference to the operational transparency of the obscene, the pornographic and the promiscuous. 'After the orgy' of sexual liberation, sex becomes a simulation of desire that awaits the mutation of human beings into sissiparous clones – the mutation that will finally mark the end of any productive antagonism between sex and politics (Baudrillard 1995a, pp. 20–5). What Foucault's writing both fails to acknowledge and provides the perfect reflection of therefore, is the descent of the political into a simulation of those 'effects' – of domination, discursive legitimation, resistance, transgression – by which power was once able to manifest its reality (Baudrillard, 1999, pp. 21–2).

Within the context of universal simulation, therefore, political parties and institutions can 'rediscover a glimmer of existence and legitimacy' only through speaking of themselves as the 'anti' of a simulated otherness – of a threat which would put the whole ethical order of society at risk (Baudrillard 1999, p. 19). The politics of ecology, to use one of Baudrillard's examples, is conducted as a thoroughgoing antitechnologism which seeks to re-establish the unity of human beings with the 'equilibrium' of nature (Baudrillard, 1995b, p. 91). For Baudrillard, however, such enactments of resistance merely confirm the fact that politics, as a 'discursive practice', has entered its death throes. Both its institutional and transgressive forms can claim authority only by becoming ghosts; simulacra which can never risk any decisive claims to truth or objective necessity:

> It is always a question of proving the real through the imaginary, proving truth through scandal, proving the law through transgression, proving work through striking, proving the system through crisis. (Baudrillard, 1999, p. 19)

The play of simulation, in other words, precipitates a circulation of autonomous finalities in which it has become impossible to determine the loci of 'real' political power. For once simulation has become the exclusive condition of the appearance of the real, the political can no longer be understood in 'discursive' terms – that is, in terms of relations of power radiating from established centres of disciplinary knowledge and practice. In the end there is only the distribution of unforeseen benefits to every simulacra of political reality – a distribution in which even the most 'objective' repression, repudiation or refutation of a particular model will eventually return as confirmation of its truth (Baudrillard, 1999, p. 16).[3]

The economy of conditions through which Foucault's power/knowledge relation is supposed to function has, therefore, become *hyperlogical*: it can no longer be conceived as a space within which there are mobile but ultimately specific sites of power, resistance and transgression. And so the question arises, of the possibility of anything approximating to an ethical politics after the collapse of the social into the play of simulacra.

The Masses and 'the Mutation of the Real'

In order to address this question properly, we need to look at the relationship which Baudrillard sets out between 'the masses' and the mass media. In *Simulacra and Simulation*, he argues:

> One must think . . . of the media as if they were . . . a kind of genetic code that directs the mutation of the real into the hyperreal, just as the other micromolecular code [DNA] controls the passage from a representative sphere of meaning into the genetic one of the programmed signal. (Baudrillard, 1999, p. 30)

We have seen that, for Baudrillard, the drift into simulation marks the passage of the real into a total exchangeability of signs – a passage in which 'the symbolic', in all its contradictory, contingent and agonistic forms, is expanded into an 'operational' version of itself. We have also seen that this drift into the hyperreal marks the end of the specular-carceral dynamics through which Foucault attempts to set out the relationships between power, identity and autonomous subjectivity. What is of fundamental importance in Baudrillard's understanding of the mass media therefore, is their coextensivity with the processes through which 'the political' has become a pure simulation of itself, and through which the masses emerge as the 'silent majorities' whose solicitation is the purpose for which this virtual politics is performed. The 'phony exactitude . . . simultaneous distancing and magnification, distortion of scale, [and] excessive transparency' (Baudrillard, 1999, p. 28) through which the real is hyperrealized, are technological processes which, for Baudrillard, become increasingly significant with the emergence of television as the primary medium of mass communication. As a 'terminal of multiple networks', television immediately plugs the masses into their own hyperreality: it takes the 'meaning' of whatever it presents (family life,[4] sex, work, marriage, love) and subjects it to sequences, breaks, codifications and juxtapositions which precipitate both its death, and its re-emergence in the acutely overdetermined phenomenon of the masses.

Within this 'telematic' system, the media do not simply demand conformity to the moral norms of the social. Their power as technologies of simulation lies precisely in the fact that they abolish the distinction between 'active and passive'; between the subject considered as the 'addressee' of social and political norms, and the state considered as their 'addressor', or sender:

> a switch [occurs] from the panoptic system of surveillance . . . to a system of deterrence, in which the distinction between the passive and the active is abolished. There is no longer any imperative of submission to the model, or to the gaze. 'YOU are the model!' 'YOU are the majority!' (Baudrillard, 1999, p. 29)

Once televisual images reach a certain level of saturation, in other words, the concept of a subject who actively receives and reflects upon the meaning of those images becomes unsustainable. For in so far as the circulation of simulacra has become 'orbital', the subject has always already been taken up into their infinite exchangeability and reversibility. There are no longer any determinate positions of power and resistance, legislation and transgression (Foucault); there is no 'aesthetic time' of the self in its relations with the objective temporality of social being (Lyotard); there is only the mutable conductivity of the norm, and the inertia of the masses that is always co-present with that conductivity.

'The precession of simulacra' touches only briefly on the social and political significance of the media: Baudrillard suggests that Marshall McLuhan's 'formula' of a progressive 'confusion of the medium with the message' marks the first serious recognition of the impact of telematic technologies on the body politic (Baudrillard, 1999, p. 30). However, this theme is developed much more fully in 'The implosion of meaning in the media', which is also part of the collection published as *Simulacra and Simulation*. Baudrillard begins the essay by suggesting three possible effects of telematic media or, more precisely, of the information which they circulate. *Either* such information 'reinjects' meaning into an increasingly meaningless social world, *or* it is 'outside the circulation of meaning strictly speaking', *or* it is 'directly destructive of meaning and signification' as such (Baudrillard, 1999, p. 79). The first two hypotheses are dismissed by Baudrillard as attempts to salvage social democracy from the effects of media saturation: the first by maintaining that the mass media are themselves productive of new technologies of free speech (a kind of 'anti-media' – CB radios, the Internet – which would talk back to the established producers of meaning and identity); the second, by claiming that the orientation of new media towards functional goals (clarity, calculability, systematicity) revives the spontaneous production of moral, aesthetic and political meanings (*ibid.*). Both of these hypotheses share an assumption that the media produce a 'surplus of meaning' without which the organization of the social bond would collapse. Yet for Baudrillard, this organization is collapsing anyway – and precisely because of the 'rigorous and necessary' correlation between information and the destruction of meaning (*ibid.*).

The information circulated by telematic media therefore, is the direct expression of this hyperreality of the social bond: it is a simulation of the agonistic, contradictory forms (family, sex, work) through which 'the social' has presented its rational-historical evolution. There is nothing 'outside' of this operational-technological staging of the real: and so we must understand the reproduction of meaning and the symbolic which is mounted through the media, as a 'deterrent function'; as that which constantly solicits the political engagement of the masses through the simulacra of social responsibility (the television 'vox pop', the radio 'phone in', the referendum).[5] Thus, as the system becomes increasingly evacuated of meaning, so the media redouble their production of the 'signs' which vouchsafe the truth of our rational-communicative democracy:

> Immense energies are deployed to hold this simulacra at bay, to avoid the brutal de-simulation which would confront us in the face of the obvious reality of a radical loss of meaning. (Baudrillard, 1999, p. 80)

This 'circularity' of the system refers us once more to the political significance of the masses. For in so far as they are constantly solicited by the telematic simulacra of communication, and in so far as this solicitation is provoked by their absorption of whatever is deployed to energize or enlighten them, we must recognize that the masses are both the condition and the failure of the social. They are both engaged by the simulacra of communication and disbelieving of them; they both conduct and shortcircuit the operational modalities which precipitate the hyperreality of the system (*ibid.*, p. 81). I will say more about this disturbing duality of the masses in a moment.

In a slightly later essay, 'The masses: the implosion of the social in the media', Baudrillard begins to flesh out the political implications of 'the confusion of the medium with the message' (Baudrillard, 1996, pp. 207–19). Again he starts by rejecting two 'conventional' theories of the media: McLuhan's account of the technological facilitation of communicative democracy and Enzensberger's notion of the media as a 'productive force' whose expansion allows, for the first time, mass participation in the production of culture (*ibid.*, p. 207). Baudrillard's own argument is an attempt to extend the consequences of McLuhan's formula beyond the technological optimism of the 'global village'. Telematic information certainly does destroy the traditional content of the social (the message), but what McLuhan failed to recognize is that mass communication also undermines the very 'communicative' potential of the media. The accelerating flow and increasing superficiality of information produces a certain redundancy of the real – a virtualization of those events which supposedly legitimize the moral claims of the media. Coverage of the catastrophes of the Third World, for example, perpetuates a logic of guilt and suffering from which Western culture derives a sense of purpose, of the need to act, which is increasingly absent from its own 'precession of simulacra'. The operational function of the media therefore, is to emit information in a way that leaves no room for unexpected or unforeseeable responses; a function which systematically destroys the possibility of their 'mediating' between one state of the real and another. If we do continue to respond to the appeals of aid organizations, if we do continue to respond to the suffering of those 'others' who are constantly presented to us as our 'sacrificial debt', these responses are no more than simulations of responsibility already inscribed in the operational codes of the media (Baudrillard, 1995b, 68-71). Politically, this truncation of the relationship between the masses and the media is extremely significant; for '[t]o give [the message], and to do it in such a way that no return can be made, is to break the exchange to one's own profit and institute a monopoly: the social process is put out of balance' (*ibid.*, p. 208). Restoration of this balance therefore, would require 'an "anti-media" struggle' which has dispensed with conventional 'technological' (McLuhan) and 'ideological' (Enzensberger) theories of the media. Is this possible?

Moral debates about the media have, according to Baudrillard, proceeded as if 'the public' continues to exist as the referent of experiences (productive labour, the inner voice of conscience, the provocations of compassion) which ought to remain independent of informatic distortion. Conventional critiques therefore, continue to invoke ideals of democratic practice that belong, genealogically, to an organization of the real and the symbolic which precedes the current primacy of simulation (Baudrillard, 1999, p. 214). And so highly mutable concepts like socialized production, civic individualism and communicative action are constantly recycled by conventional media theory – the very concepts through which the system presents itself as authorizing the individual and its rational will. The 'anti-media' theory which Baudrillard proposes, on the other hand, begins by rejecting the assumption of a classical public who constantly suffer the effects of simulation.

The loss of the dialectic of objective necessity and subjective recognition from the public sphere, means that the experience of the masses is characterized by radical uncertainty. The media's overproduction of information can only exacerbate this uncertainty; indeed, for Baudrillard, we have reached the point at which 'the social' never has time to enact the moments of negativity, mediation and recuperation through which it would unfold its historical 'truth' (Baudrillard, 1996, p. 210). Yet for Baudrillard, this very uncertainty of the masses, their simultaneous belief and unbelief in the operational simulacra of the real, opens the possibility of resistance to informatic domination. The masses receive information about themselves (through opinion polls, advertising, publicity) with a certain irony; they take pleasure in observing the spectacle of the daily fluctuations of their opinions (*ibid.*, p. 212). This spontaneous excess of the masses, however, should not be understood simply as an 'archaic residue' of those demands for sense, meaning and deliberation presented in the media, but rather as 'the effect of an offensive (not defensive) counterstrategy by the object' (*ibid.*, p. 213). The relationship between the masses, the ideals of deliberative democracy and the media responsible for the transmission of those ideals, in other words, is one in which the masses participate as a strangely destabilizing presence which constantly provokes the production of simulacra (*ibid.*, p. 215). Yet this immense labour of solicitation can only recreate the indifference that it seeks to overcome; for it is the reversion to ironic hyperconformity that is the defining 'characteristic' of the masses. Indeed, for Baudrillard, the perpetual seductiveness of this abrogation of responsibility is its communication with a deep unconscious desire to 'be relieved of choice and be diverted from one's own objective will' (*ibid.*, p. 216).

Baudrillard's most detailed discussion of the masses, *In the Shadow of the Silent Majorities*, begins with a series of puns on the term 'mass', which in French can mean 'substance', 'majority', or the negative electrical power of an 'earth' (Baudrillard, 1983, p. 1). This tactic is designed to alert us to his reservations about the political significance of the term; specifically that it might be taken, in his own writing, as designating a symbolic community, a body of active resistance or a system of shared meanings. According to the symbolic economy presented in *Silent Majorities*, however, the masses have none of these attributes. They are what absorb all the 'radiations' of the social; they are what cannot be represented in the dialogical and dialectical categories of the system of regulated political exchange (*ibid.*, p. 2).

For Baudrillard then, the constitution of the masses is not even an aggregate of punctual identities ('the unlimited sum of equivalent individuals: $1+1+1$'); for this would imply a totalization that is always under the control of certain disciplinary interventions (*ibid.*, p. 6).[6] The 'being' of the masses therefore is labile and disaggregated; it simultaneously conducts, absorbs and disperses the reproduction of the social as a kind of 'alter' process. In the end, then they are the inescapable 'double' of the simulacra through which the system stages its reality: that which demands the constantly accelerated production of signifiers which itself signifies the fatal implosion of meaning (*ibid.*, p. 3). The danger in all this, as far as Baudrillard is concerned, is that the negative stricture of his description of the masses might encourage us to believe in their political 'reality'. We might, for example, begin to believe in the rebirth of socialism in the masses; in the possibility of a unifying refusal of the simulacra which continue to alienate their proletarian identity. For Baudrillard, however, the withdrawal of the masses into their private-domestic indifference has no such radicalizing potential; their preferences and fascinations are a 'direct defiance of the political' which have no meaning beyond the evanescence of their particular events (Baudrillard, 1983, p. 39). Thus, when Baudrillard claims that '[t]he masses are a stronger medium than the media', his intention is to designate their existence as an internal limit to the pure simulation of the social (*ibid.*, p. 44).[7] The hyperreality of the economic which Baudrillard first described in *Consumer Society*, for example, cannot be adequately understood as an incremental process of reification. It is through the play of simulacra that the final dissolution of the bond between objects (commodities) and their use value is brought about; for once they have become 'signs' of a certain lifestyle, of a certain level of affordable wastage, they interlock the desires of the 'sovereign' consumer with a total integration of production and consumption (Baudrillard, 1996, pp. 43–4). Even this economic imposition of the social (the hyperrealization of exchange value), however, fails to overcome the passivity of the masses. For in the end, the 'hyperconformity' with which they shortcircuit the demands of total consumption, total medicalization, total aestheticization, total sexualization, remains an entirely 'transpolitical' effect: it follows the simulation of meaning as a kind of parody which has no 'messianic' hope or expectation.

In *Fatal Strategies*, Baudrillard begins to sketch out the limits and possibilities of the masses considered as the 'object' of political conjuration. 'When I refer to the object, and its fundamental duplicity,' he remarks, 'I am referring to all of us and to our social and political order' (Baudrillard, 1996, p. 199). Considered as the inertial body generated by the overproduction of meaning, the masses sustain a conductivity of effects that is irreconcilable with the simulacra of regulated symbolic exchange (the stakeholder citizen, the green consumer, the responsible capitalist to name a few contemporary examples). If there is a 'morality' that is appropriate to the simulation of the social, therefore, this should be understood in terms of a certain existential necessity that arises out of the strategic deployment of meaning. For Baudrillard, the political solicitation of the masses is always at its most potent as a 'first encounter'; as a pure bewildering spectacle. The Watergate scandal, for example, was far more successful in its attempt to restore faith in the political order than subsequent scandals have been – indeed, the 'Irangate' affair only succeeded in convincing a large section of the public that it was Oliver North, and not the American government, who had acted 'morally'. (History repeating itself as farce, perhaps?) The immediate complicity of the masses with the simulation of the real therefore, gives rise to a certain 'fatality': to the return of the hyperconformism which follows every 'spontaneous' reinjection of meaning. The 'almost parodic' clamour to absorb the simulacra of morality, community and responsibility runs through the masses as a seductive inertia; the desire to have done with 'objective will' that is immediately co-present with the desire for totalization in the political scene. Thus, in so far as they cannot reflect the operational expansion of the symbolic order, the experience of the masses always returns to the fact of their 'objectivity'; to the unpredictable, ironic contingencies distributed in the simulation of the real:

> What is left then but to pass over to the side of the object, to its affected and eccentric effects, to its fatal effects (fatality is merely the absolute freedom of effects). (Baudrillard, 1996, p. 205)

We are left, in other words, with a 'hypermorality' which arises from the impossibility of concluding the seduction between the 'affected and eccentric effects' produced in the inertial body of the masses, and the informatic media through which those effects become fatal. A morality which, we might say, is responsible to the masses as (no more than) the 'internal limit' of the social.

The hyperconformity of the masses then, should be understood in terms of their status as the unpresentable condition of social and political representation. Their significance as the inertial conductivity which shortcircuits the total simulation of the real, cannot enter into the system of symbolic exchange: it remains unspecifiable within the register of agentic categories – will, judgement, transgression – that are constantly recycled in the production of political meaning. However, Baudrillard's 'passing over to the side of the object' in an attempt to mark the 'fatal' contingency of the masses, is a strategy which bears directly upon the possibility of salvaging the political from the simulation of the real. Butler, in his account of *Silent Majorities*, correctly identifies this question as that of a quasi-transcendental condition (the masses) which constantly demands to be phrased in terms of the restricted economy (the symbolic order) whose possibility it opens up: 'Baudrillard wants to say "no one speaks for the masses' silence", that "the masses should not be transferred into meaning", and yet this is what he does even in saying this' (Butler, 1999, p. 136). I would suggest that this structural ambiguity in Baudrillard's account of the masses is also what informs his understanding of 'extreme phenomena' in *The Transparency of Evil*. For his speculations about the resistive effects of phenomena like AIDS, cancer, terrorism and drugs (Baudrillard, 1995a, pp. 67–8), are ultimately attempts to outplay the operational logic of simulation: to invoke the passivity of the masses as a kind of political pathos or suffering which at least redeems the system from the possibility of collapse into frictionless hyperreality.

The masses then, are a 'strange attractor': an object that remains seductive precisely because its 'being' always exceeds the logic of simulation (Baudrillard, 1995a, p. 172). And so it is their unconscious distribution of inertia and hyperconformism which, for Baudrillard, is the final provocation to theorize the hyperreality of the social. As we have seen, the simultaneous activity and passivity of the masses in relation to the production of meaning, is not something which Baudrillard is prepared to allow into the realm of political morality. The masses are without both self-identity and self-knowledge (subjectivity), the two fundamental pre-requisites for participation in the regulated exchanges of conventional citizenship. Conceived as a 'ludic' play of conductivities, attachments and defiances, however, the mass is a demand of the object to give its 'lethal pathologies' (AIDS, cancer, terrorism) the chance to redeem themselves in their unintended disruption of hyperlogical unity. In pursuing the mass therefore, theory responds to the same unpredictable 'otherness' that comes to us in the shape of 'a gesture, a face, a form, a word, a prophetic dream, a witticism, an object, a woman, or a desert' (*ibid.*, p. 174), that is to an alterity which is the inescapable counterpart of simulation.

I will argue shortly that a comparison of the political implications of 'simulation' with Derrida's notion of '*différance*', needs to concentrate on Baudrillard and Derrida's respective accounts of the presence of 'the real' (culture, law, subject) within the systematic organization of signs and representations. Indeed, I think it is fair to say that if we are to understand why deconstruction is both a modernist and an anti-modernist project, and why Derrida's political thought remains faithful to a certain 'right of reflection', it is important that we have a clear understanding of the operational logic which is set out in Baudrillard's concept of simulation. 'The mass' is obviously significant in this respect, as it represents a total suspension of the categories of will, deliberation and judgement – a suspension which is given even greater force in Baudrillard's later accounts of the fate of the social. In *The Transparency of Evil*, for example, the chapters on 'The hell of the same' and 'The melodrama of difference' are both accounts of how the mass has become increasingly subject to the 'model' of informatic communication. In the first, he describes how the cloning of human beings would be the realization of an utterly predictable identity that would have no need of the other as the mediator of its self-recognition. The genetic code (DNA), in other words, would become the operational principle of an informatic society free from the messy and disturbing demands of sex (Baudrillard, 1995a, p. 115). In the second, he examines the total overdetermination of the real through the simulacra of sexual, racial and cultural 'difference'. Racism, for example, in its 'current and definitive form', represents an 'abreaction' against the universal simulation of difference and responsibility; it has become a fetishistic pursuit of identity produced by the very logic of communicable difference which animates the system of social relations (*ibid.*, p. 130). Both of these examples then, refer us back to the masses as the referent of an increasingly 'total' simulation. Their hyperconformity, in other words, becomes ever more extreme: more inarticulate, more unreflexive, more 'ecstatic' and so more troubling for those agencies which reproduce the simulacra of the social. I will argue, however, that this economy of mass solicitation cannot, as Baudrillard claims, erase all traces of its history; and that if we are to salvage the possibility of a reflective politics from the logic of simulation, we need to pay careful attention to Derrida's account of the relationship between culture, humanity and technology.

Before turning to Derrida, however, we need to return briefly to the question of the fate of the aesthetic in 'late' – or 'post' – modernity. In so far as Baudrillard's account of the relationship between telematic technology and simulation appears to put an end to the 'disarming' spontaneity of aesthetic feeling, it is clear that he also wants to have done with the enterprise of trying to recover the speculative significance of such feeling within the escalatory logic of the social. The provocation of aesthetic feeling has, as far as Baudrillard is concerned, been reduced to pure simulation; to a 'frission of vertiginous and phony exactitude . . . of simultaneous distancing and magnification . . . of excessive transparency' that is immediately a solicitation of the mass *as mass* (Baudrillard, 1999, p. 28). We have then returned to the proposition with which we began: that there is a sense in which it is possible to read Baudrillard's work as announcing 'the postmodern' as the worst possible outcome of the Marxist critique of culture. Benjamin, Adorno and Jameson all retain some sense of the transcendent significance of the aesthetic, even within the disastrous constitution of our 'late-capitalist' modernity. Baudrillard maintains a fatal rupture in the dialectical powers of the real from which it is impossible to salvage any moral or eschatological significance of aesthetic apprehension. The postmodern aesthetic, in other words, has become hyperreal: a play of reversible trends and fashions which is utterly unhinged from the dialectics of truth, beauty and morality.

According to Lyotard, this whole discourse of the technological penetration of the masses and of the end of aesthetic transcendence, is founded upon a confusion of the stakes of two distinct genres of discourse: the sublime and the technological (Lyotard, 1993, p. 201). Baudrillard's account of the simulation of the aesthetic presupposes that the perfection of media technologies is able to 'operationalize' those feelings associated with the experience of the sublime. According to Lyotard, however, this perfection of the media is founded upon a certain sense of its own insufficiency; for the simulation of the aesthetic proceeds from sensations of disquiet and incertitude which cannot be subsumed under the escalatory logic of the social. The telematic effects of magnification, distancing and transparency, in other words, may well produce a certain labile desire in the masses, but such effects can neither complete the virtualization of the social bond (its collapse into total simulation), nor would they be able to cancel the 'disarming' relationship of the sublime to what is always beyond and before the resources of the social (birth, death, love, sex). Thus, Lyotard's defence of the aesthetic, or rather his attempt to set out the contours of a postmodern art and aesthetic experience, is an attempt to defend the spontaneity of the sublime from the technological, philosophical and aesthetic reproduction of the social bond. We need to examine the detail of his claims.

Notes

1. We have already seen how this 'ecstatic' precipitation of the social works in Baudrillard's account of the transeconomic expansion of capital. For once the logic of capital exceeds Marx's dialectical categories, we are left only with a 'catastrophic' precipitation of events into unforeseen possibilities of exploitation, annihilation and death (the 'monstrosity' of capital).

2. In his essay 'Forgetting Foucault', Baudrillard famously contends that '. . . if it is possible at last to talk with such definitive understanding about power, sexuality, the body, and discipline, even down to their most delicate metamorphoses, it is because at some point *all this is here and now over with*' (1980, p. 88, author's italics).

3. Fascism, for example, retains a certain fascination, and a certain mobilizing power, because it cannot be refuted by the utilitarian logic of liberal democracy (the economic desirability of universal rights, the bureaucratic inertia produced by racial legislation). All of fascism's postwar reversals, defeats and marginalizations, in other words, contribute to its return as an 'effect of power': to its perpetuation as a mythology of absolute truth, obedience and sacrifice (the other of simulation). (See the note on fascism with which Baudrillard concludes the essay 'History: a retro scenario', in *Simulacra and Simulation*, 48.)

4. See Baudrillard's example of the (1974) 'TV verité' study of the Louds – a middle-class American family who agreed to be filmed in their own home. Baudrillard argues that their failure to survive the ordeal – the family split up during filming – was due to the constant demand for operational perfection imposed by the presence of the camera. The Louds, in other words, could not live 'as if we were not there'; the constant demand for simulation proved fatal to the private symbolic order of the family (Baudrillard, 1999, p. 28).

5. Obviously Baudrillard's theory of the total operationalization of the social raises profound questions not only for Foucault's account of the discursive organization of power, but also for Habermas' attempt to defend the practico-linguistic bases of communicative democracy.

6. This is the basis of Baudrillard's rejection of Adorno and Horkheimer's account of the masses. For by insisting that the reification of the social produced by the culture industry has

become all but complete, they fail to recognize the 'ludic' excessiveness, the ironic hyperconformism, that is the counterpart of universal simulation.

7. It is worth quoting Rex Butler's excellent account of the relationship between the masses and the strategies of the social in full: 'The masses are not an *external* limit to the social, which the social would overcome, but an *internal* limit, a limit the social would never overcome, because it is a limit brought about by this very overcoming' (Butler, 1999, p. 61).

8

The Postmodern and the Sublime

Introduction

The question I will address in this chapter concerns Jean-François Lyotard's defence of the moral and political significance of the aesthetic within the economy of universal simulation. Ultimately, his work on the sublime is an attempt to salvage a sense of transcendence from the feelings of shock, agitation and disquiet that arise from the 'lack of reality' implicit in 'postmodern' societies. In order to understand what is at stake in Lyotard's attempt to reconfigure the relationship between culture, aesthetics and politics therefore, we need to look at:

- his configuration of the relationship between 'modernity' and 'post-modernity';
- the account of the relationship between the dissolution of the social bond, the proliferation of heterogeneous 'language games' and the end of political metanarratives presented in *The Postmodern Condition*;
- his reading of Kant's *Critique of Aesthetic Judgement*, particularly the transcription of the 'Analytic of the sublime' presented in *The Differend*;
- his attempt to trace the transformative potential avant-garde art within the capitalized, mediatized economics of culture.

Lyotard and Baudrillard

The relationship between Baudrillard and Lyotard's accounts of 'the postmodern' is not easy to specify, especially given the changes of emphasis which mark both of their intellectual biographies. If there is a communication between the two, this is initiated in Lyotard's treatment of Marx in *Libidinal Economy* (Lyotard, 1993, pp. 95–154). The general issue that Lyotard addresses here is the possibility of a 'critique' of Marx that would not attempt to complete the theoretical labour of human emancipation (*ibid.*, p. 103). Such a critique, he argues, would regard 'capital' as a limitless desire: as a 'perverse body' whose disunited effects and events could never be brought back to an 'ethical' organization of the social. Lyotard then, demands that we give up trying to designate the 'outside' of capitalism's 'libidinal economy': for in so far as every negative effect of capital is always already charged with the joy of resentment, we can never find the proper place from which to designate the 'alienation' of our essential humanity. Lyotard's initial concern with Baudrillard's work in *Libidinal Economy*, is focused on the idea of symbolic exchange as it is set out in *The Mirror of Production*. We have already seen that, for Baudrillard, symbolic exchange represents the originary moment of unregulated risk which both initiates and disrupts the economy of social meanings. In *The Mirror of Production*, this primitive economy of the gift – with its immediate expression of the 'real' stakes of exchange (death, obligation, violence) – is presented as a counter to Marx's historicization of the relationship between use and exchange value. For Baudrillard, '[t]here is *neither mode of production nor production* in primitive societies' (Baudrillard, 1996, p. 115); which means that the concept of 'use value' by which Marx characterized the 'natural' integration of primitive societies, is already a product of the rationalized – or 'castrated' – exchange which produces the monstrous expansion of capital. Yet for Lyotard, the possibility of remarking the unforeseen antagonisms, conflicts and complicities produced by this expansion, is crucially restricted by Baudrillard's concept of symbolic exchange. Primitive society, as it is conceived in *The Mirror of Production*, returns as a kind of second nature; as a resistance that constantly reassumes the 'ethical' position of the contra-culture. In the end, Lyotard's claim is that Baudrillard cannot avoid dramatizing the libidinal economy of capital through the idea of a 'good rebel nature' – a nature that returns to redeem the evil perversity of capital (Lyotard, 1993, p. 107).

I would suggest, however, that Lyotard's determination to give symbolic exchange the status of an ethical referent within Baudrillard's writing, raises serious questions about the comparison of their respective accounts of the aesthetic. Any such comparison would have to acknowledge the development which has taken place in their writing since the mid-1970s. For it is certainly true that the account of the hyperreal which Baudrillard presents in *The Transparency of Evil*, seems to encourage the kind of ungrounded critique whose precautions are initially set out in *Libidinal Economy*. Indeed, both Lyotard and Baudrillard's later work makes the general demand that theory respond to 'the real' as challenge; as a kind of *agent provocateur* which forces the established powers of the system into occupying the space of truth and reality (Baudrillard, 1993, pp. 123–5, and Lyotard, 1991a, pp. 130–57). Our immediate task then is to distinguish between what is at stake in Baudrillard's account of the theoretical 'dizziness' induced by simulation, and the 'disarming' sense of the unique, the immediate, the spontaneous that informs Lyotard's idea of the sublime.

We need to be clear that, for Baudrillard, 'the aesthetic', both in the sense of the feelings provoked by art and nature and in the sense of the mass aestheticization of our everyday experience, belongs entirely to the realm of simulation:

> What we are witnessing, beyond the materialist rule of the commodity, is the semio-urgy of everything by means of advertising, the media, or images. No mater how marginal, or banal, or even obscene it may be, everything is subject to aestheticization, culturalization, museumification . . . The system runs less

on the surplus-value of the commodity than on the aesthetic surplus-value of the sign. (Baudrillard, 1995a, p. 16)

What this means is that the 'reality' of aesthetic experience – its irreducibility to the immediate presence of the social, its transfiguration of the relations of ethical life – has become part of a complete virtualization of experience. There is no longer a discrete realm of subjective feelings to which artistic production is both a response and a provocation; there is only the ecstatic circulation of styles. Art therefore,can no longer question the established powers of the social; for the configurations through which it has sought to express the utopian, the barbarous and the aporetic forces at work in human culture, have become mere simulacra of themselves (*ibid.*, p. 18). This, of course, returns us to the politics of the mass. For in so far as aesthetic simulation is a process which constantly escalates the collapse of the real into overdetermination and self-parody, we can no longer regard any of the sensations produced by contemporary media (cinema, television, pop music) as singling out the individual subject as a point of spontaneous reflection. All there is is the parody of artistic styles circulated through the media, the hyperinflation of 'original' art objects, and the unpredictable currents of irony and hyperconformity which traverse the production of popular culture (*ibid.*, p. 19): a collapse of the real which leaves theory with the task of anticipating the catastrophic effects of simulation.[1]

Lyotard's work on the relationship between the postmodern and the sublime is both complex and extensive. After the publication of *The Postmodern Condition* in 1979, his writing began to consider the possibility of an ethical politics that could emerge from the processes of social, cultural and epistemological fragmentation which characterize post-modernity. In the essay 'What is postmodernism', he claims that the 'lack of reality' which has come to afflict social relations is an effect which originates in the dynamical processes of industrialization. His argument is that the progress in science, technology, industry and economy by which we recognize the modern epoch, depends upon a constant 'shattering' of the belief systems which have structured and legitimized the social bond (Lyotard, 1991b, p. 77). What is characteristic of *postmodernity* therefore, is the acceleration of this process of shattering, and the proliferation of the discourses, or 'language games', through which the real is distributed. The sense of a 'lack of reality' in social relations, in other words, has become the defining characteristic of postmodern experience; a characteristic which, for Lyotard, is made ever more acute by processes of technological and informatic specialization.

It is this sense of uncertainty before the proliferation of language games which informs Lyotard's understanding of the relationship between politics, postmodernity and the sublime. In 'What is postmodernism?' he remarks:

What does this 'lack of reality' signify if one tries to free it from a narrowly historicized interpretation? The phrase is of course akin to what Nietzsche calls nihilism. But I see a much earlier modulation of Nietzschean perspectivism in the Kantian theme of the sublime. I think in particular that it is in the aesthetic of the sublime that modern art (including literature) finds its impetus and the logic of avant-gardes find its axiom. (Lyotard, 1991b, p. 77)

This short paragraph anticipates a number of important themes in Lyotard's work on the sublime. First, the 'postmodern condition' should be understood as an intensification of the dynamics of modernity: as an acute lack of 'being' that comes from the collapse of the social bond into the agonism of heterogeneous language games. Second, this insubstantiality of the social bond is the condition of modernist attempts to bring the appearance of difference under the narrative structures of universal history (Lyotard, 1991, pp. 18–23). Kant, Hegel, Marx and Habermas are all cited by Lyotard as examples of the Enlightenment determination to find the 'truth' of the relationship between culture, economy and progress. Third, the technological reproduction of 'the real' functions as one particular language game within a general economy of incommensurable rules and demands. And so while it is certainly true that 'denotative' and 'prescriptive' language games (whose stakes are the distinctions between true and false and just and unjust respectively) have tended to lose their independence from the rules of technological efficiency, this 'operational' legitimation of force can only proceed through the reduction of truth and justice to particular subsets of functional integration (*ibid.*, p. 47). Fourth, even though new technologies have brought about a virtualization of the real in which efficient communication has become the predominant necessity, the very expression of this demand precipitates the agonism between informatic efficiency and justice and responsibility. The 'sublime' then, is the name that Lyotard gives to those feelings of agitation provoked by the incommensurability of different genres of discourse; by the fact that there is no universal role by which the conflict could be properly resolved. Finally, the relationship between art, politics and the sublime which Lyotard develops, is concerned with the elaboration of those 'events' through which the violence of legitimation is disclosed; events whose triviality, strangeness, alterity is expressed most powerfully by a certain 'postmodern' art (Lyotard, 1991a, pp. 181–93).

We need then, to be clear about the status of the sublime in Lyotard's work, particularly the relationship between feeling, judgement and performativity which he extracts from Kant's *Critique of Aesthetic Judgement*.

Reconfiguring the Aesthetic

I have given an extended account of Kant's third *Critique* in Chapter 4 so I will be brief in my remarks here. The 'negative pleasure' described in Kant's 'Analytic of the sublime' is produced through the simultaneous necessity and impossibility of representing ideas within the faculty of imagination. When I apprehend some overwhelming magnitude in nature, my mind is referred beyond the cognitive theoretical schemata which, in general, organize my experience of the external world. This experience of nature provokes a reaction from the faculty of reason; a reaction which conceives the greatness of the magnitude apprehended as a sign of the rational unity, or Idea, of Nature. Having subsumed my particular apprehension under this Idea, however, reason 'calls forth an effort of the mind, unavailing though it be, to make the representation of sense adequate to this totality' (Kant, 1982, p. 119). The 'fact' of the unrepresentability of nature as a whole therefore, presupposes the a priori separation of reason and imagination which Kant attempted to validate in the first and second *Critiques*. In the account of phenomenal experience which he presents in the *Critique of Pure Reason*, the imagination is conceived as the faculty which allows apprehension of a spatiality which cannot be directly schematized by the understanding. For Kant, this faculty is the basis of mathematical truth; of those propositions about quantity, relation and proportion which remain true independently of phenomenal experience. The faculty of reason, on the other hand, is concerned with the Idea of freedom, or more precisely with the pure self-determination of rational will. In the 'Analytic of the sublime', however, this separation of reason and imagination gives rise to a peculiar feeling of 'pleasure-displeasure', which is the result of the imagination's inability to find a suitable representation (analoga) for the Idea of Nature. As rational beings, we feel a simultaneous 'pleasure' in our possession of a faculty of ideas, and 'displeasure' at our inability to represent them. The conclusion which Kant draws from this sublime discordance of reason and imagination, is that the subjective faculties of human beings are organized so as to disclose – through the feeling of pleasure-displeasure – a homology between the purposiveness of nature and the historical fulfilment of the moral law as culture.

For Lyotard, however, Kant's account of the sublime is crucially disturbing for the immanent purposiveness which he attributes to the cognitive faculties. According to the third of *The Differend*'s four 'Kant notices' (Lyotard, 1988, pp. 130–5), the negative power of the sublime cannot contribute to a harmonization of natural and moral purposiveness, or more precisely, to the idea of a community of rational beings in which the contingency/otherness encountered by the moral will, would be reduced to mere appearances of its own self-identity (universal history). For Lyotard, the feeling of agitation through which the Kantian subject encounters the sublime, does not simply register a 'litigation' (resolvable difference) between the faculties of reason and imagination. Rather, it signifies the impossibility of reducing the difference between two heterogeneous genres of discourse; genres which, given their discrete rules of judgement and formation, cannot be subsumed under a 'unifying' set of rules.

We can, I think, understand the ethical significance which Lyotard attributes to the sublime by a (non-Kantian) analogy with Kant's presentation of the moral law in the *Foundations of the Metaphysics of Morals*. For Kant, the moral law derives its force from its indivisibility; from the fact that the practical demands of universal application, respect for rational humanity, and the harmony of moral ends are 'only so many formulas of the very same law' (Kant, 1985, p. 54). The 'difference' that Kant marks in these formulas, in other words, is more 'subjectively than objectively practical, for it is intended to bring an idea of reason closer to intuition . . . and thus nearer to feeling' (*ibid.*). For Lyotard, the importance of the sublime lies in the fact that it reconfigures this relationship between feeling, autonomy and moral obligation: that it calls into question the very cognitive-theoretical ground upon which Kant erects the principles of moral and political responsibility. Thus, if we were to schematize the impact of the sublime upon the Kantian subject, we would have to invoke the simultaneity of its intrusion of feeling upon the realm of cognitive universality, the necessity of judging without a determinate concept, and the constitution of a 'moral culture' whose demands are always beyond the possibility of 'objective' realization (Lyotard, 1988, pp. 165–7). It is these essentially related effects of the sublime therefore, that are intensified by the rapid fragmentation and reconstitution of moral, legal, technical and political necessity. The 'lack of reality' by which Lyotard characterizes the postmodern condition, in other words, is exactly what engenders the conflicts through which 'the subject' is called to judge between the demands of competing genres of discourse. Such a judgement, as Lyotard makes clear at the beginning of *The Differend*, ought to remain responsible to what is *absent* from the rules of every genre: that is, to the feelings of agitation and disquiet that arise from conflicts in which the party that is judged has no language in which to phrase the wrong that is done to him/her/them (*ibid.*, p. ix).

For Lyotard, the registration – or 'phrasing' – of the silences which haunt the necessity of different discourses, is always an event that can conform to none of the rules (of temporality, recognition, success) which this or that genre presents as legislative. Such events begin from a sensation – of agitation, of disquiet – which suspends the established powers of 'subjectivity', and demands an act of phrasing which is radically heterogeneous with the rules of legal, economic, political or ethical prescription. This moment of radical initiation is not restricted to linguistic performativity. Indeed, for Lyotard, 'the phrase', in its 'postmodern' significance, becomes an increasingly aestheticized form whose expressiveness is dispersed across the transgressive, dissonant and offensive gestures that are provoked by 'established' forms of artistic expression. As he puts it in the essay on 'Philosophy and painting in the age of their experimentation':

> [In postmodern art] [t]he powers of sensing and phrasing are being probed on the limits of what is possible, and thus the domain of the perceptible-sensing and the speakable-speaking is being extended. Experiments are made. This is our postmodernity's entire vocation, and commentary has infinite possibilities open to it. (Lyotard, 1991a, p. 190)

This transformative relationship between art and philosophy is developed more fully in the later essay, 'The sublime and the avant-garde' (*ibid.*, p.

196–211). Recalling Benjamin's remarks on surrealism, Lyotard attempts to register the political significance of an art that risks non-reception (by the mass, the audience) for the sake of provoking sensations which confound the reproduction of the present as tradition. Philosophical consideration of the sublime, particularly in the work of Kant and Burke, impacts upon the established canons of the aesthetic. Art can no longer be satisfied simply with perfecting its representation of 'ethical life': it becomes the transfiguration of the present through the 'shock effect'; the disruption of unity, harmony and beauty through the representation of the monstrous, the formless and the inhuman (*ibid.*, p. 202). Thus, the experiments of the avant-garde are 'micrologies', whose uniqueness is staged as a challenge to the technical conventions of representational painting. If they 'happen', they touch immediately upon the vigorous sensations which belong to the 'soul': upon the feelings of mortality, sexual difference and natal contingency that exceed every generic faculty of the human 'subject' and every 'objective' power of the social bond. The task of the avant-garde therefore, is essentially one of 'undoing the presumption of the mind with respect to time' (*ibid.*, p. 211), of depriving us of the securities of tradition and making us judge the present as the perennial return of a violent historical necessity. .

In the chapter of *Libidinal Economy* entitled 'The desire named Marx', Lyotard describes Marx's constant postponement of finishing work on *Capital* as ' . . . a totally pulsional proliferation of a network of concepts hitherto destined . . . to "finalize", to "define" and to justify proletarian politics' (Lyotard, 1993, pp. 96–7). Marx's inability to complete his description of the mode of production, in other words, disclosed something unavoidable in the general economy of capital: the fact that there is no limit to its investment of the suffering, creativity, imagination and exchange through which the system expands. The self-transcendence of capitalism therefore, is unreachable; for its 'structure in dominance' always produces libidinal effects, or 'pulsions', that exceed the point, the instant, of revolutionary praxis. Jameson's determination to treat this libidinal time as a modification of capitalism's functional-economic rationality, has led him towards a political imagination in which the aesthetic is called back to its legitimate objects: class solidarities, internationalism, ecologism. For if we are to question and oppose the global organization of capital and its postmodernist ideology, he claims that we must pursue a moral-asthetic sense of its reifying powers and of the damage these have done to human culture and historical self-awareness (Jameson, 1998, p. 131). According to Lyotard, however, such a political imagination would always lag behind the pure exigency of the present; for in so far as the perversity of capitalism is always exceeding itself (as desire, exchange, consumption, art, body, suffering), it is only through the experience and expression of the sublime that we can approach its constant disordering of 'the real'.

The obligation under which 'we', as sensing, feeling, articulate 'souls', are placed, is to remain receptive to those sublime provocations which arise from the 'objective' forms of human community (capital, economy, technology, functionality). Art, or more specifically avant-garde art, is a kind of transfiguring spontaneity, an expression of those heterogeneous moments which 'disarm' the mechanisms of universal progress. There is, in other words, an irresolvable conflict (*differend*) between the technological procedures through which art is able to recycle the imagery of the avant-garde, and the avant-garde phrasing which seeks to reconfigure the sublime. And so even after artistic production has become largely formulaic, its complicity with the development of technological means, the massification of public taste and the demands of informatic capital, remains a *silencing* of its obligation to the unpresentable (Lyotard, 1991a, p. 210). It is this fragile, aesthetic trace of ethical responsibility which, for Lyotard, cannot be forgotten or operationally discharged.[2] Even the ecstatic transformations of fashion, which Baudrillard presents as the collapse of the aesthetic into the infinite mutability of signs, cannot bring about a complete self-referentiality of the system. For where artistic production has been drawn into the repetitive logic of capital, this also sharpens the agonism between the 'economic genre', which demands that every 'occurrence' (phrase, event) conform to its demand of immediate exchangeability (Lyotard, 1988, p. 173), and the avant-garde response to the litigations through which that demand appears as an objective necessity (capital).

Sublime Provocations: Art, Politics, Capital

We have seen that, for Lyotard, the extension of our capacity to feel the sensations of the sublime is closely related to the ethical demands that arise, unsolicited and unimagined, from the incommensurability of different genres. We cannot avoid being 'summoned' by a pragmatics of power which is constantly seeking to place us within its established terms of litigation. For as human 'subjects' who must negotiate a way through the economic, technological and political rules of exchange, we are necessarily affected by the lack of reality which plays around these heterogeneous forms of discourse. Thus, the aesthetic demand of the sublime arises as an irreducible possibility from the fragmentation of the social bond. For even though we may not feel that 'something has to be phrased' (Lyotard, 1988, p. 181), the very fact of our having been 'situated' in relation to the strategic demands of exchange means that the avant-gardist impulse to express, or configure, the sublime, retains the possibility of finding a response in those subjects who would otherwise belong entirely to the necessity of the economic genre. There remains, in other words, a Benjaminian strand in Lyotard's writing; for the political demand of avant-garde art is retained in its shocking transfigurations of our 'living present'.

The Differend leaves us with the practical demand of Lyotard's radical contextualism: the demand that 'being' be allowed its aesthetic modality, or, what is essentially the same thing, that the conflicts which arise from the generic forms of community be received as 'events' that cannot be mediated within the logic of universal identity (Lyotard, 1988, p. 181). The possibility of an ethical response to the agonism of different genres therefore, is given through the sense of 'wrong' which may arise from their attempts to situate a specific party, or parties, within their heterogeneous rules of litigation. Such wrongs are, by definition, irresolvable within the terms of any particular genre. For the violence that is done to the plaintiff is immediately transformed into a 'damage', for which he/she/they can receive no more – and frequently much less – than the generically applicable form of restitution (Lyotard, 1988, p. xi). This, for Lyotard, is the operational principle of power. For in so far as the agencies which enforce the limits of the social bond (the state, the legislature, the police) can do so only on the basis of litigation, they are founded upon a refusal to allow the possibility that their forensic procedures begin by excluding the uniqueness of each particular case. Bill Readings, in his essay 'Pagans, perverts or primitives? Experimental justice in the empire of capital', cites the example of the commercial exploitation of Aboriginal homelands in Australia (Benjamin, A., 1992, pp. 168–91). His argument is that the mining companies, who sought to gain the patronage of the state by presenting the old rationale of modernization, prosperity and universal benefits, simply passed over the fact that the social economy of the Aboriginal groups who were to be expropriated, could not possibly survive their expropriation.[3] After their separation from the land, there could be no passage into the abstract humanism of progress and development; there could only be the death of a unique and untranslatable culture. This is exactly the kind of irresolvable conflict which Lyotard registers in his idea of the *differend*: for as long as the modernist/capitalist programme is determined to 'speak for' the rights of the Aboriginals to take part in the universal progress of 'white' history, they are immediately denied the possibility of registering the wrong that is done to them (Lyotard, 1988, p. 5).

There is a sense then in which Lyotard's reading of the Kantian sublime returns us to the 'critique' of epistemological hierarchy set out in *Libidinal Economy*. As we have seen, Lyotard's claim is that every form of knowledge presupposes and reproduces libidinal investment. And so what distinguishes theoretical, scientific and philosophical knowledges is not their 'neutrality', but rather the desire to objectify 'true' forms of production, satisfaction and investment. For Lyotard, however, one cannot become 'theoretically' disengaged from the *jouissance* (the simultaneity of pleasure and suffering) which invests libidinal distributions; even the extended labour of writing the perversity of capital involves a kind of pleasure in the struggle for completion. What marks the continuity between the *jouissance* of *Libidinal Economy* and the reception of the sublime expounded in *The Differend* therefore, is a certain 'affection' produced at the limits of cognitive thought. Lyotard has acknowledged that within the terms of the former, our encounter with these limits could only reproduce a 'primary process' (the libidinal band) which invests every representational form of knowledge. Our registration of the dispersal inherent in the categories of scientific and philosophical thought, in other words, would always be destined to return to the 'ontology' of pulsions and affects (Bennington, 1988, p. 50). The 'agitation' experienced by the Kantian subject in the presence of the sublime, however, points to an alterity which cannot be designated in any particular genre – even the quasi-generic tropes of libidinal economics. The sheer unrepresentability of the sublime puts the faculties of reason and imagination into suspension and provokes a judgement which, although 'subjective', demands the agreement of all sentient beings. Thus, Lyotard's transcription of Kant's 'Analytic of the sublime' (Lyotard, 1988, pp. 161–71) is an attempt to register the possibility of a political judgement that would remain sensitive to the events of difference (alterity, incommensurability) distributed among heterogeneous forms of legitimation.

Of this political judgement, or politics of the sublime, Lyotard remarks:

> Each genre of discourse would be like an island; the faculty of judgement would be, at least in part, like an admiral or a provisioner of ships who would launch expeditions from one island to the next, intended to present to one island what was found (or invented, in the archaic sense of the word) in the other, and which might serve the other as an 'as-if intuition' with which to validate it. Whether war or commerce, this interventionist force has no object, and does not have its own island, but requires a milieu – this would be the sea – the *Archipelagos* or primary sea as the Aegean was once called. (Lyotard, 1988, p. 131)

This 'objectless' judgement then, is the condition of the legitimacy of every genre of discourse; for it is only in so far as each is brought into 'war or commerce' with the other that their respective boundaries are established or redrawn. Politics, in other words, takes place through the 'passages' which occur among different genres; each holds out the possibility of 'linkages' which it is unable to foresee or to control. We have seen, for example, that the fact that 'capital gives political hegemony to the economic genre' does not mean that 'capital has been able to effect a comprehensive regulation of the differends that arise from its rules of exchange' (Lyotard, 1988, p. 141). (This, I would suggest, is Baudrillard's position: that the operational logic of capital has produced an infinitely self-referential system of simulation.) Rather, Lyotard's proposition should be understood as expressing the need to phase the damages that arise from the increasingly techno-scientific organization of capital, and indeed to phrase the *differends* that arise from the phrasing of those damages. Our ultimate responsibly as human beings therefore, is to 'the unpresentable': to the autonomy of the phrase, to the spontaneity of feeling (*sensus communis*) that arises the from the 'difference' of different genres, and to the wrongs, persecutions and injuries that occur under the dominance of any particular system of litigations.

I began by suggesting that Baudrillard's *Simulacra and Simulation* could be seen as announcing 'the postmodern' as the worst possible outcome of the Marxist critique of culture. After the collapse of the real into the logic of simulation, the aesthetic becomes hyperlogical; a play of trends, fashions and images which can never reach the point of ethical transfiguration. In terms of Baudrillard's economy of the image therefore, Benjamin and Adorno's writings give some sense of the fatality of the transition from 'the modern' (where representation functions to 'mask and denature' reality) to 'the postmodern' (where representation functions to conceal the collapse of the real into pure simulation). We have seen that their speculative Marxism is focused upon the relationships between art, technology, capitalism and culture, and upon the collapse of 'the public' into the post Enlightenment dynamics of 'the mass'. Yet the intention remains one of discerning the transfigurative potential of the aesthetic within the reifying powers of instrumental reason. Benjamin, Adorno and Jameson's respective accounts of technological reproducibility, retain an urgent sense of the distinction between the 'ideological' and the 'revolutionary' forms of the aesthetic; a distinction which, for Baudrillard, marks the return of the sacred (the messianic, the redemptive) at the point of absolute profanity (hyperlogical capital). Ultimately, however, the logic of Baudrillard's exposition demands that we understand this return as the end of redemptive aesthetics; an end in which the representation of the sacred, even as it has been made monstrous, is perpetually locked into the reproduction of the same.

Reflecting on the Adornian question of the possibility of art 'after Auschwitz', Lyotard remarked that:

> If art persists, and it does persist, it is entirely different, outside of taste, devoted to delivering and liberating this nothing, this affection that owes nothing to the sensible and everything to the insensible secret. (Lyotard, 1990, p. 44)

This is close to the idea of post-Auschwitzian art which Adorno develops in the *Aesthetic Theory* and *Negative Dialectics*. After the fact of the Holocaust, art is charged with the joint responsibility of responding to the violence of reified culture, and of opposing the forms of 'positive legality' in which the difference of the individual is effaced. Adorno's questioning of the possibility of art, politics and morality therefore, demands that we, who live within the post-Auschwitzian order, accept a certain 'pathos of the infinite': the dispersed and inescapable feeling that positive law will always perpetuate its 'incapacity to absorb what essentially defies absorption' (Adorno, 1990, p. 310), and that it is only through a 'micrological' aesthetics that thinking will be able to respond to the reifying powers of totality. Yet there is a *differend* between this Adornian conception of art and Lyotard's understanding of a postmodern responsibility to the sublime. Adorno's reading of Freud, according to Lyotard, remains too concerned with the psychical mutilations which underlie 'normal' personality types; his reading of Marx is 'too speculative', and fails to recognize the informatic trajectory of capital; and most importantly, his reading of Kant fails to make a proper distinction between the analytics of the beautiful and the sublime (Lyotard, 1990, p. 44). Negative aesthetics, in other words, is responsible to the mutilations suffered by an autonomous nature (in the form of the vulnerable, heterogeneous particular), rather than to the intensifications of conflict, agonism and damage provoked by the fragmentation of the social bond. For Lyotard, the importance of Freud's work lies in its registration of the 'unconscious affects' produced through the organization of sexual desire; the importance of Marx, in his account of the infinite mutability of the 'economic genre'; and the importance of Kant, in his registration of those 'feelings of the mind' initiated by the experience of the unpresentable. Thus, if art is possible 'after Auschwitz', and if such an art is to be responsible to the ethical and political dilemmas of postmodernity, then it must express the *sublime* affection which plays around the most 'acceptable' formulae of agonism, complexity and litigation (Lyotard, 1995, p. 159).

In *The Other Heading*, Derrida remarks that the possibility of a political judgement which is properly attentive to the violence of its origin, begins from the recognition of an aporia: that neither the 'technico-economico-scientific' powers of monopoly nor the dispersal of 'self-enclosed idioms' are adequate figurations of the experience of responsibility. Thus, Baudrillard's account of the circularity of the relationship between the masses and the simulacra of the social would have to be addressed in terms of what haunts the hyperlogical production of the real: the *différance* that makes the 'end of politics' political. Lyotard's account of the sublime, on the other hand, would raise questions about the responsibility of the artist and the intellectual. For in so far as he or she claims to respond immediately to the agonism of heterogeneous genres of discourse (*Is it Happening?*), the question of acknowledging a certain indebtedness to the 'being' of the community (which, for Derrida, is never pure, ontological violence) is immediately raised. These questions need to be addressed more fully, as they bear upon Derrida's claim that 'ethics, politics, and responsibility, *if there are any*, will only ever have begun with the experience and experiment of the aporia [of monopoly and dispersion]' (Derrida, 1992, p. 41).

Notes

1. Baudrillard makes it clear that after the collapse of moral categories into the play of simulation, there is no longer any possibility of organizing the social around the idea of 'the good'. Evil, in other words, has become dispersed across the whole range of effects – obscenity, pornography, obesity, cancer, AIDS – that are produced through the solicitation of the mass as *mass* (Baudrillard, 1995a, pp. 81–8). The provocations of theory then can do no more than oppose one catastrophic effect of simulation to another – a strategy which might at least make us aware of the fate forestalled in our current extremity.

2. In 'The sublime and the avant-garde', Lyotard maintains that under Nazism the anxiety which founds political constructions of identity is converted into a hatred of the avant-garde (Lyotard, 1991a, p. 209). The shocking apprehension of the unpresentable – the sublime –

is blocked, and converted into a politics of millennial anticipation (of the *Führer*, the *Volk*). Ultimately, such anticipation demands its absolute fulfilment: the liquidation of those who, by their very existence, threaten the 'arrival' of pure Germanic culture (see Lyotard, 1990, p. 22).

3. Readings' essay, in its attempt to register the *differend* between the narratives of 'modern' and 'Aboriginal' identity, draws upon Werner Herzog's film *Where the Green Ants Dream*. As a dramatization of the conflict between the capitalizing mechanism of modernity and tribal narrations of time, place and belonging, the film points up the 'untranslatability' of Aboriginal culture into the terms of 'Universal Humanity'. There is no tribunal which could effect such a 'translation' without immediately silencing the demands of the plaintiffs.

9

Culture, Politics, *Différance*

Introduction

In this chapter I will open up the postmodernist economies of culture, representation and aesthetics we have examined to Derrida's account of the metaphysics of presence. In particular, I want to examine his claim that deconstruction demands that we regard human cultures as 'non-identical'; as forms which constantly attract and exceed the categories of being through which the demands of political unity are sustained. Specifically, I will to look at:

- Derrida's relationship to Heidegger and the question of Being;
- the implication of culture in this question, especially the ideals of friendship, community and belonging which have organized Western conceptions of shared identity;
- the difference between the symbolic economy of deconstruction and those presented by Baudrillard and Lyotard;
- the concepts of *différance* and 'dual responsibility' through which Derrida traces the chance of the political in the time of 'tele-technological' capitalism.

Derrida, Heidegger and Metaphysics

If we are to understand Derrida's approach to culture, we first need to understand his relationship to Heidegger, or more specifically to Heidegger's account of the question. We know from Chapter 5, that Heidegger's thought is concerned with what he calls fundamental ontology: with the disclosure of Being in particular existents, with the categories through which this disclosure has been reduced to the formality of logic and epistemology, and with the historical questions which arise from Man's (*Dasein*'s) concern with his own existence. What Derrida remarks in Heidegger's earliest account of fundamental ontology (*Being and Time*), is his formulation of the question of Being in terms of the categories through which it appears in the economy of metaphysics. Thus, although we can never step outside of the 'syntactic and lexical resources' of philosophy, we must 'work to locate [its] metaphysical holds, and to reorganise increasingly the form and cites of our questioning' (Derrida, 1981, p. 10). What Derrida takes from Heidegger's critique of philosophy, in other words, is the demand that we constantly subject the hierarchical structures of our culture to the question of their present legitimacy.

Derrida's concern with the question in Heidegger's thought ultimately comes to focus on the return of the notion of spirit in his later work, particularly in *An Introduction to Metaphysics*, the *Rectorship Address* and the essay on the German poet Trakl. For Derrida, the return of spirit in Heidegger's writing demands a detailed examination of how it is articulated in his work after 1933, and how this articulation affects the economy of the question originally presented in *Being and Time*. What is ominous about this return, is that it appears to suspend the ontological necessity of the question. Spirit seems to designate certain limits to the autonomy of questioning, and to constitute its own hierarchical organization of language, culture and humanity. In his *Rectorship Address* – which is published as 'The self-assertion of the German university' (Woolin, 1998, pp. 29–39) – for example, Heidegger claims that we must understand spirit in terms of a fervent, burning illumination of Being which harks back to presocratic philosophy. Man's original departure into Being takes the form of a violent 'cutting in', whose perilous solicitation of will, fortitude and resoluteness light up the question of his existence. After its expression of this originary relationship, however, philosophy, in its Greco-Roman forms, began to reduce the idea of spirit to the level of an epistemic universal. It becomes, in other words, the formal ideality of things, the paradigmatic form of their particular existence. What is urgently demanded of our present epoch therefore, is that spirit should return to its spiritual relationship to Being, and that it should again illuminate the authentic purpose of human existence (Derrida, 1990a, p. 32). For in so far as our 'darkening world' (the West) has 'misinterpreted' its spiritual vocation, the fate of humanity becomes tied to the technological manipulation of man and nature, and to the slavish preservation of cultural norms and values.

What is of particular concern here is Heidegger's identification of the German language as that which is best able to approach the question of Being, and the German university as the institution in which 'spirit can do nothing other than affirm itself' (Derrida, 1992a, p. 33). For in so far as spirit is identified as that which imposes the 'directive rigidity of a mission', it seems that the spiritual leadership of European culture belongs uniquely – and vocationally – to the German nation and its people. For Derrida, however, Heidegger's assertion of this spiritual hierarchy should not be understood simply in terms of his support for the Nazi party during the early 1930s. The reading of Heidegger which Derrida presents in *Of Spirit*, is an attempt to show that while his use of the term 'spirit' cannot be cleanly dissociated from the Germanism of his political speeches, there was never a total abandonment of the question which would allow us to regard his Nazi associations as 'the logical outgrowth of his philosophical doctrines' (Woolin, 1998, p. 273). Thus, in the *Rectorship Address*, Derrida finds a more complex kind of complicity from the one usually attributed to Heidegger. He argues that the spiritual mission which Heidegger claims for the German university is something which must constantly question its own vocation; for the very fact that its mission relates to the authenticity of *Dasein*'s relationship to Being, means that it must confront the risks and dangers of its pronouncements – even to the extent of questioning its own spiritual-historical primacy. Nazism, then, despite Heidegger's attempts to solicit its 'inner truth and greatness' (Heidegger, 1987, p. 199), could not be made responsible to the question; for in so far as its ideals of authenticity remained biologistic and racist, the movement remained an 'ideological', rather than a 'spiritual', expression of spirit. For Derrida, however, this implicit demarcation of responsibility against the political agenda of the Nazi party remains tied to the infinite return of 'spirit's spirit'; to those transcendental/epochal forms of identity which forever lay claim to the rights of man (Derrida, 1992a, p. 41).

It is in the now (in)famous passage which Derrida placed in the footnotes of *Of Spirit*, that the question of his relationship to Heidegger is most succinctly formulated. We have seen that Derrida's primary concern in his reading of Heidegger is the fate of the question after the return of spirit in his later writings. The exposition presented in *Of Spirit* traces the tension between Heidegger's undoubted commitment to a spiritual redemption of modernity (and everything which that entailed for his political associations), and the responsibility of human beings to the question. Derrida's footnote begins by returning to the significance of language in Heidgger's critique of metaphysics:

> [In Heidegger] language is already there, in advance of the moment at which any question can arise about it. In this it exceeds any question. This advance is, before any contract, a sort of promise of originary alliance to which we must have in some sense acquiesced, already said yes, given a pledge, whatever may be the negativity or problematicity of the discourse which may follow. (Derrida, 1992a, p. 129)

In Heidegger's thought, the origin of language is thematized through the provocation to poesis through which *Dasein* responds to the overwhelming mystery of Being (Heidegger, 1987, p. 177). This means that, for language in general, the act of enunciation (the 'saying') is never simply continuous with the totality of language (the 'said'): speech begins with a relationship (to Being) which is prior to every received meaning, and to every established determination of sociality – culture, idle talk, functionality, technology. Derrida's account of the return of spirit in Heidegger's later work therefore, is concerned with the fate of this preoriginary promise of language to the question: is it utterly lost in the 'Germanism' of Heigegger's philosophy? The full complexity of his answer lies in the textual analyses which make up (the body of) *Of Spirit*. We can, however, divine the thread of his argument from his remarks in the footnote.

Heidegger's writing presents a complex economy of openings, complicities and insights; an economy which, in its ontological-existential pursuit of the question, led Heidegger into his attempt to spiritualize Nazism. Derrida's reading of Heidegger, however, while acknowledging the guilt of his political associations, refuses to follow the logic of strict cultural determinism.[1] Heidegger's critique of metaphysics, in other words, exceeds any providential reconstruction of *Dasein* – its authenticity and resoluteness – as the bearer of German *Volkish* identity. So, what is the nature of this excessiveness? Derrida alludes, very briefly, to five examples, each of which, he contends, reopens the demand of the question from within the thematics of spirit. Perhaps most tellingly he argues that, in *An Introduction to Metaphysics*, the mission upon which spirit embarks in the 'darkening world' of modernity, depends upon an acceptance of the aporias that necessarily arise from such a mission (Derrida, 1992a, p. 135). The questions concerning technology, functionality and rationalization which inform Heidegger's critique of modernity therefore, are not simply turned over to the resurgence of the Germanic spirit; they remain as ethical and philosophical demands for which traditional metaphysics can provide no adequate response.

For Derrida, the responsibility of human beings to the question of their being is always implicit in Heidegger's writing. We should not, however, take his exposition to be an uncritical acceptance of fundamental ontology. The economy of difference which is presented in Heidegger's writing, vacillates constantly between the openness of language to the preoriginary demand of the question, and the categories (authenticity, resoluteness, calling) through which that demand becomes a historical mission. To the end of his writing career, he could not avoid soliciting the 'ghosts' of spirit; the ghosts of a self-identical culture reflecting only (upon) itself (Derrida, 1992a, pp. 40–1). We must recognize therefore, that Derrida's reading of Heidegger works *within* his text, reconfiguring the conflicts, oppositions and unities through which he approaches the question of modernity. We cannot, in conscience and responsibility, return to the spiritual vocation of *Dasein*; for if we are to remain responsible to the question, we must recognize that speech (the saying) is always promised to those particular questions which exceed the established metaphysics of 'nature', 'humanity' and 'spirit'. Practically, then, this responsibility takes the form of acknowledging that the 'culture' through which we identify ourselves (as selves), is sustained by the impossibility of uniting the technological, economic and geopolitical conditions of its being.

Culture 'without Identity'

It is through this exposition of the Heideggarian question that we are finally able to return to the 'axiom' which Derrida proposes in *The Other Heading*: 'What is proper to a culture is not to be identical with itself' (Derrida, 1992, p. 9). Three points are encapsulated here which need to be made explicit. First, Derrida's axiom means that it is only in so far as we identify ourselves through the norms, values and ideals of our culture that we are able to exercise political judgement and responsibility. Second, it means that at any given time, a culture is sustained through a process of 'gathering', of giving itself a 'presence', which calls together its internal differentiations and constitutes a boundary between itself and its 'outside'. And third, it means that culture, conceived in Derrida's sense of an economy of difference, is the condition of an ethical demand: the demand that we remain open to the 'other' of our cultural identity, but in such a way that we do not simply valorize what is heterogeneous, exotic or idiomatic (*ibid.*, p. 15). If we are to act responsibly therefore, we must acknowledge that *both* 'monopoly' (commodification, mediatization, capitalization) and 'dispersion' (the locality, the province, the idiom) are essential conditions of ethical judgement. For while it is true that 'omnipresent and extremely rapid networks' (*ibid.*, p. 39) have come to dominate the production and dissemination of culture, it remains the case that the valorization of the local determines its own reactionary politics: 'self-enclosed idioms, or petty little nationalisms, each jealous and untranslatable' (*ibid.*). Ethics and politics then 'will only have begun with the experience and experiment of aporia' (*ibid.*, p. 41).

One of the recurrent issues which arise from deconstruction is the relationship of its own grammatological strategies to the resources of (Western) philosophy. In an interview with Henri Ronse, published in *Positions*, he remarked that:

> Heidegger recognizes that economically and strategically he had to borrow the syntactic and lexical resources of language and metaphysics . . . Therefore, we must work to locate these metaphysical holds, and to reorganise increasingly the form and sites of its questioning. (Derrida, 1981, p. 10)

Thus, as soon as the demand of the question is freed from Heidegger's metaphysical presuppositions, philosophy becomes that which arises from the aporetic, disjunctive time of modernity. Questions arising from the rationalization and functionalization of man, for example, cannot be referred to a putative 'darkening of the world' or to the historical mission of *Dasein*. Rather, they demand to be considered in terms of the impact of informatic, digital and prosthetic technologies on the cultural, religious and philosophical structures of modern identity. For Derrida then, we cannot escape the language of metaphysics: for a 'spectralized' humanity, whose essence is dispersed across the complex of electronic and digital technologies, demands a constant, constantly uncertain, redrawing of the boundaries between the human and the technological. Thus, the debates about euthanasia, drugs, transsexualism and cloning which arise in our modern culture, take place through the undecidability of this relationship; for it is only in so far as it constantly returns in the contradictory demands of 'monopoly' (capital, rationality, technocracy) and 'dispersal' (the 'others' of technocratic and logocentric rationality) that we can assume the ethical responsibility to the question.

Politics then, takes place through this aporia of Western culture: the fact that our present responsibility cannot be discharged through the realization of universal cultural norms and ideals, or through the rights of every cultural difference. One must therefore '*invent* new gestures, discourses, politico-institutional practice that inscribe the allegiance of these two imperatives: the capital and the a-capital, the other of capital' (Derrida, 1992, p. 44). This returns us to the question of the masses, or more precisely to the possibility of their exercising the kind of reflexive judgement demanded by the disjointed time of modernity. In Baudrillard's work, we have seen that the 'allegiance' of capital and the a-capital has collapsed; for the power of modern image technologies has become such that the a-capital (the immigrant, the woman, the locality) can appear to the masses only through its simulacra. Thus, to take one of Baudrillard's examples, media constructions of the wars and famines which continue to afflict the Third World, can do little more than provoke their own simulations of guilt and the massified, media-generated charity of Live Aid and the 'telethon'.

The question therefore, becomes whether the image technologies that are deployed by capital can erase all traces of the ethical demand from the realm of culture. For Baudrillard, we have seen that the virtualizing effects of these technologies have finally and definitively exceeded the dynamics of spirit. And so their social and political impact must be evaluated in terms which are purified not only of the Heideggerian metaphysics of *Dasein*, but also of Marxist conceptions of class struggle and Enlightenment ideals of deliberative subjectivity. It is the masses then, who are the 'shadow' which follows Baudrillard's writing: for in so far as the economy of signs (simulacra) constantly exceeds the functional, communicative, aesthetic and ethical limits which it seeks to represent, the masses do no more than absorb the novelty of their latest solicitation. The most we can say of their political significance is that they have a certain 'inertial' tendency', which means that they never quite conform to the simulacra of 'youth', 'family', 'sexuality', 'health' (Baudrillard, 1983, pp. 41–8).

This account of the technological erasure of politics and ethical responsibility returns us to Heidegger's claim that 'the essence of technology is by no means anything technological' (Heidegger, 1996, p. 311). According to Heidegger, we must understand the technocratic organization of modernity in terms of the reductivism of Western metaphysics. For it is only in so far as the 'real' and the 'true' become identical with the 'logical' and the 'consistent' that it is possible to subject the world to technocratic control. Within this generally manipulable organization of reality, *Dasein*, the being which is defined by its concern for its own existence, becomes part of the resources which sustain modernity's drive towards maximal efficiency. Yet for Heidegger, *Dasein*'s becoming part of the physical resources of modernity ('standing reserve') immediately raises the question of its responsibility; of how it is to remain faithful to the question of Being within the functional organization of time and society.

Heidegger's essay on technology concludes by claiming that the political ideologies which have grown up around the functionalization of the world, do no more than reflect the essential determination to maximize the efficiency of the social machine. And so it is only in the work of art, whose execution responds to the originary expressiveness of *Dasein*'s relationship to Being, that the non-technological origins of history, community and resoluteness are disclosed (Heidegger, 1996, p. 340). What Derrida's political writing takes from this Heideggarian critique is the idea that the technological colonization of social, ethical and political relationships, can never entirely master the questions to which it gives rise. The image technologies whose logic Baudrillard expounds with such rigour, do undoubtedly impugn the status of the real; they do, without question, perpetuate cultural norms, ideals and values which caricature the ideal of deliberative politics. Yet for Derrida, this colonization of the public sphere does not mark its final splitting off from the Enlightenment project; the total collapse of the masses into a guiltless, irresponsible conformity. Rather, we must recognize that the technological reproduction of the real by the media is always an imposition; that their contrivance of the simulacra which produce/solicit the masses proceeds through a *strategic* relationship to the 'others' of monopoly (*le Capital*). It is this relationship which returns us to the question of the question. For in so far as the 'gathering' which is effected through the technological forces of capital always impacts upon 'the gathered' (regions, cultures, ethnicities), the responsibility for the question remains implicit in the economy of cultural massification.

It is in this sense then, that we can perhaps still talk about ideas like public opinion, deliberation and responsibility. In the interview published as 'Call it a day for democracy', Derrida remarks that:

> Public opinion is not an incalculable average, but there is something of the incalculable in it. It is simply that the incalculable, *if there is any*, never *presents* itself; it is not, it is never, the theme of some scientific or philosophical objectification. (Derrida, 1992, p. 105)

The 'incalculable' to which Derrida refers in this passage is what constantly arises, spontaneously and unforeseen, from the media simulation of the real. The concept of humanity, for example, has become increasingly 'spectralized' by the technological powers of capital, and so each of us is confronted with questions about our identity which we cannot simply refer to essentialist constructions of life, nature or species being. For Baudrillard, the possibility of public reflection on such difficult and undecidable questions has already been excluded by their representation in the media. The masses are what they are because they simply absorb the simulacra of difference; each 'one' is the same as all the other 'ones' who are solicited by the hyperfunctional forms of sex, gender, health, beauty. For Derrida, however, the questions raised by the relationship of the human and the technological always exceed the simulacra through which they are presented. And so the gathering and reproduction of the masses which Baudrillard describes, is always followed by the ghosts of its own simulacra: the 'others' who are both created and solicited in the logic of mass representation. Ultimately, politics depends upon the unforeseeable events in which 'the human' returns as an impossibly ethical demand; events of violence, subjection and autonomy that constantly traverse and differentiate 'the masses'.

The Idea of the Political: 'Democracy to Come'

Derrida's idea of democracy then, turns·upon the infinitesimal, infinitely dispersed events of *différance* which demand the right of expression – '*droit de réponse*' (Derrida, 1992, p. 105). It is this right which allows the citizen to be more than 'the fraction of a passive "consumer" public' (*ibid.*), and which must, if there is to be democracy at all, be recognized by the legal and political institutions which administer the idea of justice.

It should not, however, be assumed that right of response expresses a radical valorization of the encounters and events that are precipitated by the system of monopoly capital. In Lyotard's work on the sublime, emphasis is placed on the feelings of agitation and disconcertion which accompany the heterogeneous structure of reality. The overdetermination of the real through incommensurable 'genres of discourse', in other words, gives rise to events of difference (*differends*) to which no a priori criteria of judgement can be applied. It is to those events that postmodern art, philosophy and politics are responsible: art in the sense of a transfiguring creativity which 'disarms' the mechanisms of technocratic efficiency; philosophy, in the sense that it must seek the generic rules which govern transcendental ideals of truth, justice and beauty; and politics, in the sense of the precipitation of the *differends* that arise from ideas such as citizenship, enlightenment, nationhood and democracy. What is important here, and what ultimately differentiates Derrida and Lyotard's approaches to politics, is the status of the event and its relationship to political judgement. We have seen that for Lyotard, the relationship of the singular occurrence, or event, to the transcendental forms of cognitive, aesthetic and historical apprehension can be glimpsed in Kant's account of the sublime. For it is there that he considers the way in which our cognitive faculties are disarmed by the presence of some great magnitude in nature, and the way in which this disarming necessitates that we judge (this natural phenomenon as sublime) in the absence of any determinate concept. In Lyotard's reading of Kant, this suspension of the cognitive faculties gestures not towards the inherent purposiveness of nature and history, but towards the overdetermination of the real that is characteristic of postmodernity. Thus, the feelings of disquiet and agitation that arise when we encounter the events of conflict which Lyotard calls differends, signify the impossibility of resolving such conflicts through the rules of any particular genre.

Lyotard's politics of the sublime therefore, is responsible for the events of irreconcilable conflict that arise out of the scientific, technological and economic organization of modernity. Each of us has, as a matter of fact, to conduct our lives through competing and incommensurable imperatives. Employment in the temporal economy of capital, for example, gives rise to a multiplicity of questions about risk, health, familial obligation and class solidarity which cannot be made to conform to the logic of economic independence and fiscal responsibility. However, as the technological powers of capital expand and condense the experience of time into one of simultaneous requital, it seems as if the possibility of receiving and reflecting upon such questions is foreclosed. Lyotard's response to this totalizing necessity is to argue that the economy of effects produced by capital always exceeds its functional resolution of *differends*. As the turnover of capital becomes ever more efficient (cybernetic, informatic), so the suppression of its 'others' becomes ever more complete. Politics therefore, arises out of the fact that we, as human beings, are responsible to the violence of generic necessity; a responsibility which arises not from any shared sense of human essence, but from our capacity to receive and express what is unique and uniquely heterogeneous in particular events (Lyotard, 1988, p. 181).

Ultimately, Lyotard's reading of Kant is concerned with the question of whether it is possible for a unified, transcendental subject to 'have' aesthetic feelings. For in so far as these feelings arise from the suspension of the cognitive faculties, it seems as if their demand (that this object or phenomenon be judged beautiful or sublime) refers to a community of souls whose sensibility exceeds their formal structures of recognition (Benjamin, A., 1992, p. 22). The community towards which this aesthetic sensibility gestures therefore, cannot be brought into the realm of determinate cognition; for it cannot be made subject to the generic rules (of scientific, economic or technological necessity) through which the social bond is presented. This 'unrepresentable' community from which political judgements arise is, of course, very close to Derrida's understanding of our preoriginary responsibility to the question. Both Derrida and Lyotard emphasize the impossibility of 'realizing' the demands of an ethically responsible politics, and the necessity of responding to unique and unforeseen events of injustice. Yet for Derrida, there remains in Lyotard's writing a tendency to precipitate political judgement towards the demands of the absolutely unique and the heterogeneous. His claim that political responsibility can arise only where 'culture' (in the Kantian sense of aesthetic apprehension) responds to the pure singularity of the event, tends to present the spontaneity of ethical and aesthetic praxis as radically independent of the question of being.

For Derrida, the 'community of the question' which arises from the economics of cultural identity, is responsible not only to the dispersion of localized and idiomatic forms (regions, ethnicities, sexualities), but also to the universal structures through which truth and reality are maintained (capital, nation, the people). The promise to which we, as human beings, are responsible therefore, is the return, or reinscription, of the origin in the institutions which comprise our community. This does not mean, as Lyotard argues in his essay on Heidegger, that Derrida is unable to register the play of disparate intensities which characterize postmodern temporality (Lyotard, 1990, p. 73). Rather, it entails a 'dual responsibility', in which each of us is responsible *both* to the promise of democracy maintained in the institutional organization of the social (this would include the informatic 'channels' which Baudrillard consigns to pure operational necessity), and the events of silencing and exclusion through which the question (of being) is constantly reopened. For Derrida then, the most pressing question of our day is whether Western culture remains more faithful to the ideals of the Enlightenment by 'cultivating the difference-to-oneself that constitutes identity or by confining oneself to an identity wherein this identity remains gathered' (Derrida, 1992, p. 11). It is to this question that I will turn in the final chapter.

Note

1. Such a logic maintains that Heidegger's thought is not only analytically incoherent, but also that his ontological-existential categories – authenticity, calling, resoluteness – should be conceived as the metaphysical reconstitution of a shattered Germanic identity. His association with Nazism then becomes the necessary consequence of a philosophy which, from its inception (in *Being and Time*), is dogmatically 'German' (Woolin, 1998, pp. 1–22).

3

Postmodernism and the End of History

10

Derrida, Fukuyama and the 'New World Order'

Introduction

When Derrida remarked of deconstruction that it would have been 'impossible and unthinkable' outside of a Marxist space (Derrida, 1994a, p. 92), his proposition concerned the relationship which Marx designated between the technological effects of capital and the conflicted, contradictory time of the present. For Derrida, Marx's writing on the ideological construction of the masses, on the relationship between time, capital and machine technology, and on the mechanical enhancement of human labour power, discloses an economy of technological reproduction that constantly, and without exception, ruptures the religious, philosophical and political ideals of democracy. For Derrida therefore, the spirit of Marx's critique is disclosed in its registration of the conflictual development of capitalism, and in the fact that idealist configurations of enlightenment, ethical life and moral progress begin from a concept of humanity that is abstracted from its socio-economic and socio-technological relationships. It is in the context of this reading of Marx therefore, that I will examine the following issues:

- Francis Fukuyama's enunciation of a liberal capitalist end to the ideological struggles of human history, and his consignment of Marxism to a former epoch in which the emancipatory potential of the free market was insufficiently developed;
- whether the development of global capitalism has really been achieved through the moral enlightenment of productive humanity, and whether, as Fukuyama claims, it is possible to discern the *inevitability* of this development in the historical events of our day;
- the return of the old Marxist concerns about free market economics, unequal development, international law and structural unemployment that is determined by the global-technological organization of capitalism;
- the ways in which new media and cybernetic technologies redetermine philosophical questions about time, human freedom and political responsibility;

- Derrida's inheritance of Marx's 'revolutionary promise': the way in which he reconfigures political responsibility through the idea of democracy to come.

Capital and Technology

From the beginning of *Spectres of Marx*, Derrida is fascinated by the figure of Hamlet and his relationship to the ghost of his murdered father. So what, we must ask, is at stake in this fascination?

In Shakespeare's play, the ghost of Hamlet's father returns to the ramparts of Elsinore to demand that Hamlet purge the murder and adultery that were committed against him by Claudius, his brother, and Gertrude, his queen. For it is not until their sovereignty over the kingdom of Denmark is brought to an end that he can be released from his time in purgatory. His address to Hamlet begins: 'I am thy father's spirit / Doomed for a certain term to walk the night / And for the day confined to fast in fires / Till the foul crimes done in my days of nature / Are burnt and purged away' (*Hamlet*, I.5). The return of the ghost to Elsinore therefore, is a demand which is made directly to Hamlet: the fatal and insane demand that takes his fragile existence and makes of it the instrument of justice. And so, when he exclaims, 'The time is out of joint / O, cursed spite / That ever I was born to set it right' (*ibid.*), his realization is that the present which it is his fate to inherit is so disordered that it threatens the very concepts of humanity, time and history.

Hamlet then, inherits the 'malediction of the law' by his birth; for it is the rottenness of the state of Denmark which destines him to put time 'back on its hinges'. He must struggle with his disturbed and disjointed present by taking on his responsibility to the ghost of his father, and by challenging the spectres of holy writ, oedipal love and feudal absolutism that confuse and disarm him (Derrida, 1994a, p. 21). The question he confronts then is the question of the righteous inheritor: the question of who one is to be, of who one is to recognize and of how one is to think and reflect upon the present (dis)order of things (Derrida, 1994a, p. 23).

In the end, the possibility of Hamlet's discharging his responsibility to his father depends on the time's being 'out of joint'. For as the violence of the law becomes ever more barbarous (more dispersed, unregulated and incalculable), so the responsibility of the inheritor becomes a question of remaining faithful to the promise of a democracy to come. It is this promise, the very one which Hamlet confronts in his soliloquy (*Hamlet*: III.1), which brings us to Derrida's reading of Marx. Hamlet's relationship to the corrupt and disordered state of Denmark discloses an irreducible configuration of the present: the fact that its being between past and future must always summon the ghosts of the past (those old conflicts and revolutions in which the idea of the human was in play) to the hegemonic powers of the day. Derrida's claim therefore, is that if we are to remain faithful to the spirit of Marx's revolutionary promise, we must recognize that his critique responds to a conflictual economy (capitalism) whose scientific, technological and ideological powers constantly intensify the disjointedness of time. As the idea of the human becomes increasingly dispersed (spectralized) through prosthetic and telematic technologies, we, as the inheritors of Marx, are thrust upon the aporetic structure of the present: for the law, in its promise of universal recognition, is always 'out of joint' with the de facto processes through which humanity is used in the global turnover of capital.

We must be careful then, to distinguish between what Derrida understands as the 'spirit' of Marx's writing from what he conceives as the 'spectres' raised by Marxism as a historico-political force. The entry of Marxism into the conflicts determined by the mode of production is always done through the strategic action of particular proletarian organizations. The history of Marxist politics therefore, is a history of 'spectres', of those forms of political activism (Leninism, Stalinism, Maoism, Trotskyism) which have arisen from the conflict between state authority and the masses. The spirit of Marx's critique, however, remains distinct from the particular struggles through which it appears. For it is only in so far as that spirit is irreducible to any of its historical manifestations that it can remain a provocation to pursue the idea of democracy. It is to this spirit, which is both concealed and revealed in the procession of spectres, that Derrida refers us in his account of Hamlet's encounter with the ghost. For the spectral figure of his father can only command him as long as it remains a faceless voice, a spirit which speaks through and beyond the armed and catastrophic struggles of the day (Derrida, 1994a, p. 8).

The 'messianic' power of Marx's critique therefore, lies in his disclosure of the relationship between capital and technology. For Derrida, the categories through which Marx expounded the temporality of capitalism (fixed and organic capital, surplus value, the general rate of profit) are contemporary with a certain level of technological development; one in which the commodity is already mass produced, electric communications are already becoming influential upon the turnover of capital, and the mass media, in the form of newspapers and magazines, are beginning to invent the sphere of popular taste. Now, for Derrida, Marx's writing is characterized by a tension between his commitment to a humanist ontology, and his registration of capitalism as a technological disordering of every established ideal of humanity, identity and justice. In Marx's own political texts, this tension tends to be resolved in favour of the eschatological forms of socialized production, proletarian justice and the emancipation of productive humanity. Indeed, it is these forms that haunt the political history of Marxism. Derrida's point, however, is that this designation of the political tends to force the aporetic structure of the present into a *programmatic* determination of the future. Thus, in so far as the present can never be identical to itself, our political responsibility to the day is constantly transformed through the disordering, unforeseeable effects of technological capitalism. We need to ask then, what the nature of this disordering is: how it has come about, and what its consequences are.

Derrida makes it clear from the start of *Spectres of Marx* that remaining faithful to the promise of Marx's critique (the promise of justice and emancipation) involves a fundamental questioning of the relationship between capital and technology. In order to understand the nature of this questioning, we need first to specify the technological effects which have produced the temporal dislocation of our historical present. One of the fundamental ideas that has informed deconstruction since the publication of *Of Grammatology* in 1967 is originary technicity. In essence, Derrida's claim is that it is impossible to disintricate the concept of humanity from the technological supplements which have, from the beginning, accompanied human culture and civilization. There is, in other words, no description of an original point (Rousseau's 'state of nature', Marx's 'primitive communism') or ontological identity (Heidegger's account of *Dasein*) which can avoid opposing the pure, non-technological essence of humanity to the ultimately corruptive influence of technology. To this extent we can see that Derrida's critique of metaphysics (his determination to trace the logic of supplementarity in essentialist constructions of man, woman, life, nature) and his idea of originary technicity, are part of the same attempt to radicalize our understanding of the present. It is in the context of these two heterogeneous yet originally related notions, that we should conceive the relationship between capital, history and time.

What Marx says in the *Communist Manifesto* is, for Derrida, a crucial anticipation of new technologies and the unforeseen consequences this techno-evolution will have for a revolutionary critique. So, what are these technologies, and how have they impacted upon the temporal economy of capitalism?

Digital and informatic technologies   The increasing sophistication of computer systems is, of course, one of the central concerns of postmodern theory. On the one hand, there are those who consider the revolution in information technology as a potentially democratizing force; one which places information at the disposal of all, and which increases the potential for local resistance to global strategies (see, for example, some of Marshall McCluhan's more optimistic accounts of the 'global village'). Derrida's concern with informatic technologies, however, is focused on their potential for technocratic control. At its simplest, this notion can be understood as the hyperextension of functional necessity: each individual is conceived in terms of retrievable bits of information which defines his or her utility to the socio-economic system. This informatic reduction of the individual has a distinctive temporality. For in so far as its functional principle is the rapid transfer of information which controls the influx and outflow of capital into different sectors of the global economy, we must recognize that traditional ideas of nation, state, class and production have lost the basis of their authority. Corporate capital, in other words, becomes increasingly autonomous: increasingly able to produce massive social and political dislocations through the speed of its shifting between the 'developed' and 'developing' worlds (Derrida, 1994a, pp. 93–4). The effects of informatic technologies on the reproduction of capital therefore, should be conceived in terms of the loss of the socio-historical reality (colonial power, nation state, civil society) which has supported our experience of community and ethical life. The idea of the human has become 'spectralized' (ghostly, insubstantial), and we are faced with the responsibility of trying to remain hospitable to 'the other' while the substance of our own (Western) identity has become radically uncertain.

The mass media   As we saw in the previous chapter, the mass media and its effects are one of the central concerns of postmodernist theory. In Baudrillard's work, for example, the spectralizing effects of the media are theorized in terms of the concept of simulation. Very briefly, his claim is that as the technological means of representation became increasingly sophisticated (TV, video, virtual reality), the image attains complete autonomy from its object, its referent. The 'real', which Baudrillard variously identifies with the unpredictable contingencies of bodily reproduction, racial and sexual difference, and the old Marxist dialectics of scarcity, is lost in its technological simulation, and all that remains is a play of representations (simulacra) which constantly modifies the popular reception of the true, the beautiful and the ethical. Baudrillard therefore, conceives the masses as the structural counterpart of this play of simulacra; they are the labile, undifferentiated consumers of images who have passed beyond the possibility of reflection on the real (Baudrillard, 1983, pp. 1–9). As we have seen, this relationship is theorized in terms of a structural dependency: the masses consume the meanings produced by the media without 'radiating' any sign of change or recognition, and so the media must continue to produce new simulacra in order to retain the interest of the masses as voters, citizens, consumers. The temporality of simulation therefore is radically disordered. For in so far as it is the ruin of providential history (the cumulative enlightenment of rational humanity), we are left only with an infinite recycling of signs and meanings, all of which are transient, reversible, and escalatory (*ibid.*, p. 41–8).[1]

Ultimately, then, Baudrillard's account of simulation announces the 'hyperfunctionality' of the social. The spiritual unity which idealist histories attribute to the institutions of social life is ruptured by the production of images which present 'the real' (sex, gender, love, death) as a solicitation of consumption, economy and capital. There is no ethical necessity in social life; there is, for Baudrillard, only the escalation of social reality beyond its putative limits. This disordering logic of simulation is undoubtedly part of what Derrida conceives as time's being 'out of joint'; for the regulative idea of 'the human' becomes increasingly dispersed through the technological means of representation. However, we must also recognize that the procession of simulacra through which the masses are

141

solicited, even though it is constantly intensified through media technologies, takes place within the general economy of self-identification, or culture. We know that for Derrida the possibility of self-identification depends upon the concepts of agency, individuality, responsibility and recognition that are inscribed in the normative and legislative structures of social integration. It is in this sense that we are all inheritors of the violence of the law. We also know that for Derrida, what is 'proper' to a culture is 'not to be identical with itself', that its designation of the ideals of justice and democracy should be conceived as a provocation to receive those 'others' who remain unrecognized and unincluded (Derrida, 1992, p. 9). Baudrillard's account of the relationship between the masses and the media therefore, is complicated by Derrida's claim that culture, even in its hyperlogical production, returns in the traces of universal recognition through which 'we' (Western Europeans) experience our identity and difference. To this extent, then, the play of cultural and political simulacra always reopens the chance of an unforeseen reaction; a reaction which springs from the dissonance engendered between the promise of Enlightenment ideals of justice and democracy and their simulation. It is these unforeseen instances of conflict which, for Derrida, mean that we cannot be justified in treating 'the masses' *simply* as the negative effect of simulation. They always sustain the possibility of receiving the reality of the other, and of responding to his/her suffering as it exceeds the disordered temporality of simulation. I will return to the possibility of this response when we come to look at Derrida's understanding of Marx's revolutionary promise.

Genetic and prosthetic technologies　Finally, we must include the effects of genetic and prosthetic technologies on the temporality of the present. The ethical and political ideals which have informed Western culture involve certain basic assumptions about the integrity of the human 'being': the primacy of the will and rational deliberation, the unity of body and soul, the ontology of sexual difference. Thus, in so far as genetic and prosthetic technologies (here we can include recent innovations like intelligent prosthetic limbs, cochlear implants, and genetic therapies and modifications) are already starting to threaten this theological-metaphysical integrity of the human, we need to consider their impact on the political organization of the present.

Donna Harraway, in her essay 'A manifesto for cyborgs', approaches the question by arguing that biologistic, psychoanalytic and religious accounts of the essential characteristics of humanity, are in fact limiting of the emancipatory potential offered by prosthetic technologies. Indeed, Harraway claims that cybernetic enhancement of the human body, and its potential to liberate humankind from the political ontologies of 'feminism' and 'anti-feminism', 'racism' and 'anti-racism', must be taken up as *the* political demand of our epoch. For in so far as these technologies determine both the possibility of emancipation and the threat of complete technocratic control, the demand which is placed upon us now, in the present, is to envisage how a cybernetic humanity might inhabit the future. What is demanded then, is a literature which anticipates the infinite extension of physical and mental powers; a literature which questions and exceeds the political ontology of 'the human' (Harraway, 1985).

Baudrillard's view, on the other hand, is that technological utopianism of this kind takes a far too simplistic line into the future. As we have seen in his account of fourth-order simulation, the technological production of the real has exceeded the logic of reification. Even the traces of a damaged humanity which Adorno made out in the rational organization of capital have disappeared (or have themselves become simulacra), and there remains only 'eccentric singularities' whose exchange has collapsed into an ironic escalation, recombination and revocation of effects. The clone, for example, is the paradigm of fourth-order simulation. It is brought into existence not through the violent and seductive alterity of sexually heterogeneous beings, but from the replication of a genetic code (DNA). Such 'sissiparous' reproduction has no historical or dialectical significance: it cannot, in principle, be made to conform to the logic of differentiated exchange which characterizes both Marxist and non-Marxist accounts of the symbolic order of the social (Baudrillard, 1993, p. 117). Ultimately, therefore, the genetic technologies which make cloning possible are themselves forms of simulation; for in their reproduction of the real, the substantive differentiations of class, race, gender are erased from the temporal economy of exchange. Thus, as the material 'perfection' of the human being, the clone discloses what Mike Gane calls the 'bathos of technology': the constant expansion of the processes of 'esotechnological' supplementation (prostheses) which progressively consumes the 'sub-stance' of the symbolic order (Gane, 2000, p. 59).

So what are the consequences of this 'bathos' of technological reproduction? For Baudrillard, the amorality of capital is far from antithetic to this expansion of the processes of simulation: indeed, the virtualization of debt, profit and exchange which they produce allows a more subtle form of control than was possible within the strictures of fiscal responsibility (Gane, 2000, p. 62). Yet it would be misleading to argue that for Baudrillard the 'logic' of simulation is ultimately just an extension of rational capitalism. As we have seen in his account of 'the masses', the solicitations through which the state has now to produce conformity have moved beyond the relatively stable forms of commodification described by Adorno and Horkheimer in *Dialectic of Enlightenment*. The pathos of the human particular has been displaced by a system of fetishized differences ('viral racism' for example), through which 'the will of the people' is constantly formed, dispersed and reformed. The masses, in other words, are without culture and memory; they have no sense of the violence of their own conformism (its aversion to extremes and to the fate of others), or of the futility of their positive attachments (to the simulacra of political ideals, football teams, movie stars) (*ibid.*, p. 63).

For Baudrillard then the apocalypse has already happened. The dialectics of history have collapsed into the technological procedures of simulation and prosthesis, and there remains only the infinite 'perfection' of humanity in the evanescent, reversible forms through which it is simulated. Consequently, he maintains that the relationship of theory to this implosion of the real should be that of a mobile, unpredictable provocation; a counter-simulation (of truth, reality, coherence) which insists that the simulacrum present the grounds of its 'objectivity' (Baudrillard, 1993, p. 123). Derrida's notion of originary technicity, however, demands that we conceive the effects of prosthetic technologies slightly differently.

If, as Derrida claims in *Spectres of Marx*, we cannot conceive the relationship between humanity, technology and capital in terms of the cumulative alienation of 'our' productive essence, then we must seek the conditions of political responsibility in the dispersion, intensification and recombination to which the concept of the human has been subjected. The difference between Baudrillard's ideas of 'simulation' and Derrida's account of 'spectralization' hinges on how this economy is understood. Baudrillard, we have seen, sets out a kind of disordered genealogy, in which fourth-order simulacra finally consume every trace of the real in human culture and present the 'bathos' of an infinite recirculation of signs. Derrida's idea of spectralization, however, belongs to the originary promise of humanity to the question of its being; that is, to the cultural and institutional forms in which Enlightenment ideals of subjectivity, recognition and justice are inscribed. Thus, if 'the future belongs to ghosts', the appearance of these ghosts (of nature, progress, internationalism, communism) constantly reopens the question of justice (Bennington and Derrida, 1993, p. 349). For in so far as their spectral presentation of 'the human' takes place within the conflictual economy of the present, their complicities with the technocratic organization of capital and the discursive conditions of the law constantly reconfigure the ethico-political demand of the other. The figure of the clone, to return to Baudrillard's example, does not simply stand for the collapse of the real into the logic of infinite, undifferentiated replication. Rather, its possibility raises questions about difference (between 'viviparous' and 'sissiparous' beings) which, in the end, refer to our originary promise to the question of being. As we will see in a moment, it is in the light of this promise that Derrida pursues the spirit of Marxism.

Spectres of Marx – and Their Return

Time ('this' time, 'our' time, and all times in which one attempts to say 'our time') is 'out of joint': it promises no providential or messianic redemption of humanity (Derrida, 1994a, p. 49). Yet for this very reason, the 'being' of time, the disjunctive being suspended between past and future, is always hospitable to spirits: it is the 'virtual body' of spirit which summons the ghosts of the past to the violence and strife of the present. Today, as we have seen, media and communications technologies have made the identification of 'the political' as a determinate sphere or set of relations[2] impossible; and so the present is more than ever a place of spectres, of old conflicts summoned to the present. So, which are the most important of these spectres? Clearly, the ghosts of fascism, nationalism and racism still haunt the new European order. For even if we discount the ethnic cleansing carried out in the former Yugoslavia, there remains the populist appeal of the far right in France, Germany and Austria. Also, the dissolution of the Eastern bloc and the abandonment of Marxist-Leninism in Russia has not put an end to Marxism as a political ideology. Indeed, one of the spectres raised by the social and economic disorder caused by the end of the old regime is that of authoritarian socialism. For in so far as the transition to the 'free market' has yet to come up with the promised social and economic benefits, the 'old guard' (who return anew with every generation) keep an ominous watch over the formation of liberal democracy. I will return to these ghosts in a moment. For now, however, I want to look at the return of a particular spectre; the one which, for Derrida, is summoned by the earnest wish of those capitalist states who dominate the world economy to bury the remains of Marxism.

The spectre to which Derrida refers is bourgeois liberalism, the ghost that has worked within the discourses of the free market (Smith, Ricardo, Say), providential history (Kant, Hegel) and cosmopolitanism/globalization (Beck, Fukuyama) from their very beginnings. Today, this spectre has become the simulacrum of capitalism; for it announces, in its latest forms, the moral, ethical, religious and political finality of liberal democratic states and their institutions. We can, through the miraculous, transfiguring power of the ghost, make out the signature of rational enlightenment in the political history of the later half of the twentieth century: the destruction of fascism in the Second World War, the dissolution of the Eastern bloc in the late 1980s, the emergence of the European Union, the UN, UNESCO – all of these attest to the progress of 'the greater part of humanity' towards liberal democracy (Derrida, 1994a, p. 57). For Derrida, however, this triumphalist reworking of providential history must be conceived as a 'conjuration' of Marxism; as an attempt to maintain the moral finality of the free market in the face of its global exploitation, dislocation and expropriation of humanity. As Derrida puts it:

> If this hegemony [of liberal democracy/capitalism] is attempting to install its dogmatic orchestration in suspect and paradoxical conditions, it is first of all because this triumphant conjuration is striving in truth to disavow, and therefore to hide from the fact that never, never in history, has the horizon of the thing whose survival is being celebrated (namely, all the old models of the capitalist liberal world) been as dark, threatening, and threatened. And never more 'historic' by which we mean inscribed in an absolutely novel

moment of a process that is nonetheless subject to a law of iterability. (Derrida, 1994a, p. 52)

We need then, to look at the nature of this conjunction of Marxism, and at its relationship to our historical present.

For Derrida the 'old models' of the capitalist world depend, at least in part, on their being 'represented by a dominant rhetoric or ideology' (Derrida, 1994a, p. 54). And so the fact that the cultural identity of the West *still* coheres around notions of self-reliance, possessive individualism, fiscal responsibility and the limitation of government intervention can be traced to three specific factors: the pervasiveness of liberal ideals in the official language of liberal democracy; the liberal democratic appropriation of digital and communications technologies; and an academic culture that refuses its responsibility to the Marxist inheritance. In *Spectres of Marx* Derrida presents Francis Fukuyama's *The End of History and the Last Man* (1992) as effective in each of these spheres of ideological hegemony.

The theoretical underpinning of Fukuyama's book is a reading of Hegel which is taken from Alexandre Kojève (Kojève, 1969). What Fukuyama found attractive in Kojève's account of Hegel's *Phenomenology of Spirit* was the emphasis he placed on the dialectics of recognition, particularly in the extended discussion of the master-slave dialectic which comprises the first chapter of his *Introduction to the Reading of Hegel*. Essentially, Kojève attempted a detailed analysis of how the absolute domination of the slave by the master institutes a set of social relations in which the demand for universal recognition is already at stake. This demand is, of course, implicit; for it is only in Hegel's recapitulation that we, as the inheritors of the concept of ethical life (*Sittlichkeit*), are able to make out the development of universal recognition in the concrete relations of slavery. We, in other words, are able to recognize that the master's removal from the sphere of work, and his constitution as pure consumer of what is produced by the slave, is ultimately the negation of his rational autonomy. The master exists as a pure ego, absorbed in its own desires, while the slave, as the self-consciousness which mediates between nature and the egoity of the master, is transformed (universalized) by the hard, continuous demands of work performed on pain of death. For Hegel then, the very concept of self-consciousness demands universal recognition; and in so far as this is denied in the concrete relationships of ethical life, these remain subject to the historical demand of spirit – the ideality of rational freedom.

For Kojève, the essence of the *Phenomenology of Spirit* is Hegel's depiction of the relationship between freedom and social actuality. In the master–slave dialectic, the slave, who lives in primordial fear of the master, is unable to gain recognition of his transformative activity, and so the outcome of this feudalistic organization of worldly existence is the 'Unhappy Consciousness' that gives itself over to a religious abnegation its work, satisfaction and desire. From this point on, the *Phenomenology of Spirit* sets out the dialectics of misrecognition through which self-consciousness develops. 'The law of the heart, and the frenzy of self-conceit', 'Virtue and the way of the world', and the abstract forms of rational individualism which Hegel terms 'Individuality, which takes itself to be real in and for itself' (Hegel, 1967a, pp. 413–53): all of these forms are inadequate expressions of the concept of rational autonomy. For in so far as they fail to integrate the practical activity of self-conscious individuals into a system of mutual recognition, they fail to bring the world into conformity with the idea of freedom (Kojève, 1969, p. 52). The historical significance of the French Revolution therefore, lies in its attempt to realise the principles of universal freedom and equality, and to establish the conditions under which work would transform both the exteriority of the world (its 'otherness') and the self-recognition of human consciousness (*ibid.*, p. 53).

The 'end of history' to which Fukuyama refers in *The End of History and the Last Man* is essentially a reassertion of transformative power of reason in history. In the demand that human beings should not be forced to submit to the irrational traditions of monarchical rule and that absolute subservience is an offence to the concept of self-conscious humanity, he claims that it is possible to discern the formal conditions of universal freedom:

> The Battle of Jena marked the end of history because it was at that point that the vanguard of humanity ... actualized the principles of the French Revolution. While there was considerable work to be done after 1806 – abolishing slavery, extending the franchise to workers, women, blacks – the basic principles of liberal democracy could not be improved upon. (Fukuyama, 1989, p. 5)

The French Revolution, in other words, is the beginning of the end of history, for it marks the point at which the 'rights of man' emerge as an ethically and politically transformative demand. The labour which Fukuyama undertakes therefore, is to show that the historical events which have taken place since the Revolution, and particularly those of the latter half of the twentieth century, have demonstrated the superiority of liberal democracy over every other form of political ideology. In his essay 'The end of history?', Fukuyama summons two dangerous old ghosts for exorcism: fascism and communism. Fascism, he claims, 'was destroyed as a living ideology by World War Two' (Fukuyama, 1989, p. 9). The volkish mythology which lay at the core of the National Socialist movement, for example, meant that the German nation was destined to exemplify the impossibility of founding the state on an explicitly racist ideology. The constant provocation to wars of conquest and subjugation, and the drive to exterminate the eternal 'other' of the *Volk* (the Jew), mark *the* definitive repudiation of fascist ideology. In his analysis of the failure of Russian and Chinese versions of communism, Fukuyama claims that there is a direct relationship between the chronic under-productivity of their respective economies and the state's denial of individual rights of ownership and self-determination. Indeed, his argument, which predates the publication

147

of *The End of History and the Last Man* by three years, is that the economic reforms introduced by Gorbachev in the Soviet Union were essentially liberal democratic in their conception and effects. Gorbachev's version of Leninism, in other words, could not easily be distinguished from the 'welfare capitalism' of many Western countries.

In 1989, Fukuyama was still relatively pessimistic about the chances of Gorbachev's reforms bringing about the transition of the Soviet Union into a liberal democratic society:

> The Soviet Union could in no way be described as a liberal democratic country now, nor do I think that it is terribly likely that perestroika will succeed such that the label will be thinkable at any time in the near future. But at the end of history it is not necessary that all societies become successful liberal democracies. Merely that they end their ideological pretensions of representing different and higher forms of human society. (Fukuyama, 1989, p. 13)

Fukuyama's subsequent remarks on the end of history, however, leave us in no doubt that we should understand the fall of Soviet communism as a sign of the universal progress of humanity. Indeed, the precipitous collapse of the Eastern bloc simply confirms that the cultural and economic conditions established in the liberal democratic West penetrated the ideological life of the USSR more quickly than Fukuyama envisaged. Derrida, however, argues that the providential history set out in *The End of History and the Last Man*, constantly slides between the enumeration of actual events (the fall of the Berlin Wall, for example), and the appeal to a natural finality ('Nature') whose principles transcend the conflicts and contradictions of empirical history (Derrida, 1994a, p. 63). The teleology presented in Fukuyama's work, in other words, functions as an eclectic gathering of signs from the disordered temporality of the present. For where the facts (the persistence of Third–First World exploitation, the maintenance of mass unemployment, the dependency of the world economy on the arms trade) contradict the finality of the liberal capitalist ideal, they are consigned to an 'empirical history' which is destined to peter out in the general progress of wealth, prosperity and freedom.

According to Derrida, it is precisely this empirical history that demands our attention; for it is the new techno-scientifico-mediatized development of capital which again (and again) solicits the spirit of Marx's critique (Derrida, 1994a, p. 69). He argues that Alexander Kojève's ironical conclusion that American capitalism had fulfilled Marx's demand for socialized production (i.e. the suspension of the gap between need or desire and its fulfilment) is misrepresented in Fukuyama's account of the end of history. Fukuyama's claim is that the dialectics of recognition that Hegel set out in the *Phenomenology of Spirit*, point to the fulfilment of humanity in the prosperous, utilitarian integration of liberal capitalist societies (Fukuyama, 1989, p. 19). For Kojève, however, the question of a capitalized-commodified conclusion to the dialectics of need, immediately gives rise to questions about the future of man (Kojève, 1969: footnote, 159-162), and about his reinventing himself (as 'pure form') in ways which challenge and oppose traditional concepts of politics, ethics and autonomy. As Derrida puts it:

> There where man, a certain determined concept of man, is finished, there the pure humanity of man, of the *other* man and of man *as other* begins or has finally the chance of heralding itself – of promising itself. In an apparently inhuman or else a-human fashion. (Derrida, 1994a, p. 74)

The end of one order of history, in other words, immediately reopens the question of the future, and of our messianic responsibility.

Thus before we begin to specify this relationship between messianic responsibility and the spirit of Marxism, we need to look at Derrida's enumeration of the effects of capital which continue to affect the progress of liberal democracy. For Derrida, our time's disjunction with itself is not just another crisis, a stage in the historical evolution of liberal capitalism or of socialized production. Rather, the political crises of our day have something of the 'state of emergency' about them which Benjamin described in his 'Theses on the philosophy of history' (Benjamin, W., 1992, pp. 248–9). They do not take place 'in time' (that is, within the dialectical organization of history), but serve to threaten the temporal organization of historicity as such:

> Electoral representability or parliamentary life is not only distorted, as was always the case, by a great number of socio-economic 'mechanisms' but it is exercised with more and more difficulty in a public space profoundly upset by techno-tele-media apparatuses and by new rhythms of information and communication, by the devices and the speed of forces represented by the latter, but also and consequently by the new modes of appropriation put to work, by the new structure of the event and of its spectrality that they produce . . . (Derrida, 1994a, p. 79)

The concept of democracy (in the sense of *res publica*: public space, deliberation, reflection, judgement), in other words, is fundamentally threatened by the amplificatory effects of media technologies.[3] And so in order to understand the out of jointness of the present, we must understand how these media-technological effects contribute to the 'civil international war' which defines our historical present.

Derrida specifies 'ten plagues' which afflict the global-technological organization of capital (Derrida, 1994a, pp. 81–4):

1. *Homelessness*. Increasingly, nation states define themselves as realms that sustain their social, legal and cultural identities through those who 'belong' and those who are 'foreigners'. Justice, then, is restricted to those who are recognized in the putative geopolitical origin of the state.
2. *Economic War*. The economic conflict within the European Union, the conflict between the European Union and the United States, and the conflict between the EU, the US and Japan is impossible to subsume under Fukuyama's liberal democratic teleology. For Derrida, this economic war is fundamentally important because 'it controls the

practical interpretation and an inconsistent application of international law' (Derrida, 1994a, p. 81).

3. *Unemployment.* New forms of 'telework' (call centres, data entry jobs, for example) which are not easily specified in terms of wage labour (the factory, the product, class solidarity) bring with them a new form of repetitive and unpredictable unemployment, one which suffers all the more for being deprived of the traditional forms of expression and solidarity.

4. *The contradictions of the free market.* The logic of the 'free market' is based on an unequal distribution of economic power, and so Western capitalist states are able both to protect their nationals from the threat of cheap foreign labour and to exploit that labour when it is expedient to do so.

5. *Foreign debt.* The expansion of the global market does not, as Fukuyama claims, lead to an equalization of prosperity. Rather, it tends to increase Third World debt and exclude the greater part of humanity from the democratic rights that are the counterpart of economic prosperity.

6. *The arms trade.* The trade in both conventional and the most sophisticated 'teletechnological' weapons has become so much a part of the world economy that it is now virtually inconceivable that it could function without the legal and illegal commerce in weapons.

7. *Nuclear weapons.* Nuclear weapons are traded by the very nations who claim that they want to prevent proliferation. Thus the principle of democratic convergence expounded by Fukuyama is hopelessly threatened by the arming of every national interest.

8. *Inter-ethnic wars.* With the spread of global media the originary 'ontopological' significance of the locality (territory, city, native soil) is intensified. For in so far as the space of the locality is increasingly threatened, the virtual significance of original identity becomes increasingly important: the 'archaic' demands of 'blood and soil' constantly return through technological processes of representation/ simulation. Thus it is not only time that is out of joint, 'but space, space in time, spacing' (Derrida, 1994a, p. 83).

9. *Mafia and drug cartels.* 'These phantom states invade not only the socioeconomic fabric, general circulation of capital, but also the statist or interstatist institutions' (*ibid.*, p. 83). The turnover of capital, in other words, is increasingly influenced by an extra-legal commerce which is beyond the control of the regulative structures of the international market.

10. *International law and its institutions.* Deconstruction, we have seen, demands a certain fragile 'perfectibility' in the established institutions of international law. To give up their promise of justice would, for Derrida, be to fall into nihilism. However, we must recognize that their organization of international justice takes place under two unavoidable limits: (1) they cannot be dissociated from 'certain

European philosophical concepts'; and (2) 'international law in its application, [remains] largely dominated by particular nation states. Almost always their techno-economic and military power prepares and applies, in other words, carries the decision.' (Derrida, 1994a, p. 83)

It is through these effects of 'teletechnological capital' then that our living present solicits the spirit of Marx, the spirit that would respond to what is 'out of joint', 'not going well', in the world.

In Fukuyama's account of the end of history, we can, according to Derrida, glimpse the spectre of 'Old Europe' (the alliance of state, religion and capital) returning to exorcise the ghost of Marx once and for all. For under the disguise of a peculiarly bourgeois Hegel, the categories of liberal democracy are presented as essential forms of human self-recognition. Thus, in so far as Marx attempted to set out the 'material' conditions presupposed by possessive individualism, abstract morality and the fetishism of commodities, Fukuyama claims that his thought represents a fatal abandonment of the emancipatory potential of civil society and its institutions. Marx's critique of capital, in other words, marks the beginning of a profound involution of the human spirit: an abandonment of its practical ingenuity in the demands of economic subsistence (Marxism), the repression of 'deeply hidden sexual urges' (Freud, Jung, Lacan), and the pointless relativism of Heidegger and Nietzsche (Fukuyama, 1992, p. 333). Ultimately, however, the political ideologies which emerge from this Western malaise (most notably fascism and Marxist-Leninism) become part of a historical development in which the free, self-directed activity of the human spirit demonstrates both its economic utility and its moral necessity.

One of the fundamental insights of deconstruction, as we have seen in the preceding chapters, is Derrida's account of the metaphysics of presence. In general, his work is characterized by a complex expository approach to the resources of philosophy, which is concerned with the way in which the 'spirit' of humanity has been deployed as true, essential and beyond question. It is within this textual economy of metaphysics that the categories of deconstruction produce their effects. Derrida's notion of 'the trace', for example, appears as the simultaneous condition and revocation of humanity's spiritual identity. It is that which marks the constant deferral of spirit's presence to itself; the fact that its 'being there' is always sustained within an economy of supplements which can never realize the certainty of its origin. Now for Derrida, the spirit of Marx's writing lies in the immediacy of his response to the amorality of capital; in fact his deployment of the categories of surplus value, profit and exploitation respond to the disjunctive temporality of his own historical present (Derrida, 1994a, p. 13). This spirit cannot be ontologized, for it is only in so far as it is immediately reborn from 'all that is not going well' in our time, that it can retain its revolutionary-transformative promise.[4]

The demand that Marx's writing makes upon us then is that we seek constantly to revise his critique of capital, to pursue the promise of 'democracy to come' through the techno-scientific intensification of our disordered time. Fukuyama's account of the end of history is what Derrida describes as a 'conjuration' of this promise, a dogmatism that constantly reannounces the death of Marx and the banishment of his ghosts (Derrida, 1994a, p. 56). As we have seen, Fukuyama's reading of Hegel emphasizes the historical affirmation of liberal democracy which is made in the French Revolution. After the battle of Jena in 1806, Europe begins two hundred years of ideological conflict from which the principles of liberty and equality emerge as essential to the moral and economic progress of humanity (Fukuyama, 1989, pp. 4–5). Yet it is clear from his remarks on the descent of the Revolution into the terror of the Jacobin regime, that Hegel is far less sanguine about the principles of abstract individualism than Fukuyama contends. Indeed, one of the spectres which constantly haunts Hegel's concept of ethical substance is the chaos of individual self-seeking and the forms of subjective conscience which legitimize it (Hegel, 1967b, pp. 89–90). The relationship between state and civil society which Hegel presents in *The Philosophy of Right*, for example, maintains that the ethical necessity of the state, while arising out of the rights of particular individuals, retains a *coercive* necessity which legitimately enforces the authority of the universal. It is the origin of this necessity which Marx began to question in his 'Critique of Hegel's Philosophy of Right'. From this point on he maintained that the realm of abstract individualism (civil society) which Hegel sought to bring back to the 'Idea' of the state had an 'empirical existence' which functions independently of the concept of ethical mediation (Marx, 1977d, p. 27). The logic of capital accumulation, in other words, ruptures the temporality of spirit; and so Marx's categories of surplus value, profit and exploitation, in so far as their effects cannot be incorporated into the structures of mutual recognition, exceed the dialectical-synchronic time of Hegel's political philosophy.[5]

It is in this impious materialism that Derrida, paradoxically, finds the spirit of Marx's writing. Time, or more specifically the time of technological capitalism, is 'out of joint', and so it is our responsibility, as the inheritors of Marx, to respond to the amorality of capital as it is manifest in our own historical present:

> One must *assume the inheritance of Marxism*, assume its 'living' part, which is to say, paradoxically, that which continues to put back on the drawing board the question of life, spirit or the spectral, of life-death beyond the opposition between life and death. (Derrida, 1994a, p. 54)

A political response to the forms of exclusion and violence which accompany the expansion of capitalism, in other words, cannot simply revive the recuperative dialectics of Hegel's spirit. (Certainly Baudrillard's account of simulation ought to alert us to the effects of such a revival upon the linearity of historical time.) Rather, it should respond to the economy of liberation and control which is proper to technological development, and to the ghosts of (human) nature, authenticity and community which haunt the disjuncture of our living present. I need to specify the political effectiveness which Derrida attributes to this response.

Marx's Revolutionary Promise

A couple of years before the publication of *Spectres of Marx*, Derrida wrote that:

> Responsibility seems to consist today in renouncing neither of these two contradictory imperatives [monopoly and dispersion]. One must therefore, try to *invent* gestures, discourses, politico-institutional practices that inscribe the alliance of these two imperatives, of these two promises or contracts: capital and the a-capital, the other of the capital. That is not easy. (Derrida, 1992, p. 44)

In this quotation, which comes from *The Other Heading*, Derrida sketches the concept of ethical responsibility which informs his reading of Marx. His claim is that 'we' who inhabit the structures, institutions and ideals of Western cultural identity are charged with a 'dual responsibility'. On the one hand, we cannot continue to maintain that the ideals articulated in Enlightenment philosophy will, by force of rational necessity, become legislative for all humanity. Yet it is equally irresponsible simply to pursue the heterogeneous movements and sovereignties that are produced in the technological expansion of capital. The recognition of difference (alterity), in other words, has no practical significance if it is not referred to the legal economic and political institutions of Western liberal democracy. Derrida's tracing of the dual responsibility through which ethical obligation *might* be enacted therefore, prefigures some of the central themes of *Spectres of Marx*. First, the distinction which he makes between 'le capital' (capital in the economic sense) and 'la capitale' (the capital city of the nation state) in *The Other Heading*, points to the relationship between capitalism and the law which is the focus of Derrida's 'New International'. For in so far as 'la capitale' stands for the ethical responsibilities constituted in the 'enlightened' culture of the West, it is simultaneously that which is threatened by the amorality of 'la capital'. Indeed, for Derrida, their relationship has been such that the material exploitation of the non-Western ('developing', 'Third') world, has in general assumed the spiritual legitimacy of enlightenment and redemption. Second, as inheritors of Marx we must recognize that the processes through which the other is determined in its alterity are always already processes of capital. The multiplication of sovereignties, ethnicities and political movements which is valorized in certain strands of postmodernist theory, for example, should be understood in relation to grossly unequal levels of scientific, technological and economic development. Third, digital and telematic means of mass communication have a logic which exceeds any transcendental demand of human culture. Thus the relationship between 'the West' and the 'others' whom it has constituted through the capitalizing logic of spirit, tends to be increasingly 'spectral'. Only the barest traces of their alterity are visible in the temporality of global communication.

The 'New International' to which Derrida refers in *Spectres of Marx* concerns a 'profound transformation, projected over a long term, of international law, of its concepts, and its field of intervention' (Derrida, 1994a, p. 84). It adheres to a certain spirit of Marxism, one which constantly criticizes 'the *de facto* take-over of international authorities by powerful nation states, by concentrations of technoscientific capital, symbolic capital, and financial capital, of state capital and private capital' (*ibid.*, p. 85). For Derrida, this critique excludes a commitment to conventional Marxist notions of class, state, party and revolution. For in so far as these notions ontologize the spirit of revolutionary critique, they always return to practices of autarky. The New International, however, attempts to respond directly to those 'others' whose suffering and subjection is unregistered in the present organization of international law. It is a community that is ethically pledged to the question of a democracy to come.

Our time's disjunction with itself, we have seen, is not just another 'crisis': a stage in the dialectical evolution of capitalism towards its revolutionary transcendence. Rather, the political crises of our day are characterized by a certain technoscientific urgency; that is, by the fact that their happening serves to threaten the temporal organization of history as such (Derrida, 1994a, p. 77). For Derrida, then, remaining faithful to the spirit of Marx's critique involves a complex intertwining of two opposed and incommensurable positions, both of which are broadly Marxist. The first of these positions maintains that, despite the evil which is present in the world, in its organization and events, there is still a discernible ideal which ought to guide the critique of international law, citizenship, globalization, patriarchy. The second position maintains that the very concept of 'the ideal' is inapplicable to our historical present. For in so far as the effects of technological capitalism are heterogeneous, hyperlogical and disjunctive, it would be impossible to derive any providential significance from the events of the day. This proscription would extend to analysis of every sphere of 'bourgeois ideology': liberal democratic theory, human rights, feminism, 'free market' economics. Thus, remaining faithful to the spirit of Marx's critique involves 'not choosing' between these two positions: the first would lead to a dogmatic eschatology in the face of the world's evil, the second to a 'sort of fatalist idealism' (*ibid.*, p. 87).

This 'not choosing' is a necessity that arises from the temporal economy of the present. As we saw in Derrida's analysis of Fukuyama, the technological expansion of capital produces effects which exceed the logic of moral finality. And so it is in the impossibility of schematizing those effects (virtual capitalization, technocratic and cybernetic control, frictionless exchange of information) eschatologically, that we encounter the disjuncture of our historical present. The question arises then as to how we, as inheritors of the Marxist promise, are to respond to the events of our day. To take a contemporary example, the fall of Soviet communism has summoned an array of competing and conflictual possibilities to its occurrence: the world beginning its final convergence upon liberal democracy, the collapse of a system which betrayed the true principles of Marxism, or the opening of a primitive 'industrial economy' to the demands of scientific ecologism. For Derrida, all of these finalities adhere to the logic of providential history: that the ideal, however it is conceived, can be realized in historical time, and that its 'ideality' acts as a kind of engendering power in the economy of the present. If we are to respond ethically to the events of our day, however, our response must forego the temptations of political eschatology; we must begin with the aporetic experience of having to apply metaphysical conceptions of humanity to conditions that constantly render those conceptions inapplicable. This, for Derrida, is the messianic demand of Marx's work: the fact that the utopianism of his critique is always ruptured by the 'storm of progress', the catastrophic amorality of technological capitalism. Our responsibility to the spirit of Marx then, cannot be dissociated from 'not choosing' between the absolute cynicism of capital registered in Marx's materialism, and the unrepresentable idea of democracy to come ontologized in Marxist humanism. For it is in this undecidable 'contretemps' that the possibility of justice, of bearing witness to the plight of the other, is sustained (Derrida, 1994a, p. 88).

In its relationship to Marxism, then, deconstruction constantly seeks the promise of emancipation that is co-presented in the dynamics of historical materialism:

> This [deconstructive] thinking cannot operate without justifying the principle of radical and indeterminable infinite (both theoretical and practical) critique. This critique belongs to the movement of an experience that is open to the absolute future of what is coming, that is to say, a necessarily indeterminate, abstract, desert-like experience that is confided, exposed, given up to its waiting for the other and for the event. In its pure finality, in the indetermination it requires, one may find yet another essential affinity between it and a certain messianic spirit. (Derrida, 1994a, p. 90)

Derrida, therefore, in his acknowledgement of the present as the place of spectralization (as the return of ghosts to the point at which time is 'out of joint'), opposes any metaphysical distinction between the 'real' and the 'ideal'. The present is always a conflictual economy in which the past (wars and conflicts) is solicited through what is 'of the day', and the future is glimpsed as a responsibility (promise, pledge) that lies beyond what our traditional categories, whether Marxist or liberal, can schematize. The question of the spirit of Marxism, therefore, is the question of hospitality to the other; of remaining open to the economy of conflict, silencing and exclusion that is determined by the powers of technological capitalism.

Such hospitality is only possible through a certain sensitivity to ghosts, to those who return, like Hamlet's murdered father, to demand that their suffering should not be forgotten in the ideologies of our day. If those who died in the Holocaust or in the genocides in Cambodia and Rwanda have any 'power' over our own time, this power can only take effect in so far as it haunts/interrupts the discourses of racial, cultural, economic and technocratic hegemony. The past generations of 'political' dead, in other words, return to us as a messianic demand for 'new effective forms of action, practice [and] organization' (Derrida, 1994a, p. 89); forms which are always pledged to the possible emancipation of the other.[6]

For Derrida, as for Levinas, the provocation of the other always returns us to the concept of infinity: to the relationships through which its alterity can affect us as an ethical demand, and to the possibility of our assuming an effective, practical responsibility for his/her existence. We have seen that, for Levinas, the concept of the infinite is inscribed in the face of the other; for it is the likeness of the human face to the face of God which gives ethical force to the suffering of any and every individual. The responsibility which I, as a sentient being, have to other sentient beings is without gender or race; its demand is originally independent of the economic, technological and ideological powers through which these basic categories of difference are circulated and reproduced. Levinas' conception of the relationship between the infinitude of the ethical demand and the construction of human sociality therefore, registers a certain excessiveness of the other: an alterity which both demands and defies inclusion in the totality of legal, economic and political relations. For Derrida, however, this excessiveness cannot be understood as a transcendental-phenomenological quality of the human subject. For in so far as the condition of its historicity is the disjuncture of the present, we, as inheritors of the spirit of Marx, must respond to the fate of the other as it is designated, silenced, excluded and erased through the technological powers of capital.

We have seen that, for Derrida, deconstruction would have been 'impossible and unthinkable' in a pre-Marxist space. The infinite contemporaneity which he identifies as the spirit of Marx's critique, therefore, proceeds from two basic axioms. First, that the logic of the mode of production was never purely systemic: that there was always a troubling, excessive dissemination of humanity through its techno-scientific powers. And second, that this logic cannot be understood simply in terms of the reification of humanity, nor simply as its technological enhancement (Beardsworth, 1996, p. 147). Derrida's reading of Marx then, demands that our critical attention is focused on the *relationships* between technocratic control, technological supplementation and the promise of universal recognition inscribed in the law. This, of course, returns us to the metaphysical question of the other: the problem of those whose fate within the global-technological organization of the present (biogenetic exploitation, cultural and geographical expropriation) goes unrecognized in the body and institutions of international law.

Spectres of Marx bequeaths a spirit of Marxist critique which is promised to the aporetic structure of time. The fact that this spirit cannot be realized in the political ontologies of Marxism is precisely what, for Derrida, discloses its relationship to the absolute future, to a democracy to come. It is in this sense that we, the inheritors of Marx, remain responsible to the idea of humanity, to receiving the traces of its concept as they are disclosed in the effects of technological capitalism (Derrida, 1994, p. 75). It is the spectral figure of the other, therefore, the *arrivant* who unexpectedly disturbs the measured, legitimized violence of the system, that provokes Derrida's idea of messianic justice: the demand that every epistemic, technological or metaphysical schematization of the present is brought back to the transcendental horizon of the future. In the final two chapters then, I want to look at how this deconstructive responsibility impacts upon contemporary debates about the politics of risk and the global economy.

Notes

1. Baudrillard's account of 'extreme phenomena' in his *Transparency of Evil* is a registration of the catastrophic nature of total simulation. Essentially, his account of effects such as AIDS and cancer, presents their 'extremity' as a kind of intrusion of the real upon the system; as afflictions which at least have the 'virtue' of staving off even more disastrous (and unforeseeable) effects of simulation.

2. See Hegel's concept of ethical life (*Sittlichkeit*), or Marx's account of the political significance of class relations.

3. Among the effects of this amplification of the spectralizing effects of media technologies, we would have to include: the increased mobility of capital and the decline of national politics; the loss of the 'eventness' of events (their collapse into repetition/iteration); media dissemination of Third World catastrophes and the commodification of guilt; and the collapse of the 'locality' in global networks.

4. As early as 1971 Derrida had maintained that: 'In what I have begun to propose [i.e. deconstruction], I attempt to take into account certain . . . determined incompletions in the orders of philosophy, semiology, linguistics, psychoanalysis . . . Now, we cannot consider Marx's . . . texts completely finished elaborations that are simply to be applied to the current situation. In saying this, I am not advocating anything contrary to Marxism, I am convinced of it. These texts are not to be read according to a hermeneutical or exegetical method which would seek out a finished signified beneath a textual surface. Reading is transformational' (Derrida, 1981, p. 63).

5. Gillian Rose, in her *Hegel Contra Sociology*, argues that the historical temporality of Hegel's idea of ethical life cannot be reduced to such a simple 'sychronic' unfolding. The 'real actuality' of ethical life is sustained in the relationship between its 'Idea' (concrete mediation), its objective organization (state, economy, civil society) and the subjective forms of consciousness (conscience, morality) which are reinforced in bourgeois art, culture and philosophy. Rose's exposition of Hegel makes the explicit demand that we recognize his critique of abstract individualism (Rose, 1981, p. 208). For in so far as pre-Hegelian philosophy posited conscience and morality as the truth of ethical life, it is the task of the 'speculative' philosopher to concentrate on how contemporary forms of subjective culture contribute to the dominance of 'liberal capitalism'. To ask, in other words, how notions like 'possessive individualism' or the 'stake holder citizen' have come to stand in for the spiritual demand of our fractured, contradictory *Sittlichkeit*. For Rose, the problem with Marx is that his critique of capital remains complicit with this kind of abstract thinking (*ibid.*, p. 219). His failure to recognize the way in which the contradictions of the economy are mediated

through the transformation of satisfaction and desire (especially in art and the aesthetic sphere), the subjective forms of morality and the universal demand of the law, means that Marxism, as a political culture, has tended towards ideological autarky rather than transformative critique. A critical (post post-Hegelain) Marxism then, would acknowledge that: 'a presentation of the contradictory relations between capital and culture is the only way to link the analysis of the economy to the comprehension of the conditions for revolutionary practice' (ibid., p. 220). What separates Rose and Derrida's responses to Marx therefore, is Derrida's determination to pursue the technological effects of capital on the concept of humanity (its 'spectralization'), rather than assuming that these effects will reproduce themselves in the regulated forms of 'misrecognition' (Conscience, Morality, the Beautiful Soul).

6. In his essay 'Spirits armed and unarmed', Warren Montag argues that the spirit of Marxism which Derrida seeks to disclose in *Spectres of Marx*, ends up as a kind of Kantian critique which is promised to the transcendental (that is, undeconstructable) idea of justice. His claim is that Derrida's account of the historical conflict in which Marxism has acted as a configuring power tends to valorize the work of a transcendental spirit (Marx's originary promise) over the demands of contemporary political struggle. Derrida's pursuit of a spirit of Marxism which is always already beyond its contemporary organization, in other words, leads him to underplay the (Foucauldian) economy of force, resistance and conflict into which the body of Marxism must always enter (Sprinker, 1999, p. 80). This claim that Derrida's reading of Marx slides back into a kind of Kantian reformism, however, fails to acknowledge his insistence that the temporal economy of the present *includes* the strategic oganization of the left. The political demand of *Spectres of Marx*, in other words, is that the strategic pursuit of emancipation should always, no matter how difficult this might be, remain open to questions of difference, exclusion and silencing.

11

Science, Technology and Catastrophe

Introduction

The 'question concerning technology' is fundamental to any consideration of postmodern politics, as it bears directly on how we experience ourselves as subjects (men, women, citizens, workers), and on how we orientate ourselves within the technological systems of society. The question itself, as Heidegger's now famous essay makes clear, is not just about the unfolding of technological progress (Heidegger, 1996, p. 312). It should not, for example, be understood simply in terms of an accumulation of social and economic benefits, nor indeed in terms of the new challenges (space exploration, cloning, gene therapy) that result from technological innovation. Technology, as a way of relating to the world and to the being of others, always reopens the question of *Dasein*'s 'spiritual' vocation, of its capacity to engage with the fundamental questions of its own existence. Thus, if Heidegger's vision of European modernity on the brink of spiritual extinction still speaks to us, it is perhaps through the questions that he has bequeathed to modern debates about science, technology and philosophy. The expositions of Beck, Giddens and Derrida presented in this chapter, therefore, all proceed from the following Heideggarian questions:

- What is the effect of technology on our experience of 'being in the world': on our experience of having certain existential relationships with self, other and world? (This question, as we will see, has a particular resonance in Beck's account of the ecological foundation of reflexive modernity.)
- How is technology related to our experience of time: that is, of our relationship to the ethical and political demands of past, present and future? (In general, as we will see, the sociology of risk is concerned with trying to bring our collective responsibility to future generations into the realm of public debate, and to promote a reflexive awareness of the consequences of continuing to use technologies like nuclear power.)
- What can remain of philosophical and political reflection once its cultural and institutional forms are subjected to the demands of technological functionality? (Both Beck and Giddens are concerned to show how the public sphere can be regenerated through the technological systems upon which modern societies increasingly depend.)

- Does the increasingly pervasive nature of technology entail a total 'enframing' of humanity; a loss of our capacity to address the ethical, aesthetic and spiritual questions that belong to the question of being? (Derrida's account of this question in *Spectres of Marx*, revitalizes the old Marxist concerns about capital, inequality and exploitation; concerns that are, perhaps, avoided in Beck and Giddens' work.)

I want to begin by looking at the relationship between science, technology and reflexive modernization that Ulrich Beck presents in his *Risk Society*, and then proceed to the notions of trust and anxiety that Anthony Giddens sets out in *The Consequences of Modernity* and *Modernity and Self-Identity*. Finally, I will examine Derrida's approach to the question of technology, and the consequences this approach may have for Beck and Giddens' sociologies of risk.

Beck and 'World Risk Society'

As we have seen, one of the fundamental claims set out by Beck his *Risk Society: Towards a New Modernity*, is that as the industrial revolution increased the productivity and material wealth of Western capitalist societies, the relationship between scientific knowledge, technical innovation and economic demand became increasingly close. Under the conditions of 'primary industrialization', in other words, the economy became the principal determinant of scientific research. For unless a particular area of theoretical knowledge was seen to offer the possibility of technical innovation in the production of commodities (that is, to increase the rate at which surplus value could be produced in a particular productive enterprise),[1] it was likely to remain relatively impoverished and undeveloped. This relationship marks the emergence of a transactional logic, in which science, contrary to the universal scepticism of its method, is forced to present its findings as infallible knowledge that awaits conversion into increased productivity, higher profits and a general reduction of material scarcity. What is significant here, according to Beck, is the contradiction that developed between the 'method' and the 'ideology' of science; that is, between the self-critical, self-reflexive procedures through which empirical testing of hypotheses was carried out, and the rhetoric of certainty through which results were presented to the 'consumers' of scientific knowledge (Beck, 1996a, p. 164). For in presenting itself as the true foundation upon which industrial modernity could set about resolving the problems which nature's insufficiency had bequeathed to humankind (poverty, disease, scarcity, war), science entered into a dangerous complicity with the mechanisms of capital accumulation. Civil society, in other words, as the legally sanctioned sphere of individual rights and bourgeois economic activity, assumed an exclusive responsibility for the deployment of scientific knowledge, and for the progress of the human species towards its technological liberation from the constraints of nature. For Beck the danger inherent in this subordination of science is that the political sphere, that is, the state's potential for critical reflection on the consequences of technological innovation, is ultimately reduced to 'rubber stamping' the developments in medicine, agriculture, industry and warfare, which confront it as the accomplished facts of a necessary and legitimate progress (Beck, 1996a, pp. 187–90).

This increasing disempowerment of the political sphere is one of Beck's principal concerns in *Risk Society*. For since parliamentarianism has become an irrelevant charade in which parties argue endlessly over whose policies are best attuned to the needs of technological progress, questions about the course which that progress ought to take are excluded from the sphere of legitimate political discussion. This means that throughout the development of primary industrialization, it is economic and professional institutions who have decided which forms of technology are 'objectively' necessary to the continued progress of humanity, what constitutes an 'acceptable risk' in the deployment of such technology and, consequently, who will be most immediately exposed to those risks. Until recently, of course, the logic of primary industrialization has dictated that exposure to risk is something that increases the lower down the class structure one goes. Yet for Beck, this class-based model of risk is no longer adequate to comprehend the catastrophic damages that new technologies (especially nuclear power) are capable of visiting on humanity. And so we need to frame a new conception of risk which emphasizes the 'globality' of the threats posed by nuclear, chemical and medical technologies: threats which, through the closed system of the Earth's biosphere, affect the whole (cosmopolitical) body of humanity (Beck, 1996a, pp. 37–8). It is this enclosure of human beings within the fragile economics of nature which is schematized in Beck's account of 'the solidarity of living things', and which is present as an implicit consensualizing power throughout his analysis of the shift from 'industrial' to 'risk' society. I will return to this presence of organic life to itself in Beck's ethical and political theory in a moment.

We have seen that, for Beck, a contradiction develops between the method and the ideology of science during the development of primary industrial society. His contention is that science, considered as an instrument of critical inquiry becomes increasingly sceptical and self-reflexive in its research practices, while at the same time being forced by the general dynamics of the economy to hold on to the ideology of infallibility. What is important here is that, the emergence of technologically produced 'side effects' that can be confined neither to the spatial extent of the nation nor to the present generation who have gambled on the safety of nuclear power and gene technologies, is what ultimately precipitates the emergence of a 'scientized' politics of risk. As genetically mutable, biologically contaminable beings, we are all susceptible to the effects of radiation and chemical poisoning;

and it is this shared vulnerability that, for Beck, becomes the focus of a 'democratic' resistance to the techno-economic powers which have, until now, monopolized the control, development and deployment of technology. Most of the damage caused by radiation leaks or chemical discharges does not occur through spectacular and highly publicized events like the Chernobyl or Bhopal incidents. Rather, it tends to take the form of an invisible and pernicious accumulation of 'effects' upon nature and the human community. Given the institutional power of those corporations who have invested heavily in a 'nuclear' or 'agrichemical' future for modernity, and allowing for their ability to muster and present the 'infallible' research of science in support of such futures, it is unsurprising that evidence of culpable contamination adduced by affected communities, has tended to be dismissed as simply anecdotal and unscientific.

Beck, however, claims that the established relationship between efficient causality (event A is the cause of event B, A→B) and the legal standard of proof of responsibility (a standard which requires a massively comprehensive adduction of evidence concerning specific acts of negligence, definitions of 'acceptable levels' of contamination, and the co-implication of other natural and human conditions in the vicinity of the pollution) can no longer be sustained (Beck, 1996a, pp. 63–4). The kind of damages incurred by human beings through the accelerated development of technology (cellular and genetic mutation, multiply resistant bacteria, the accumulation of toxins in the body's organic structures) refer, from the beginning, to science for their cognition, definition and evaluation as 'risks'. In primary industrial societies, according to Beck's argument, the colonization of science by those enterprises which control the generation and distribution of capital (industrial corporations, finance capital, the military), determined a general blindness to technological risks that allowed human and environmental damages to be consigned to the category of 'side effects'. Yet with the increasing extent and frequency of such harm, the power of science to enforce its official assignment of particular exposures, contaminations and irradiations to this politically deactivating category, begins to breakdown. Within what Beck conceives as the emergent 'sub-politics' of risk society – a politics of opposition, contestation and mediation which industrial society has precipitated through its pursuit of technological solutions to the side effects of technology – science begins to emerge as the facilitator of a critical dialogue among opposing societal interests (Beck, 1996a, pp. 172–3). Thus, in their function as the only discourses through which technological risks can be properly determined (Beck makes it clear that, in general, the risks which define our 'new modernity' are non-intuitable and require both conceptual and instrumental designation), scientific knowledges begin to shake off their ideological attachments to 'system necessities' and 'objective economic constraints', and to open up newly democratic practices of forensic evaluation, dispute settlement and the cosmopolitical articulation of civilization risks (Beck, 1996a, pp. 231–5).

The concept of the political which runs throughout *Risk Society* is informed by a particular notion of science and its relationship to modernity. Obviously, the idea of a global community of risk – a community whose possibility would depend upon the mobilization of a sense of reflexive anxiety – can retain its ethical force only for as long as the future has not *already* been determined as humanity's technological self-attrition and ultimate self-destruction. Thus, the imperative of determining the extent of the biological, genetic and ecological damage which modern technologies are doing to present and future generations, is presented as a unifying 'interest' inscribed in both the natural and the social sciences – one that begins a critical dialogue between their respective rationality claims. The emergence of this dialogue, which Beck describes as 'a still undeveloped symbiosis' (Beck, 1996a, p. 28), performs two important functions in his account of the politics of risk. First, it opens the possibility of a socio-scientific consciousness of risk; a consciousness whose responsibility to the future is given through the 'present' necessity of bringing the normative-evaluative resources of the social sciences to bear upon the data produced by the natural sciences. Second, it is the activation of this debate about civilization risks that rejuvenates a political sphere that has been progressively disempowered by the independence of corporate capital and professional organizations from the state. For Beck, the emergence of such a pervasive 'risk consciousness' brings about a crucial change in the orientation of social democracy. The rights that are enshrined in the legal constitution of the state cease to be the abstract guarantees which allow 'non-political' organizations to press on with the labour of technological progress, and become the ethical framework through which citizens are able to recognize the violence to which this labour has subjected nature and humanity (Beck, 1996a, p. 193). The 'implicit ethics' which has begun to haunt the formal autonomy of 'business, the natural sciences and the technical disciplines', in other words, becomes explicit in a 'reflexive' political sphere which would: (1) encourage research in the direction of alternatives to the existing 'system necessities'; (2) protect and expand the highest established levels of social and democratic rights; (3) create institutional spheres in which 'interdisciplinary' evaluations of risk could be subjected to public scrutiny (Beck, 1996a, p. 235).

It is this articulation of a scientific rationality whose socio-historical development is to be translated into legitimate spheres of political judgement, legislation and action which brings us to the relationship of *Risk Society* to the claims of Habermas' critical theory. In *Justification and Application*, Habermas specifies a crucial difference between those forms of knowledge which allow us to make ethical judgements about the conduct of others engaged in the lifeworld, and those which allow us to refine our understanding of physical nature:

> The empirical sciences adopt a critical attitude toward the kind of everyday institutions on which we immediately rely in our moral judgements. On the

other hand we would destroy our ethical knowledge by submitting it to scientific examination because scientific objectification would dislodge it from its proper place in our life. (Habermas, 1995a, p. 22)

In terms of Habermas' designation of the interests proper to ethical and scientific knowledges, science determines an 'objectifying' power which threatens the institutional resources of socio-linguistic consensus. And so considered as an 'expert culture' whose rationality is both increasingly distant from the interpretive structures of the everyday life, and increasingly powerful in its influence over the 'steering mechanisms' which control the technico-economic future of society, science enters into the political dynamics of the lifeworld as a force whose methodological, epistemological and theoretical procedures always require communicative reinterpretation. Now, it should be clear that for Beck, Habermas' designation of science as a sphere of knowledge that remains external to the practico-communicative rationality of the lifeworld, fails to acknowledge the processes of self-criticism initiated and developed through the discipline of scientific research. Habermas' differentiation of 'the empirical sciences' from the communicative functions which ought to inform the legislative practices of government, in other words, would conform to the ideological phase in which the development of science as an 'autonomous' critical practice depended directly upon its ability to present itself as the provider of a technologically infallible expertise. Thus, for Beck, if there are 'discursive' functions that are proper to the political sphere, and if these functions result from an incremental process of 'social learning', then it is science, as the imminently universal language of risk assessment, that opens the possibility of the 'reflexiveness' from which a truly democratic consensus could arise.

The salvation of technological modernity is, for Beck, made possible by the emergence of an increasingly critical, increasingly sceptical science. The distinction which Habermas postulates between the objectifying rationality of empirical science and the communicative potential of the lifeworld, is seen by Beck as a reflection of science's ideological phase. For in so far as it is the critical articulation of technological damages which marks the emergence of a reflexive public sphere, we must look to an increasingly interdisciplinary, increasingly ethical science for the revitalization of social democracy. Giddens, however, is rather less convinced of the reversion of science to the open, critical community of ideas presented in *Risk Society* (Beck, 1996a, pp. 165–6). As we will see in the following section, his account of the relationship between modernity and self-identity focuses on the dynamics of trust: on the necessity of maintaining faith in the experts who design, build and operate the technological systems upon which we all rely. Thus, for Giddens, the technological trajectory of civilization demands that we reconsider the relationship between autonomy and solidarity; or more specifically, the possibility of maintaining a sense of security within the reflexive demands of risk evaluation. As we will see in a moment, Giddens argues that the only way to resolve this question is to reconsider the relationship between the self-identity of modern subjects and the technical systems through which they are transformed, recombined and redistributed. The impact of these systems on the bodily and psychical constitution of individual subjects, he argues, cannot be thought of in terms of the emancipatory demands of sociological theory, including Habermas' account of communicative reflexivity. We cannot, in other words, lay down the conditions under which human beings would realize their essential freedom: for the relationship between humanity and technology is now such that the personal resources of the individual have become inextricably bound up with the transformative powers of technical systems. The task of the social theorist, therefore, is to register the new and unforeseen patterns of reflexive practice which arise within the technological body of society.

We need then to look more closely at Giddens' account of the relationship between personal autonomy, system necessity and political responsibility, and to examine the points of divergence between his version of reflexive modernization and the one presented by Beck.

Giddens and Life Politics

Contemporary discussions of risk have tended to group Anthony Giddens' work on risk together with Beck's account of reflexive modernity. The reasons for this are obvious enough. Both are interested in risk as a concept which has a distinctively modern genealogy; both are concerned with the role of risk in the transition from 'traditional' to 'reflexive' forms of social organization; and both have focused on the relationship between the globalization of risk and the emergence of new forms of social awareness and political participation (see Lupton, 1999, p. 72). There are, nonetheless, significant differences between Beck's and Giddens' theories – differences which, I will argue, are best understood in terms of the limits of normative sociology in relation to the moral, existential and political questions raised by the notion of risk. Before addressing these questions directly, however, I need to make some introductory remarks about the significance of risk in Giddens' work on reflexive modernity.

In *The Consequences of Modernity*, Giddens sets out a seven-point definition of the 'specific risk profile of modernity' (Giddens, 1997, p. 124):

(1) *Globalization of risk* in the sense of *intensity*: for example, nuclear war can threaten the existence of humanity;

(2) *Globalization of risk* in the sense of the *expanding number of contingent events* which affect everyone or at least large numbers of people on the planet: for example, changes in the global division of labour;

(3) Risk stemming from the *created environment or socialized nature*: the infusion of human knowledge into the material environment;

165

(4) The development of *institutionalized risk environments* affecting the life chances of millions: for example, investment markets;

(5) *Awareness of risk as risk*: the knowledge gaps in risk cannot be converted into 'certainties' by religious or magical knowledge;

(6) The *well distributed awareness of risk*: many of the dangers we face collectively are known to wide publics;

(7) *Awareness of the limitations of expertise*: no expert system can be wholly expert in terms of the consequences of its adoption of expert principles.

Clearly, the first four propositions of Giddens' 'risk profile' refer to the kind of objective increases in danger that are specified in *Risk Society*. For Giddens, as for Beck, the proliferation of 'high-consequence' risks is something which is intrinsic to late modernity. The ecological networks through which organic life is sustained are made subject to the techno-scientific form of control which has, in general, come to define the modern epoch. Thus, the increasing number and intensity of the risks to which 'we', as human beings, are vulnerable is a direct result of the transform-ation of nature into a manipulable resource. For both Beck and Giddens, the high-consequence risks that emerge in late modernity are of an entirely different order from those which characterized traditional and early industrial forms of social organization. In traditional societies, with their relatively low level of technological development, risk was largely deter-mined by the vulnerability of agrarian communities to the vicissitudes of the natural environment. In the primary stages of industrialization, on the other hand, the burden of risk was borne by wage labourers who had to work with the crude technologies of early mass production. However, the technologies which have arisen out of the relationship between capital and scientific innovation, threaten outcomes which fundamentally undermine the hierarchy of suffering presented in Marx's early writings (see Marx, 1979b, pp. 66–80). For in so far as the widespread use of nuclear technology determines a potentially catastrophic threat to organic life as such, human beings are forced to acknowledge that 'the global intensity of certain kinds of risk transcends all social and economic differentials' (Giddens, 1997, p. 125).

Giddens' specification of the risk profile of modernity, therefore, begins by following Beck's account of the objective reality of civilization risks. The use of nuclear, genetic and bio-technologies, gives rise to a destructive potential which cannot be understood in terms of differential exposures to risk. The fate of the entire human species, in other words, depends upon a collective determination not to destroy our material environment. This globalization of risk is compounded by the extension of 'abstract systems' of knowledge to the organization of social and economic relations. For in so far as these systems always determine a degree of unpredictability in their functioning, every local organization is made subject to events which can neither be foreseen nor influenced. To use Giddens' example, national GDP has become increasingly vulnerable to the mobility of global capital, and so it is now the case that the organization of local economies around multinational investment always involves exposing those economies to the risks of downsizing, relocation or wholesale changes in investment strategies. Beck also examines the risks that are determined by structural changes in the labour market (Beck, 1996, pp. 139–49). His contention is that the 'flexibility' which has become the norm in contractual relations between employers and employees, while allowing an expansion of the time available for personal development, exposes individual workers to the risks of poverty which are attendant upon long-term underemployment. As with ecological risks, then, the expansion in the number of 'contingent events' to which we have all become subject is an essential characteristic of late modernity.

The last three propositions of Giddens' risk profile shift the emphasis away from the 'objective' determinants of risk towards a specification of the way in which risks are characteristically perceived. Initially, Giddens maintains that the modern experience of risk is such that it cannot be 'converted into "certainties" by religious or magical knowledge' (Giddens, 1997, p. 124). What this means for the practical consciousness of human beings is that there is no possibility of avoiding a certain 'calculative' attitude towards the risks that are run in every aspect of social life. Secondly, Giddens contends that this calculative attitude has become the defining characteristic of the public sphere, and that there is an increasingly acute awareness of the risks generated by the operation of abstract systems. Finally, this public recognition of the uncertainty, produces a general sense of scepticism with regard to the authority of expert knowledges – a scepticism which, we will see, is central to Giddens' account of a reflexive 'life politics'.

The configuration of Giddens' 'risk profile' with its co-implication of subjective and objective factors in the *definition* of reflexive modernity is significant for a number of reasons. Firstly, it accents the relationship between his understanding of risk and the theory of stucturation which is the starting point of his account of 'reflexive modernity'. Secondly, Giddens' profile assumes a certain kind of 'dialectical' relationship between the high-consequence risks that arise from abstract systems and the formation of the 'reflexive self'. Thirdly, his profile also assumes that it is possible to contain the moral, existential and political questions raised by the notion of risk within the terms of this dialectical exchange between structure and subjectivity. These questions, I will argue, do not just mark the points of antagonism between Beck's and Giddens' sociologies of modernity but also open the possibility of a deconstructive critique of the politics of reflexive anxiety. I will return to this in a moment.

At the beginning of *The Consequences of Modernity*, Giddens proposes that, in order to understand the dialectics of security and risk which are characteristic of the modern epoch, we must first come to a clear understanding of the discontinuities between modern, early-modern and pre-modern societies. Essentially, his analysis is concerned to develop an 'institutional diagnosis' of those characteristics which distinguish modernity from all previous forms of social organization (Giddens, 1997a, p. 12). Drawing on the work of Marx, Durkheim and Weber, he argues that the central question regarding the *uniqueness* of the modern epoch concerns the sources of its dynamical expansion. For Marx, the primary agency in this process is the drive for profit inherent in the capitalist mode of production; for Durkheim, the expansion of modernity is governed by the complex interrelatedness of industrialism; and for Weber, the dynamism of modern institutions is produced by the universal adoption of bureaucratic rationality. According to Giddens, however, the evolution of modernity now demands that 'we make good some of the limitations of the classical sociological perspectives' (*ibid.*, p. 12). For in so far as neither Marx nor Durkheim nor Weber could foresee the complex relationships that would develop between capital, industrial organization and systems of bureaucratic and technocratic control, their respective accounts of modernity require substantial supplementation and reworking.

Giddens' claim is that while it is no longer possible to designate the unitary cause of the dynamism of modern societies (capitalism, indusrialism, bureaucracy), the classical sociological perspectives allow us to recognize the distinctiveness of the processes through which modernity has reached its contemporary 'reflexive' form. For Giddens, the continued development of the interconnections between capital, industrial organization and bureaucratic control, have produced three effects which relate specifically to the dynamical nature of modern societies: *the separation of time and space*; the disembedding of social systems; and the reflexive ordering and reordering of social relations (Giddens, 1997a, pp. 16–17). The first of these processes – the separation of time from both the cyclical changes of nature and from the localized concerns of particular communities – is of course implicit in all of the classical sociological accounts of modernization. However, Giddens' argument is that the consequences of this separation of the spatial and temporal dimensions of society force us to rethink the social dynamics of modernity. For the enforcement of a universal (mechanically measured) standard of time subsumes the spatial differentiation of each particular 'locality' under homogeneous regimes of social production. Each locality, in other words, is plotted on to an abstract 'space', which is coordinated through a temporal standard that remains independent of all particular locations. This separation of time from locality ('place') is important for three reasons: (1) its contribution to the 'disembedding' of social relations (that is, the opening up of society to abstract systems which function through the establishment of universality, homogeneity and predictability); (2) its provision of the 'gearing mechanisms' through which modern institutions are able to connect the local into the global web of capital and information flows; and (3) its constitution of a unitary 'pre-modern' past, from which modernity has emerged as a universally progressive, 'world-historical' epoch (*ibid.*, pp. 18–19).

We need to look a little more closely at Giddens' account of the disembedding of social relations. We have seen that this process is closely associated with the separation of time from the geographical differentiation of locality. As Giddens puts it:

> By disembedding I mean the 'lifting out' of social relations from local contexts of interaction and their restructuring across indefinite spans of space and time. (Giddens, 1997a, p. 21)

The two primary mechanisms in this process of 'lifting out' are the constitution of a money economy and the emergence of the expert systems which have come to define technological modernity. Giddens argues that the 'symbolic tokens' through which the money economy emerges are essentially 'a means of bracketing time and so lifting transactions out of particular milieux of exchange' (*ibid.*, p. 24). Unlike systems of barter, for example, the exchange of monetary tokens is not related to a locally established system of equivalence. And so by allowing credit and debt to break free from the restrictions of such systems, money contributes to a universal disembedding of the relationships between value, locality and social recognition (*ibid.*, p. 25).[2] In the case of expert systems – which Giddens defines as 'systems of technical accomplishment or professional expertise which organize large areas of [our] material and social environments' (*ibid.*, p. 27) – disembedding is brought about by the fact that the guarantees which underpin our faith in the relative security of our social existence, no longer belong to the 'immediacies of context' (*ibid.*, p. 28). For example, my willingness to use air transport is not based upon the personal guarantee of any particular individual; it is rather a question of my being satisfied that the principles of avionics are sound, that the design and construction of the aircraft has been carried out in accordance with publicly established standards of safety, and that the air crew are competent to fly the plane. The pervasiveness of expert systems therefore, gives rise to social relations which are founded upon a faith in technical and professional expertise which, in general, cannot be fully justified. We cannot *know* that all of the above conditions have been satisfied when we board the plane, and yet we continue to *trust* the claims to safety presented by the airlines, aircraft manufacturers and public regulatory bodies.

This notion of trust is central to Giddens' understanding of reflexive modernity. His claim is that, in its contemporary significance, trust is best understood in terms of the *lack of information* which has become endemic to modernity (Giddens, 1997b, p. 33). As the systems of expert knowledge which control our social and material environments become more complex, we are all put in the position of having to trust that those systems are being devised and run with the appropriate level of safety. Thus, we should understand the kind of 'disembedded' social relations which are characteristic of modern societies, as formed through the *contingency* that remains part of all abstract systems, and as confronting that contingency with a subjective conviction that, in general, such systems are worthy of trust (*ibid.*). Giddens, then, defines trust as confidence in the reliability of a person or a system regarding a given set of outcomes or events, where that confidence expresses a faith in the probity or love of another, or in the correctness of abstract principles (technical knowledge). (Gidden's, 1997b, p. 34)

As the 'transformative scope of human action' is increased by the powers of abstract systems, therefore, a relationship between risk and trust emerges which is central to Giddens' conception of reflexive modernity. As social agents, human beings are constantly called upon to apply moral, scientific and statistical criteria to events whose general designation is that of 'risk' – risk to one's employment, risk to one's friendships and intimate relationships, risk to one's health and longevity. A decision to undergo certain forms of cancer treatment, for example, would be understood by both patient and doctor as a calculated risk rather than a symbolic or religious intervention which places the life of the patient in the hands of *fortuna*. The perception of risk *as risk*, therefore, produces a form of secularized faith, or trust, in the abstract systems which control our social and material environments. This is important because the relationship between risk and trust is essential to the 'reflexive modernity' which emerges from the separation of space and time and the disembedding of social relations. For in so far as 'the experience of security usually rests upon a balance of trust and acceptable risk' (Giddens, 1997a, p. 36), the everyday lives of individuals are related directly to processes and decisions that are global in their effects (the use of nuclear power, GM technologies). We are all, as Deborah Lupton points out, required to be 'much more challenging of expert knowledges, requiring of them that they win [our] trust' (Lupton, 1999, p. 77).

We are now beginning to approach the central questions raised by Giddens' idea of a reflexive life politics. According to *The Consequences of Modernity*, traditional forms of social organization are characterized by their situation of 'the present' within the structured repetition of local temporalities (Giddens, 1997a, p. 37). Their transcriptions of traditional narratives of identity, while involving a textual designation of past, present and future, remain tied to conventions which are essentially fixed and unchanging. With the advent of modernity, however, reflexivity is no longer a question of simply recapitulating the past: it has become 'the very basis of system reproduction such that thought and action are constantly referred back to one another' (*ibid.*, p. 38). It is in this sense then, that modernity 'is itself deeply and intrinsically sociological ' (*ibid.*, p. 43). For in so far as the analysis and publication of information about social relations promotes reflexivity at an institutional level, it also impacts upon those 'lay individuals' who are part of an increasingly reflexive public sphere. Giddens cites the example of divorce statistics (*ibid.*, p. 42-43). It is now a well documented fact that divorce rates in most Western societies are high and continuing to rise. Given the pervasive attitude of calculative risk assessment in those societies, it is unsurprising that men and women, in the light of this information, are becoming increasingly cautious in their attitudes to marriage. After all, the legal and financial consequences of divorce would only add to the emotional costs incurred in the breakdown of intimate relationships.[3]

There is a sense in which the transition from pre-modern to modern societies which Giddens describes, repeats the Habermasian concern with the impact of expert cultures on the communicative traditions of the life-world. The abstract systems through which technocratic control is exerted over the social and natural worlds are both alienating and deskilling (Giddens, 1997b, p. 137). The pre-existing forms of local control, through which substantive relationships between knowledge and action were maintained, are crucially undermined by the expert systems which have invaded every aspect of social life. This, of course, raises questions about the relationship between knowledge authority and political participation. For in setting up 'modes of social influence which no one directly controls' (*ibid.*, p. 138), abstract systems function to produce the high-consequence risks which have become a 'fact' of late modernity. Yet for Giddens, this process of local disempowerment should not be thought of as a unilateral process, through which expert systems will simply go on eroding the moral and political resources of the lifeworld. The level of technocratic control established through abstract systems presupposes an increasing involvement of lay individuals in the servicing, running and administration of those systems. And so while it remains the case that the diversification of expert knowledges has undermined local practices of control and self-determination, the growth of these knowledges has also brought about a diffusion of specialist skills and capabilities across the entire public sphere. As Giddens puts it:

> As a result of processes of reappropriation, an indefinite number of spaces between lay belief and practice and the sphere of abstract systems are opened up. In any given situation . . . the individual has the possibility of a partial or full-blown reskilling in respect of specific decisions or contemplated courses of action. (*ibid.*, p. 139)

Implicit in the development of modernity therefore, is a 'dialectical connection' between expropriating effects of abstract systems and the reflexive powers which mark the autonomy of the public sphere.

In the final chapter of *Modernity and Self-Identity*, Giddens gives a formal definition of what he understands as life politics:

> Life politics concerns political issues which flow from processes of self-actualization in post-traditional contexts, where globalizing influences intrude deeply into the reflexive project of the self, and conversely where processes of self-realization influence global strategies. (Giddens, 1997b, p. 214)

This interconnection between the self conceived as a 'reflexive project' and the 'globalizing influences' of abstract systems can emerge only after a certain level of social and political emancipation has been achieved. Once the self is freed from the fetters of traditional societies, however, the essentialist tenets of Enlightenment thought concerning the nature of humanity are called into question by the increasingly transformative power of human action. From this perspective therefore, life politics is about the 'debates and contestations' that arise from the engagement of a deontologized self in the project of sustaining its 'authenticity'; a project which is carried out in relation to the choices and demands imposed by abstract systems and expert knowledges (*ibid.*, p. 215).

As the subject of abstract systems and expert knowledges, the self has become a 'reflexive achievement', which is sustained through the constant reintegration of local involvements, systemic necessities and global concerns. Thus, the threat of a pure technocratic control of the human subject is always dialectically mediated by the practical consciousness which arises from the manipulation of the body–self relationship. Giddens argues that under the conditions of high modernity, the body has become a 'thoroughly permeable "outer layer" through which the reflexive project of the self and externally formed abstract systems routinely enter' (Giddens, 1997b, p. 218). For example, the medical and biological sciences have already reached the point where contraceptive techniques and fertility treatments are increasingly influential upon birthrates, where prostheses (artificial limbs, cochleal implants, pacemakers) are more and more 'integrated' into the physical body, and where the theoretical basis for cloning and 'gene therapy' are well established. For Giddens, this means that the reflexively organized systems which seek to manipulate the body, inevitably give rise to 'questions' which impact upon the individual both in the form of life choices and as moral and existential dilemmas (*ibid.*) One cannot, in other words, separate the realm of subjective experience from the political questions raised by increasing technocratic specialization and control.

A way out of the 'internally referential systems of modernity' therefore, is offered by the reflexive, 'life political' project of the self. As modernity develops, the extension of control over both the natural and social environments begins to approach its dialectical limit. The abstract systems which have determined the technocratic trajectory of modernity, give rise to fundamental questions about the nature of self-identity, the finitude of individual existence and the authenticity of one's particular life project. As Giddens would have it:

> Life-political issues supply the central agenda for the return of the institutionally repressed. They call for a remoralizing of social life and they demand a renewed sensitivity to questions that the institutions of modernity systematically dissolve. (Giddens, 1997b, p. 224)

It is the very extensiveness of modernity's abstract systems therefore, which reinvigorates the moral and political life of society. The manipulation of biological reproduction, for example, gives rise to basic questions about our own mortality, and the global nature of high-consequence risks demands that we consider the ethical implications that arise from our own acquisitive individualism. In the end, then, the more closely the manipulation of nature and society approximates to the demand for complete functional integration, the more acutely the Heideggerian question of 'how existence itself should be grasped and lived' is experienced in everyday life (*ibid.*).

I began this section by suggesting that the differences between Beck's and Giddens' theories of reflexive modernity are best understood in terms of the limits of normative sociology. I need therefore, to make some brief remarks about those limits, and about their significance for the politics of risk.

One of the defining features of Giddens' account of risk, is the relationship between the demands of ontological security and those of reflexive modernization. We have seen that the significance of risk in the transition to reflexive modernity lies in the fact that it pervades every aspect of social, economic and personal existence. As social agents, in other words, we have all become risk evaluators: individuals who will, in general, apply a logic of contingent utility to the different risk environments in which we participate (the economy, work and employment, sexual and intimate relationships, public health care). The basic question which arises from Giddens' sociological analysis of risk then, is how such a calculative subjectivity can retain a sense of social belonging. For in so far as risk assessment has become the model of subjective volition, it seems as if the unity between individual consciousness, the systemic integration of society and the experience of ontological security has been crucially interrupted. Giddens' answer to this question is to argue that after the traditional narratives of collective being have been displaced by the dynamical processes of modernity, the selfhood of the individual emerges as a 'reflexive project'. The fact that all of us are touched by the uncertainties generated by abstract systems and specialist knowledges, means that the relationship of the self to the institutional forces of society has moved beyond the 'organic' interdependence envisaged in Durkheim's sociology.[4] Rather than contributing to a transformation of the 'conscience collective', the reflexivity produced in modern technological societies is understood as initiating a 'life politics' concerned with transforming and mediating the 'internally referential systems of modernity' (Giddens, 1997b, p. 223).

So, what is the nature of this life politics? In Giddens' work, the question of ontological security is referred to in Goffman's notion of the *Umwelt*.[5] Under the conditions of late modernity, this 'moving world of normalcy' (Giddens, 1997b, p. 128) is constituted through a certain desensitization of the individual to the high-consequence risks endemic to our technological present. In order to function as social actors, in other words, we have to be able to 'filter out' these disastrous possibilities and to remain focused on the personal and institutional demands of everyday existence. This filtering process then is extremely important. For without it, there could be no possibility of the life political processes (self-reflexion, self-realization, self-authentication) through which technocratic necessity can be mediated and transformed. Indeed, for Giddens, the fact that the public sphere has come to include the moral and existential questions which Heidegger characterized as the foundation of *Mitsein* ('being with') is due to the basic functions of the *Umwelt*. There could, in other words, be no reflexive deployment of the self without a basic level of trust in the expert systems which sustain modern social relations.

This insistence upon conceiving risk in terms of its transformation of ontological security signals a crucial difference between Beck and Giddens. For Beck, the relationship between risk and the political changes which mark the emergence of reflexive modernity, is based upon the exposure of the natural environment to the effects of technological civilization. Such effects, according to Beck, are essentially cumulative: genetic mutations, the accumulation of toxins in organic tissue – all have the character of damages which are already impacting upon the 'community of living things'. This community, we have seen, is not limited by social, economic or geopolitical barriers and constitutes a demand for responsibility that is both global and transgenerational. For Beck therefore, the high-consequence risks which Giddens presents as the background to a politics of reflexive self-expression, expose humanity to an absolute risk which is co-present with every technological extension of modernity.

In the end, Beck makes the possibility of transforming the political sphere dependent upon the loss of ontological security. The formation of political institutions which are to act as a check upon the development of technocratic control depends upon the articulation of those damages which are already being done to the material environment. This, we have seen, is how Beck understands the emergence of the sub-political groups which contest the established legal and scientific definitions of damage. For as the effects of poisoning, irradiation and environmental pollution are felt by a growing number of communities, the traditional processes of pluralism and sectional interest are displaced by a sophisticated contestation between the forces of technoscientific control, and those who are damaged by its 'side effects'. It is through this process of contestation that science passes out of its ideological phase and becomes the model of critical reflection which is to rejuvenate the political functions of the state.

The difference between Beck and Giddens then, is best understood in terms of their accounts of the impact of risk upon the traditional structures of social integration. For Beck, the damages that are continually being done to the material environment, have fundamentally undermined our experience of security. Indeed, the logic of Beck's account of risk demands that we conceptualize 'the political' in terms of the impact of chronic anxiety upon the organization of social solidarity. He argues that it is still unclear how this perpetual confrontation with danger will operate as a 'binding force', and that we cannot even be sure that the critical-scientific construction of risk will be sufficient to hold the forces of irrationalism, extremism and fanaticism in check (Beck, 1996a, pp. 49–50). Giddens, on the other hand, is far less willing to confront the presence of absolute risk within the social and political relations of modernity. His account of life politics is mainly concerned with 'self-reflexivity': the personal transformations that are made possible by the disembedding of social relations and the containment of risk within the filtering mechanisms of the *Umwelt*. Ultimately, the question of 'how existence itself should be grasped and lived' (Giddens, 1997b, p. 224) presupposes a kind of functional reduction of risk: a 'bracketing out' of the anxiety which would make expressive transformations of the self and the public sphere impossible.

For Giddens, there can be no politics without self-reflexivity, and no self-reflexivity without the ontological security provided by the *Umwelt*. For Beck, on the other hand, the impact of civilization risks upon the experience of security is such that the whole concept of the personal upon which Giddens' account of reflection depends is called into question. The notions of 'life style' and 'life choice', through which Giddens character-izes the transformative power of the reflexive self, are made secondary to the political demands of absolute risk. For while Beck would undoubtedly agree that the social and economic organization of modernity is increasing-ly reflexive, he would also maintain that the heterogeneous forms of risk evaluation which arise in different spheres of activity (employment and economy, family and intimacy, etc.), can have no legitimate independence from the global imperatives of risk. Ultimately then, our ethical and political responsibility *as human beings* is to the 'natural whole' of which each of us is a fragile and contingent part (Beck, 1996a, p. 74).

These two sociologies of risk give rise to a number of important issues. As I suggested at the beginning of the chapter, Beck's account of the relationship between civilization risks and the progressive democratization of the public sphere is problematic. In general, the political consensus produced through the processes of scientific contestation is possible only on the basis of Beck's originary opposition of 'the human' and 'the technological'. Risk *as such*, in other words, is that which is manifest in the technological damages that afflict the 'community of living things'. For Beck then, the sphere of political mediation and reflection develops as a response to the demands of organic life, demands which are revealed through the analytical quantification of damage to the material environ-ment. There is a sense in which it is possible to read Giddens' understanding of the relationship between risk and modernity as an attempt to pluralize the impact of risk upon reflexive social actors. His account of the filtering powers of the *Umwelt*, and of the dialectical relationship between technocratic systems and the reflexive self, seeks to establish risk evaluation as a mobile and transformative agency within the structures of social integration. Thus, the life politics which Giddens sets out at the end of *Modernity and Self-Identity* is focused on the engagement of the self with particular abstract systems and risk environments. However, I would suggest that Giddens' claim to have brought the Heideggarian 'question of Being' to bear upon the structural and systemic dilemmas of modernity gives rise to its own particular difficulties. I have argued that Giddens' account of the moral and existential questions which become part of the 'reflexive project of the self' presuppose a certain functional reduction of risk. Thus, while it is certainly true that Beck's theorization of risk gives rise to problems concerning the nature of political legitimacy (its origin, extent and translatability), it is also true that Giddens' notion of reflexive selfhood cannot be effectively disengaged from the demands of technocratic control. For as long as self-reflexion is organized through the fundamental concept of ontological security, the risks to which we respond as moral and political agents lack the danger and unforseeability of Heidegger's question of Being.

It seems then, that we are stuck with an aporia: either we accept Beck's theory of absolute risk with its attendant problems of legitimacy, or we come down on the side of Giddens' life politics, with its problems concerning the critical relationship between the self and expert systems of control. In the final section, I will argue that this aporia is the result of two distinct *sociological* presentations of risk: one where the concept of 'the organic' functions as the absolute foundation to social and political life (Beck); the other where the right of reflection lacks any real sense of impending disaster within the systemic organization of the social (Giddens). I will also argue that Derrida's understanding of the relationship between the future as absolute risk and the 'right of reflection', allows us to maintain a sense of the plurality and heterogeneity of risks, without losing the sense of exigency which belongs to the question of Being.

Justice, Democracy and the Politics of Risk

Beck's account of reflexive modernization is in the end an appeal for the radicalization of social democracy: a radicalization in which the scientific recognition of risk would initiate forms of global participation, contestation and autonomy that exceed the old national-parliamentary and state-communist models of political responsibility. As he puts it in *Risk Society*:

> As awareness of the dangers [posed by modern technologies] spreads, the world risk society becomes self-critical. Its bases, co-ordinates and pre-stamped coalitions are thrown into a state of turbulence. Politics breaks out in a new and different way, beyond the reach of formal responsibilities and hierarchies. (Beck, 1996b, p. 24)

The democratic potential of risk society therefore, is both destructive and constructive: destructive of the old corporate and geopolitical hierarchies of power, and constructive of a culture of differentiated, sub-political autonomies. It is worth drawing attention here to a certain Kantianism in Beck's work. For Beck, as for Kant, the goal of a cosmopolitan world-state is an ideal, a 'guiding thread' which remains transcendent of all the historical 'signs' that attest to the purposiveness of human history. According to Kant, the conflicts determined by the empirical constitution of nation states ultimately produce the 'technical' conditions (the political, economic and legal differentiation of civil society) upon which the moral culture of humanity is dependent. And although such a culture can never realize the ideal of rational autonomy, it does at least offer the chance of resolving peacefully the conflicts that arise from the heteronomous constitution of particular nation states. For Beck, on the other hand, nature enters into the development of 'world risk society' as the shared vulnerability of living things: an organic universal whose political significance emerges through the scientific quantification of damage. Thus, although Beck attempts to distinguish his politics of risk from idealist accounts of natural necessity, the legal, economic and technological relationships through which nature is increasingly socialized are still able to return, via the practice of critical science, to its universal demands.

The assurance of this return of the organic is important because of the relationship it determines between risks that are currently present and the absolute risk/contingency of the future. For Derrida, Kant's deployment of a teleological nature as the guarantor of the ideal of cosmopolitan democracy, contradicts the right of autonomous philosophical reflection. The historically achieved configuration of independent republics makes 'the future' (of cosmopolitan democracy) into a 'modality of the *living present*' – a modality in which all reflection on what is to come is restricted to the refinement of established moral and political ideals (Derrida, 1994a, p. 65). Beck's account of the relationship between the present risks posed by nuclear, chemical and genetic technologies and human responsibility to future generations, repeats the Kantian modalization of time: a modalization which 'decides' that the future will be like the present in so far as humanity has finally recognized the exigencies which define legitimate political authority. For Derrida, however, if we are to take the ethical and political responsibility that is opened by the future seriously, we cannot assume the regulative power of any logical modalization of time. For the uniqueness of the 'living present' (the general economy of violence deployed in the discourses of community, identity, humanity) is such that it exceeds every possible projection of politics on to *an* absolute risk which defines the future. Thus, Beck's claim that a scientifically regulated politics of contestation would be finally and uniquely responsible to future generations, fails to recognize this aporetic structure of time: the fact that each moment places us before a future which demands to be 'invented' from within the disjuncture of an ununifiable present. As Derrida puts it in *Spectres of Marx*, we are 'promised' to the future as:

[a] messianic opening to what is coming, that is, to the event that cannot be recognized as such, or recognized in advanced . . . to the event as foreigner itself, to her or him for whom one must leave an empty place, always, in memory of the hope – and this is the very place of spectrality. (Derrida, 1994a, p. 64)

We need then, to look at the ideas of memory, inheritance and return (of the other, the alter, the ghost) deployed in this politics of spectrality, and to make some provisional remarks about how such a radicalization of responsibility might bear upon the concept of reflexive modernization.

Beck and Derrida share a common concern with the 'Marxist inheritance' of contemporary theory – although, as we have seen, this concern leads them in quite different directions. For Derrida, the questions concerning technology, ideology and economy that are bequeathed to us in Marx's writings have complex metaphysical histories which forbid the simple consignment of historical materialism to the history of failed political ideas (see Fukuyama, 1992). Thus, the relationships between humanity, economy and productive technologies which Marx presents in *The Economic and Philosophical Manuscripts*, and later in *Capital*, begin to sketch the dynamics of a process which, for Derrida, becomes the defining characteristic of our historical present: the spectralization of the human. For even though Marx was determined to write the relations obtaining between the machine and the wage labourer as processes which deepen the estrangement of the latter from his/her creative essence, his apprehension of the technological body of capitalism opens the possibility of a critique which would respond to the processes of 'iterability, non-uniqueness, synthetic image [and] simulacrum' through which the concept of the human is constantly disestablished (Derrida, 1994a, p. 141). This spectralization of humanity then becomes the most urgent political question of our time. For if we can no longer rely upon the metaphysics of natural humanism,[6] nor upon the demands of system efficiency, to provide a programmatic orientation within the exigencies of technological civilization, then the possibility of judging what is unjust or unethical must take place through the *experience of impossibility*. I will return to this in a moment.

The technological origin of spectrality is crucial in differentiating the idea of risk which informs Derrida's most recent presentations of the political, from that which is set out in Beck's account of reflexive modernity. We have seen that, for Beck, the rejuvenation of the state depends upon its emergence as a discursive authority which mediates the *de facto* powers of techno-science over the social, biological, genetic and economic constitution of modernity (Beck, 1996a, pp. 187–90). Such a rejuvenation, according to Beck's argument, can take place only through the appearance of the sub-political contestation that is produced by the spread of organic damages and the consequent scientization of risk awareness. Thus:

> While the battle over particular interests and view points rages and should rage in business (and also in the sciences), politics could lay down the overall (juridical) conditions, check the general applicability of regulations and produce consensus. (Beck, 1996a, p. 235)

The idea of the *de facto*, that is, of the establishment of the power of technology over the organic and its demands, is pivotal here. The historiography which Beck presents in *Risk Society*, maintains that the transition from industrial to reflexive modernity occurs through a critical recognition of the damages that an unregulated use of technology has done to the organic conditions of life. And so the concept of the political which emerges from the sub-politics of risk, is ultimately a scientization of damages which allows – or rather *necessitates* – their inclusion within the juridico-administrative authority of the state. But what if the distinction between 'the organic' and 'the technological' upon which this discursive authority is founded has no foundation? What if 'the living present' is always already a spectralization of humanity that has occurred, and is recurrent, through the co-implications of consciousness, rationality and technology? Clearly, this is one of the major political implications of Derrida's deconstructions of Rousseau, Freud, Heidegger and Marx: for in each case, his analysis is careful to point out the ways in which 'the transcendence of the human' (the legislative necessity of 'the universal' that is announced in the metaphysics of nature, primal desire or the existential self-affection of *Dasein*) originates in the 'supplementary' powers of technicity. 'Prosthesis', in other words, belongs to human consciousness even in its most primitive differentiations from 'nature'. For as Richard Beardsworth points out, *homo sapiens'* first wieldings of the flint stone initiated a co-determination of consciousness and technology that continues through to the advent of digitization and the computerization of memory (Beardsworth, 1998, p. 79). Thus, there is no determinate break between 'civilization' and 'techno-civilization', simply because there is no possibility of presenting the conditions under which human consciousness would have affected itself as a pure, non-technicized spontaneity. This is important because it means that in judging the consequences of technology (its dangers, benefits, evils), we must recognize that those consequences cannot be modalized simply through the regulative finality of 'the organic'.

The question we are now beginning to approach then, is that of the possibility of an ethical institutionalization of legislative ideals. For Beck, we have seen that the new institutional structure of state politics will take the form of 'producing consensus' on the material damages that are caused by modern technologies, and that the structuring and restructuring of this consensus as a political demand is regulated by a developing 'symbiosis' of scientific and social rationalities.[7] What is important here is that this relationship is presented as the 'reflexive' mediation through which the state is able to 'constitute' itself as a legislative power whose rights (of administration, prohibition, intervention) rightfully exceed the aporetic temporality of the living present. Conceived deconstructively, such a state, in its determination to articulate the politics of consent from their proper 'postmetaphysical' conditions, would be prone to losing both the sense of its original conditionality, and of the contingency which the future presents to the organization of political necessity in general.

In *Spectres of Marx*, Derrida claims that in order to understand the economic and political conflicts that continue to afflict the global economy

'... a problematics from the Marxian tradition will be indispensable for a long time yet ... and why not for ever?' (Derrida, 1994a, pp. 63–4). We could, for example, cite the current state of geo-economic inequality as a condition which demands to be theorized in terms of its mutability and persistence, rather than its production of a qualitatively new relationship of humanity to its organic life conditions. Thus the World Summits that, during the last decade, attempted to come to international agreement about 'acceptable levels' of pollution have, as a matter of fact, been unable to do anything more than postpone the ratification of consensus to some indeterminate future – a future in which the social, economic and technological antagonisms that continue to structure the geopolitical constitution of the world will presumably have come to an end.[8] This failure is not, as the logic of Beck's arguments would entail, a matter to be addressed in terms of the temporary inability of authority structures which hold sway in the 'developing' world (the persistence of theocracy, the 'authoritarianism' of war and famine management), to receive the cosmo-politan demands of world risk society. Rather, this present lack of consensus over the 'true' necessities of political organization is precisely what Derrida understands as the 'aporia of time' – the co-presence of names, identities and legislations whose agonism cannot be schematized through any universally regulative ideal. Indeed, the political stricture of this economy is that we rethink the very concept of institutionalization: for the impossibility of announcing the universal right and the universal good from their established 'places' of self-identity (the state, the nation, the cosmopolitan federation of nation states), entails a fundamental questioning of the administrative functions that could legitimately fall within the bounds of a cosmopolitical authority.

The events which arise from the technical and institutional supplement-ations of 'the human' are, for Derrida, the moments of radical contingency which open and reopen our responsibility to the *différance* of the living present, and thus to the undecidability of the future. Such events, we have seen, occur within an economy of violence which both presupposes and exceeds Marx's analysis of the technological and ideological body of capital: 'exceeds' because the Marxist ontology of difference (between the human and the machine, the revolutionary and the ideological, the bourgeois and the proletarian), originates in a metaphysics of productivism which demands that 'the future' is modalized through the apophatic necessity of 'socialized production'. Derrida's relationship to the Marxist inheritance therefore, is pertinent to our present discussion because of its disclosure of a certain 'messianic' responsibility to the future; a responsi-bility which, in all its displacements into the technological, economic and cultural forms of totality, remains open to the unforeseeable events in which (the concept of) 'the human' returns to the present. Three important questions arise from this notion of the messianic: (1) how is this returning of the human possible? (2) what kind of ethical and political strictures does it place upon us in 'the living present'? (3) what is its significance for the concepts of justice and autonomy? (Abbinnett, 2000, p. 120).

The relationship between techno-science and the idea of the human that is developed in Derrida's writing is one in which the latter is increasingly subject to processes of medical, cybernetic and digital spectralization – processes whose rapidity of change, innovation and replacement urgently demand that the right of philosophical reflection be preserved against the powers of technocratic control. Indeed, this process of spectralization is precisely that which impacts fatally on Beck's notion of an organic commonality of human beings. For in so far as the integrity of 'the organic' is increasingly called into question by prosthetic and cybernetic technologies, we have reached the point at which 'the body' must be understood as the possibility of dispersed, particularized registrations of the inhuman, rather than as the locus of a universal experience of physical vulnerability. What differentiates Beck's and Derrida's respective accounts of the politics of modernity, therefore, is Derrida's insistence upon the aporetic structure of technological time: a structure which belongs to the spectralization of humanity in virtue of the events of *différance* precipitated by the loss of the organic as a defining attribute of the human. For Derrida, these events occur as radical singularities; and as such, they demand that we remain 'universally hospitable' to the disturbances, locutions and unforeseen interjections of 'otherness' through which the *possibility* of justice is disclosed. This disjointedness of the living present is defined in *Spectres of Marx* as a responsibility to those 'who are no longer or who are not yet *present and living* ' (Derrida, 1994a, p. xix); for political reflection upon the spectrality of the human is immediately related to the sufferings of the dead within the mechanisms of totality, and thus to the unknowable, unavoidable risk that marks the experience of the future as such. Thus, it is the figure of the ghost, the *arrivant*, who unexpectedly disturbs the measured, legitimized violence of the system, that schematizes Derrida's idea of messianic justice: a justice which demands that every epistemic, technological or metaphysical organization of the present is brought back to the transcendental horizon of the future.

If there is to be a politics of risk therefore, we must acknowledge that the condition of that risk (our originary promise to the transcendental horizon of the future) cannot be presented as an 'absolute' in any of the generic discourses of science, technology, epistemology or metaphysics. For Derrida, the discipline of messianic justice is precisely that its stricture cannot be exemplified in any positive organization of the present, and must 'risk' precipitating events (of alterity) whose consequences it cannot foresee. Thus Beck's modalization of risk through the established 'commonalities of organic life', remains complicit with a legislative politics in which: (1) the institutional-administrative functions of government tend to accumulate in a way that is increasingly insensitive to the technicity/spectrality of the human; and (2) the concept of 'globality' has emerged as a legislative demand to be deployed from its cognitive centres (Europe,

America, Japan) into the technically, economically and politically 'under-developed' nations of the world.

The deployment of organic nature in *Risk Society* then is strategic: it constitutes an attempt to organize the *totality* of humankind through their shared vulnerability to civilization risks. This, as we have seen, raises questions about what is actually shared in this commonality, and whether it can function as grounds for the 'preserving, settling, discursive' functions of global politics (*ibid.*, p. 235). However, Beck does at least theorize the notion of risk in terms of its radical disruption of established structures of social and political identity (nation state, civil society, family). Giddens, on the other hand, begins from the assumption of a much more restricted economics of risk: its assimilation into the norms, values and ideals of the *Umwelt*. According to Giddens, risk, and the reflexive self-consciousness which is its counterpart, is an issue that should be understood in terms of its impact on the organization of ontological security. His argument is that the shared values and expectations which constitute the *Umwelt*, have come to include risk as the mediator between personal autonomy and political responsibility. The 'life politics' which Giddens sets out in *Modernity and Self-Identity* therefore, concerns 'political issues which flow from processes of self-actualization ... , where globalizing influences intrude deeply into the reflexive project of the self, and conversely where processes of self-realization influence global strategies (Giddens, 1997b, p. 214). As agents who operate within the technological systems of society, we all, as a matter of fact, reflect upon the political implications of our life choices (*ibid.*, p. 215). Now, for Giddens, this technological connectedness of the modern self marks the emergence of a kind of Heideggarian politics: one in which the question of personal authenticity is immediately related to the functional-systemic organization of human society (*ibid.*, p. 224). However, Giddens' invocation of Heidegger is misleading. From *Being and Time* onward, Heidegger makes it clear that 'authenticity' belongs to the fundamental ontology of *Dasein* – to the basic structures of care, mortality and finitude which mark the existential condition of 'being-in-the-world'. Thus, in so far as truth is something which is disclosed in particular moments of exposure to the transcendence of Being, the engagement of the self in the technological reproduction of society is an inevitable loss of authenticity (Heidegger, 1983, p. 267). This, we have seen, is the problem to which Heidegger attends in 'The question concerning technology'. For after he has argued that technological modernity, and its reduction of *Dasein* to the level of a 'standing reserve', has endangered the fundamental vocation of man (Heidegger, 1996, p. 338), his recourse is not to politics (in the sense of the administration of technological relations), but rather to the transformative power of art in its revelation of the technological fate of Being (*ibid.*, p. 341).

What is important here is that Giddens' attempt to render the concept of authenticity in terms of Heidegger's question of Being, reveals some-thing of the complex relationship between technology, politics and time.

For Giddens, the fundamental question raised by techno-scientific systems concerns the relationship between the self, whose limits have been infinitely extended through the interface of the human and the technological, and the normative standards expressed in the *Umwelt*. In *Modernity and Self-Identity*, he argues that we should understand this engagement of the self with technological systems as a progressive articulation of what it is to be a 'person' or a 'human being' (Giddens, 1997b, p. 217). New reproductive technologies, for example, open up a whole range of unforeseen possibilities for individual social agents: possibilities which make the body the focus of constantly shifting reflections on the nature of gender, sexuality, love and familial attachment. Heidegger's essay, on the other hand, traces the reductive power of modern technologies: the way in which they complete the objectification of Being as a resource, as 'standing reserve'. From this perspective it is impossible to separate the political organization of the state from the functional-administrative organization of humanity. For in so far as *Dasein* has already suffered the fate of technological utilization, its authentic relationship to Being remains outside of the ideological movements which direct the massification of humanity.

This opposition brings us back to Derrida. As we have seen, Derrida's relationship to Heidegger is complicated, and has been the subject of a great deal of critical attention. In *Of Spirit*, he is concerned with the fate of the question of Being in Heidegger's work. The fundamental ontology of *Dasein* which Heidegger sets out in *Being and Time*, includes an implicit critique of idealism conceived as the phenomenology of 'consciousness in general' (Heidegger, 1983, pp. 246–52). Heidegger's claim is that as an existentially differentiated being-towards-death, *Dasein* cannot be understood as a totalizable being, which is able to find completion in the universal attributes of human subjectivity. Among these attributes we should include the fundamental categories of western philosophy: the soul, self-consciousness, personality and spirit (Derrida, 1990a, p. 15). What is important here is that for Heidegger, all of these categories neglect the basic fact of *Dasein*'s 'thrownness': its originary concern with the question of Being as it is given through the experience of its own finitude ('being-towards-death'). Thus, the thread which links Descartes to Hegel and Hegel to Husserl in the history of philosophy is the 'spiritual' characteristics of consciousness (selfhood, soul, personality) which enclose *Dasein* within the historical unfolding of humanity as such. The unification of mind and body, subject and object, *as spirit*, in other words, dissimulates the question of Being. For by presenting the history of *Dasein* as co-present with the history of the enlightened self-consciousness, philosophy has determined a certain indifference to the ontological dilemmas which arise from the techno-scientific organization of society (*ibid.*, p. 20). Thus, for Heidegger, the 'thrownness' of *Dasein* has a double significance. It opens the possibility of an historical relationship of humanity to its being as a 'standing reserve' (one which would question the technical processes of medicalization, psychologization, informatics), while at the same time precipitating the structures of the 'they' by which the technological enframing of humanity is maintained.

Derrida's reading of Heidegger in *Of Spirit* is an attempt to mark the return of the idea of spirit (*Geist*) in Heidegger's work after *Being and Time*. This, of course, raises a number of truly momentous questions – about the relationship between the uniquely 'spiritual' vocation of the German language and people in preserving the historicity of *Dasein*, and about the significance of Heidegger's membership of the NSDAP – which it would not be appropriate to address in this chapter. However, it should be clear from what has gone before that *Being and Time* initiates an opposition between the existential structures of *Dasein* (falling, thrownness) and the technological development of modernity. Indeed, Heidegger's claim that 'the essence of technology is by no means technological' (Heidegger, 1996, p. 311) is essentially a clarification of *Dasein*'s responsibility to the question of Being. For in so far as what is presented in *Being and Time* is an ontology of being-in-the-world, *Dasein*'s 'authenticity' remains bound up with its original (pre-technological) experience of care, anxiety and death (Heidegger, 1983, pp. 304–11). Now, for Derrida, we have seen that the most urgent questions concerning technology – the spectralization of the human, the loss of natural-biological integrity, the genetic completion of systemic modernity – take place within the textual economics of nature, humanity and the social. This economy, however, does not presuppose (in Heidegger's sense of presupposing) *Dasein* as an originary and endangered form of self-presence. For Derrida, what Western metaphysics, including Heidegger, has presented as the universal form of human consciousness is originally 'technological'. The very idea of 'hominization' (the evolution of characteristics which distinguish human beings as such) entails a supplementation of consciousness, which, even at its most primitive, exceeds every existential or phenomenological description of the origin.[10] What is important here is that the technological development of modernity, in which the concept of the human becomes increasingly 'spectralized', cannot be understood in terms of an absolute danger to the authentic historicity of *Dasein* (Heidegger, 1996, p. 331). Rather, we must recognize that the economics of technological supplementarity demands a response which remains open to the alterity of the other (his/her recombination, replication, destruction), to the necessity of institutional recognition (the right of response) and to the play of technological liberation-domination. Thus, for Derrida, the 'impossible' stricture of the ethical response is constantly reopened by the disruptive temporality of technological innovation.

If Derrida has alerted us to a certain anti-technologism in Heidegger's thought (one which becomes more articulated in the works which follow the publication of *Being and Time*), then we should be careful to note that his concept of spectralization involves a very different account of 'reflexivity' from the one presented in Giddens' work. At the end of

Modernity and Self Identity, Giddens describes the conditions under which abstract technological systems bring about a 'remoralizing' of social life (Giddens, 1997b, p. 224). He argues that although there is a tendency for these systems to operate 'self-referentially', the fact that social agents are, in general, engaged in the running and administration of such systems means that the circle of this self-referentiality is broken. In so far as each of us has been integrated into the technological order of society (both physically and cognitively), we have achieved a level of reflexive risk awareness which goes beyond the functional requirements of the system. The personal self-realization which has been made possible by new technologies therefore, is immediately engaged with, and productive of, the moral questions which arise from the proliferation of abstract systems. As Giddens puts it:

> Widespread changes in lifestyle, coupled with a de-emphasis on continual economic accumulation, will almost certainly be necessary if the ecological risks which we now face are to be minimized. In a complicated interweaving of reflexivity, widespread reflexive awareness of the reflexive nature of the systems currently transforming ecological patterns is both necessary and likely to emerge. (Giddens, 1997b, p. 222)

Giddens also argues that this moral reflexivity is likely to give rise to a new form of emancipatory politics. For if it is the case that we in the West are increasingly aware of the global consequences of our life choices, then such an awareness cannot, in principle, be separated from a commitment to those others who are oppressed by the mechanism of global capital (*ibid.*, p. 230).

Risk, as it informs Giddens' ideas of autonomy (reflexive awareness) and solidarity (the shared assumptions of the *Umwelt*), is insufficient as a characterization of the ethical and political dilemmas of technological modernity. Giddens' account of risk proposes that the instrumental rationality imposed by technological systems, is progressively desystematized within the life-political projects of rational social agents. For in so far as technological society becomes increasingly complex – each subsystem coming to include a reflexive awareness of its function, development and possible risks – those involved in its operations become aware of themselves as subjects who must actively determine their personal goals and commitments. This pursuit of self-realization, we have seen, is intensified by the technological porosity and mutability of the individual self: each of us is confronted with life choices (existential questions about who we are and how we want to live) whose significance is both ethical and political. Yet these patterns of reflexivity presuppose that the specialization of technological systems is inherently reflexive; and that as such, they cannot sustain the massifying and exploitative consequences theorized in Adorno and Heidegger's accounts of modernity. Giddens' analysis, in other words, tends to subsume the dilemmas of techno-scientific development (genetic manipulation versus biological integrity, information versus reflection) under the established *sociological* necessity of a reciprocal relationship between technological evolution and reflexive self-recognition.

In the end then, the concept of the *Umwelt* which Giddens expounds as the normative regulation of social reflexivity (Giddens, 1996b, pp. 127–8), confines the risks of technological civilization to the 'high-consequence, low-probability' dangers generated by technological systems. Thus, in so far as the reflexiveness of such systems promises both a reduction in the objective probability of catastrophe and an increase in the subjective culture of human beings, the general tendency of technological moderniz-ation remains within the parameters of rational Enlightenment. This sociological concept of risk, however, determines what we might call a fore-closure of the present. We have seen that, for Derrida, the 'now', of the present is constituted as an economy of 'spectralizing' effects (the biogenetic organization of the social, the prosthetic supplementation of the human body, the informatic temporality of the media), and that the political demand of this spectrality is responsible to a future which is constantly, and unforeseeably, impending. The social consequences of mapping the human genome, for example, cannot be known in advance. And so despite the general optimism about cancer therapies and the elimination of congenital diseases, questions about the fungibility and operational modification of human beings return in ever more urgent forms (see Baudrillard, 1999 and 1995a). The 'democracy to come' of which Derrida speaks in *The Other Heading*, therefore, is responsible to a concept of risk which cannot be adequately schematized from within the horizon of the present. The possibility of the political (conflict, negoti-ation, response, institutionalization), in other words, is given as a 'messianic' obligation; a responsibility to future generations which remains attentive to the disastrous violence of the past (Derrida, 1994a, p. xix). Such an obligation is determined within and beyond the dialectics of techno-scientific progress. For in so far as it demands reflection upon 'absolute danger', it cannot allow that danger to appear as part of the restricted economy of risk evaluation.

I want to conclude by returning briefly to the question of the relationship between ecological responsibility and the politics of differ-ence. In *The Other Heading*, Derrida has argued that the political obligation which comes with 'being European' must find its way 'experi-mentally' between the claims of 'monopoly' (as they are expressed in the conceptual categories of Marxism, 'free market' economics or tech-nologism) and those of 'dispersal' (as they are expressed in certain postcolonialist and postmodernist theories of difference).[11] This 'dual responsibility', in other words, takes place *between* the ideals of universal democracy determined in Enlightenment philosophy, and the impending 'otherness' against which European culture has prosecuted its representa-tions of humanity. For Derrida then, the possibility of cosmopolitanism is co-present with the demand of translation; with the stricture of com-municating the significance of something (a gesture, a story, a custom, a tradition) which has appeared to our socio-linguistic culture as unfathomably alien, without annulling its strangeness, its alterity. Thus 'the example of the international institution' (UNESCO) which Derrida addresses in his essay on the right of philosophy (Derrida, 1994b), functions to underline a general deconstructive point about the relationship between politics, reflection and institutionalization: that the 'autonomy' of any particular institution (the state, the university, international charities) must be understood in terms of its acknowledgement of the alterity against which its legislations are written. The institution which has acknowledged the impossibility of its enunciation of universal justice, in other words, would be just autonomous enough to respond to 'the other' as an immediate, spectral demand for the precipitation for democracy to come.

Beck's account of risk society develops a concept of critical science in which the organic/ecological foundation of politics is disclosed with increasing clarity. And so questions concerning human identity (the universal necessities that bind us into a 'world society'), the relationship between humanity and technology (the definitive specification of 'good' and 'bad' technologies), and the cultural assumptions implicit in the designation of 'civilization risks', are immediately referred to the epistemic resources of a dynamical consensus. In Giddens' work, we have seen that the regulation of technological risk takes place within a much more restricted economy than the one presented in Beck's account of reflexive modernization. The structuring necessity of the *Umwelt* is interposed between the critical-scientific provocation of anxiety, and the life projects of reflexive social agents. Despite Beck's opening up of the dynamics of collective anxiety, however, his scientific ecologism still begs the question of its own political necessity. For if 'the political' is that which occurs in the gaps between legislative necessity and the alterities that it seeks to appropriate, then the persistence of real obstacles to 'global consensus' (the obsolete nuclear technologies that still provide for large parts of the former Eastern Bloc, the reliance of many Third World countries on the 'dirty' manufacturing processes of primary industrialization, the proliferation of nuclear rivalries around the globe), cannot be understood simply as temporary moments within a general historical teleology. The 'risk' of Beck's 'world risk society' then, would be that its political organization would tend to accumulate legislative functions in such a way as to endanger the demand of 'the other' as it exists outside of the cognitive centres of risk evaluation. Those nations who are suddenly charged with endangering the whole 'community of living things' in virtue of their poverty and technological underdevelopment, in other words, would surely become far more threatening to the future of humankind when considered as the residue of an absolute ecological necessity.

What deconstruction leaves us with in regard to the ethical and political ideals presented in Beck's work, therefore, is the stricture of attending to the 'system of implications' (teleology, eschatology,

187

elevating and interiorizing accumulation of meaning, a certain type of traditionality, a certain concept of continuity, of truth) which govern the universality of ecological risk (Derrida, 1981, p. 56). Such a stricture cannot be gathered into the construction of 'lineal time', and demands that we attend to the heterogeneous histories and temporalities of nationhood, technicity, culture and religion, that *necessarily* exceed the global-ecological management of risk. Practically, this would mean seeking to establish cosmopolitical institutions that would respond to the *dispersal* of risks across the uneven and conflictual development which underlies the 'new world order'. These institutions would try to sustain a kind of 'messianic' relationship with the present; for it is only in so far as 'things are going badly' and the epoch is 'out of joint' with itself, that the impoverished and the dispossessed can return as the immediate singularities to which justice *as such* is responsible (Derrida, 1994a, pp. 22–3). Clearly it is the recognition and precipitation of this 'messianic' justice that Bennington has in mind when he remarks of the 'reflexive' institution: '[it] should be sensitive enough to the event of this alterity [of the other] to undo and reconstitute itself at a very rapid rhythm' (Bennington and Derrida, 1993, pp. 258–67).

The danger inherent in Beck's idea of 'reflexive modernity' therefore, is that his account of 'civilization risks' assumes that it is possible to transpose scientific calculation of possible damages to the natural conditions of life, on to the speculative idea of a 'community of living things'. Such a community, however, with its constitutive assumption of an emergent consensus that is to become the universal form of political judgement (Beck, 1996a, p. 235), cannot exist. Its realization is always pre-empted by the violence, antagonism and force which is played out in the economy of the 'living present'. Conceived deconstructively, civilization risks must always be referred to the infinite complexity of this economy – a complexity whose political demand originates in the recognition that the most impoverished and endangered 'singularities' (nations, tribes, indigenous peoples, refugees), cannot be 'justly' subordinated to the demands of any universal rationality. Despite its compelling analysis of the ever increasing risks of technocratic control, therefore, Beck's scientific ecologism remains complicit with a certain cumulative-teleological enlightenment which limits the demands of the other upon established ideals of political recognition. For even if these ideals are presented only as the *formal* conditions of democratic risk evaluation, it remains the case that the 'community' to which they refer has already excluded the absolute risk which haunts the economy of our living present. If the politics of risk society really is the politics of impending catastrophe (Beck, 1996a, pp. 78–80), then justice demands that we acknowledge the infinite dispersal of that catastrophe. I will return to the issues of globalization and cosmopolitan responsibility in the following chapter.

Notes

1. For Marx's account of the socio-economic necessity of this process, see *Capital, Volume One* (1977a, chapter 8), and *Capital Volume Two* (1978, chapter 9).

2. Giddens' analysis of the 'disembedding' power of 'symbolic tokens' owes much to Georg Simmel's account of the loss of appropriate relationships between things and social purposes that results from the expansion of the money economy. See Simmel (1991).

3. For an extended discussion of the changes in sexual and familial relations characteristic of reflexive modernity, see Giddens (1992).

4. See Durkheim (1964), pp. 111–32.

5. The term *Umwelt* refers to Erving Goffman's account of *Relations in Public*. Giddens translates the idea as 'a "moving" world of normalcy which the individual takes around from situation to situation' (Giddens, 1997b, p. 128). Under the conditions of reflexive modernity, this world has come to include awareness of the high-consequence risks that are generated by abstract systems.

6. See particularly Derrida's account of 'The inscription of the origin' in *Of Grammatology* (1976, pp. 242–55).

7. Derrida's critique of the 'human sciences' is important here, particularly his contention that structuralist, realist, cognitivist, etc. approaches to social phenomena share a debt to philosophy which cannot be discharged simply by re-operationalizing ideas of subjectivity, autonomy, community or identity. (See, for example, *Of Grammatology*'s account of the relationship between Rousseau's presentation of the regulative integrity of nature, and the structuralist 'science' of Levi-Strauss' anthropology.) Thus, Beck's account of the 'implicit ethics' of methodological scepticism, implies that the pronouncements of the human sciences on the social, political, economic and technological dilemmas raised by 'world risk society', are *comprehensively and exclusively* legitimized by the dynamical procedures of 'scientific' contestation.

8. The reductions in levels of environmental pollution stipulated in Agenda Twenty-One of the 1992 UN conference in Rio di Janeiro were agreed 'in principle' by all nations who attended. Refusal to be formally bound by these stipulations, however, was not confined to the so-called 'developing' nations. Significantly, the US maintained that it would not be in its interests to enforce the reductions in emission levels agreed at the conference.

9. There are passages in *Risk Society* where Beck comes close to admitting that the anxiety produced by a scientized risk consciousness refers 'the political' to a much more general economy than that which is articulated in his concept of reflexive modernity. See, for example, 'From the solidarity of need to solidarity motivated by anxiety', where he states: '[I]t is still completely unclear how the binding force of anxiety operates, even whether it works. What motives and forces for action do they [anxiety communities] set in motion? . . . Will anxiety drive people to irrationalism, extremism, fanaticism?' (Beck, 1996a, pp. 49–50).

10. See, for example, *Of Grammatology*'s account of the logic of supplementarity which operates in Rousseau's writing (Derrida, 1976, pp. 141–64). Particularly instructive is Derrida's quotation of a passage from *Reveries of a Solitary Walker*, in which Rousseau describes the 'catastrophic' impact of mining technologies upon the natural equilibrium between humanity and nature (*ibid.*, p. 148). For Rousseau, the technological supplement, which began with the discovery of iron and the application of metal implements to the agrarian economy, has always been a threat to the natural origin of community, morality and virtue.

11. See my 'Politics and enlightenment: Kant and Derrida on cosmopolitan responsibility' (1998).

12

Capitalism, Globalization and Cosmopolitanism

Introduction

In *Spectres of Marx*, Derrida enumerates a list of the maladies that continue to afflict the global organization of capitalism: statelessness, economic conflict, unemployment, the amorality of free market investments, Third World debt, arms trading, inter-ethnic wars, international crime, the inadequacy of international law and its institutions (Derrida, 1994a, pp. 81–3). Now, one of the principal aims of Derrida's reading of Marx is to register the impossibility of reducing these effects to vestigial phenomena that will, in the long run, be overcome by the moral and distributive justice of liberal capitalism. As we have seen, the temptation to preach the good news of the end of history and the triumph of the enlightenment over its secular and religious enemies is a persistent one in Western political thought. Francis Fukuyama's *The End of History and the Last Man*, for example, has attempted to read the morally transformative power of possessive individualism (the power which Hegel identified as both the danger and the necessity of the French Revolution) into his account of the prosperity of liberal capitalist societies. The 'spirit' of world history, in other words, alighted in Europe, migrated to the cultural melting pot of America, and now awaits recognition by the Islamic hordes who would hold back the universal progress of humanity. My primary concern in this chapter therefore, is to examine the ethical and political issues that arise from such Eurocentric constructions of the friend and the enemy; for it is only through their designation of the *différence* between the place of Enlightenment (Europe, the West), and the backward, fundamentalist civilizations of the East that we will be able to register what is at stake in the economic and technological processes of globalization.

As we have seen, Derrida's pursuit of a cosmopolitan ethics is informed by his idea of hospitality; the concept of an unconditional openness to those 'others' who arise from the technological powers of global capitalism. The possibility of this openness cannot be mapped onto the metaphysical discourse of rights, duties and obligations (the logos); for such designations of humanity are, for Derrida, always complicit with the history of legal, economic and cultural exclusions that have sustained the geopolitical dominance of the West. If there is to be hospitality to the other who comes from beyond the West, therefore, this must come through the events of cultural homogenization, national displacement, media simulation and technological exploitation (of the other) that determine the 'disjointed' time of global capitalism. For it is through the *unforseeability* of such events (their spontaneity) that we are charged with the responsibility of thinking beyond the established referents and representations of our cultural identity.

In the chapter that follows then I will situate Derrida's approach to the politics of globalization in the context of the following questions:

- What is the relationship between the global organization of capitalism and the cultural, economic and political structures of the nation state?
- What is the relationship between the present geopolitical domination of the West and the historical construction of 'Orient' and 'Occident' as opposed, unequal and antagonistic identities?
- Are the categories of European Enlightenment philosophy originally and necessarily racist?
- How has the collapse of geographical space into the instantaneous communication of media technologies affected ethical recognition of the other?
- How are questions of friendship and enmity, unequal economic development, and the global-technological determination of capitalism related to the theories of modernity and postmodernity we have examined?

The Destruction of Locality

In the introduction to his *Globalization: The Human Consequences*, Bauman sets out the basic premise of his critique of transnational capitalism:

> The centres of meaning and value production are today extraterritorial and emancipated from local constraints – this does not apply, though, to the human condition which such values and meanings are to inform and make sense of. (Bauman, 1998, p. 3)

The relationship between 'locality' and 'community', in other words, is originally sustained through the spatial limits of physical interaction between people. Thus, where technological development had yet to reach the stage where local relationships are disembedded by the intrusion of universal standards of time and rationality, the meanings sustained within localities conformed to the organic space of love, conflict and obligation (Bauman, 1998, p. 16). This traditional experience of proximity, however, has been progressively displaced by the technological means through which 'conflicts, solidarities, combats, debates and the administration of justice' are stretched beyond the locality (*ibid.*, p. 9). Bauman specifies these technological means as: (1) the panoptical organization of space through which industrial modernity begins to reduce the moral density of particular communities; and (2) the imposition of cybernetic space on the physical networks of communication (roads, railways), and its consequent erasure of 'physical obstacles and temporal distances' (*ibid.*, p. 17). Space therefore, collapses into instantaneous communication: humanity is finally liberated from the constraints of locality.

This liberation, however, is unequal and polarizing: for it is only extraterritorial corporations whose capital is not fixed in the lifeworld of particular communities that can enjoy total withdrawal from the ties of the locality. By deliberately cutting themselves off from the normative life of 'the place', such corporations leave themselves completely free to dissipate the resources of meaning and obligation that structure the ethical life of particular communities. Those who *must* live within the physical confines of place no longer have the power to generate their own normative codes, for their interactions and encounters have all been overtaken by extraterritorial necessities (efficiency, reduction of labour costs, maximization of profit) that are fatal to the duties of justice and responsibility: 'No room is left for local "opinion leaders"; no room is left for local opinion as such' (Bauman, 1998, p. 26).

Within this global economy the nation state is progressively stripped of its power to discipline, control and administer its territorial space. The sovereignty of the nation depends upon its ability to regulate its economy, to maintain armed forces capable of defending its territorial borders, and its capacity to produce cultural norms and values that create a shared sense of identity (Bauman, 1998, p. 62). During the Cold War, the logistical demands of this sovereignty were such as to limit the number of viable states: for the number of 'new nations' capable of mustering the military, economic and cultural resources necessary to demand international recognition was determined by the geopolitical interests of the two superpowers. What has happened since the end of the US–Soviet domination of world affairs, however, is that the capacity of states to exercise sovereignty over their own cultural norms, economic resources and national security has been compromised. The passing of economic power in to the hands of corporate bodies who have no local affinities has meant that even the most powerful states have become subject to the chaotic effects of globalization. The movement of capital into and out of particular locations is dictated by the demands of efficiency and profitability alone, and so the fate of national economies and the local communities they support, has come to depend on the vagaries of an unpredictable global market. This, in essence, is the meaning that Bauman attributes to globalization: the shifting of economic rationality (in so far as the chaotic transactions of global capital can be 'rational') out of the realm of civil society and into the extraterritorial space of global exchange (*ibid.*, p. 60).

The worst effects of this extraterritorial mobility of capital are, of course, felt by those new nations whose economies depend upon the exploitation of one or two resources; for in so far as their bargaining position vis-à-vis global corporations is weak, the primary function of such states is to provide the minimum level of security required for corporate exploitation to take place (Bauman, 1998, p. 68). The ideology of globalization maintains that the destruction of local restrictions on the movement of capital will result in a more productive world economy from which all nations will benefit. The reality, however, is that once capital is released from the fetters of local restrictions – the restrictions which, for Bauman, bind it to the productive life of local communities – it actively promotes the proliferation of weak, repressive sovereignties that cannot hope to feed, educate, house or defend their populations. These localities are, of course, permanently vulnerable to the new mobility of capital; for the resources they offer can, at any moment, be rendered worthless by fluctuations in the global market or changes in the geopolitical stability of the region. Capital, in other words, has no ethical investment in the locality; it always retains the option of pulling out and leaving the locals destitute and without hope of regeneration (*ibid.*, p. 75).[1]

As the power of extraterritorial corporations expands, the demand for a flexible labour force becomes increasingly determining; only those localities are chosen for investment whose workers are without rights, without representation and without alternative forms of employment. The whole world, in other words, is forced to conform to this corporate model of flexibility; to sacrifice the collective and sustaining experience of work, to tolerate the unforeseen destruction of one's livelihood, and to wait without hope for the rejuvenating power of the global corporations. Thus, for Bauman, modernity has drifted not just into moral indifference, but into a totalitarian enforcement of immobility. The prisons which, in Western societies, hold increasingly large numbers in unproductive stasis reflect a global tendency towards enforcing immobility on those who are surplus to the present needs of capital (Bauman, 1998, p. 113). And so if we are to understand the cycle of famine which repeats endlessly in the Third World, we must recognize that it is determined by the extraterritorial corporations who constantly uproot the material and symbolic relations of already impoverished localities.

Globalization therefore, has taken the most urgent questions of our epoch (how we are to frame a more inclusive international law, a more equitable distribution of power, a more equal access to wealth and resources) well and truly beyond the basic ethical resources of humanity. The uncorrupted Eden where the bonds of care sprang immediately from the proximity of the other has gone forever, and we are left with the task of finding order and meaning in a world that has been turned over to the amorality of the global market. In his recent book of conversations with Keith Tester, Bauman is at pains to point out that the loss of the nation state as a meaning-creating agency and the emergence of an ultra mobile, extra-territorial form of capital, demand that we rethink the basic concepts through which we approach the question of politics (Bauman and Tester, 2001, p. 139). We can no longer prosecute a critique of modernity on the basis of the 'totalizing' powers of panoptical states, for in so far as global capital has broken the political ideological relationship between the state and its industrial base, modernity has become increasingly uncertain, increasingly marked by the ephemerality of cultural, aesthetic and economic relations. It is this globalizing trend which necessitates a fundamental rethinking of the relationships between economy, technology and culture; for if there is to be a politics of global responsibility, it must respond to the complex intrication of these spheres which Bauman calls 'liquid modernity'.

The question I would ask of Bauman, however, is what form his proposed 'rethinking of totality' is to take. Much of what he says about the destructive relationship between global capital and local communities, valorizes the normative relationships that he traces back to the 'organic' constitution of human space. Those relationships which have grown out of the moral proximity of human beings, in other words, function as exemplary forms of care, and as such, they institute a critique of globalization that is founded on the loss of the narrative capacity of local space. This, I have argued, crucially limits the project of rethinking the politics of globalization (Abbinnett, 1998b). For in so far as the drift into liquid modernity takes place against the background of an originally ethical space, it seems as if the technological and economic effects of capitalism can be recounted only in the idiom of loss, waiting, stasis and ambivalence.

Derrida's' political writing, however, moves between the critique of origins presented in *Of Grammatology, Speech and Phenomena* and *Writing and Difference*, and the critique of capital he inherits from Marx. The technological processes through which capitalism has become increasingly monopolistic (digitization, informatics, computerization), also intensifies the spectralizing economy that Derrida traced within the structures of culture and metaphysics. The necessity of this reciprocal movement is what, for Derrida, designates the political space of the text; for within our living present it is precisely the question of how we are to respond to the dispersal, replication and supplementation of the other that opens the question of cosmopolitical responsibility. This economy then, moves us decisively away from the transcendental demand of the other (the demand which Bauman pursues in his account of the 'human consequences' of globalization), towards the heterogeneous and undecidable events in which his or her alterity is disclosed. I will say more about the issues of power, translation and recognition that arise from these events in a moment. For now, however, we need to look in more detail at the logics of cultural production and cultural identity which open the politics of cosmopolitan responsibility.

Culture, Economy, Difference

In general, Bauman's account of the global economy intertwines the logic of adiaphorization (the erasure of the moral response and the drift into indifference) with the expansion of the economic and technological powers of modernity. The 'human consequences' of global capitalism are conceived in terms of a double bind, in which the more complex and exploitative the dominant economies of the world become, the more removed from the register of moral feeling are those 'others' who resource the ever expanding needs of Western-style consumerism. Ultimately therefore, the economic and political power of Europe, the USA and Japan determine a legal-contractual model of responsibility, one in which 'developing' or 'Third World' nations figure only as subjects of debt repayments, labour costs or aid programmes. What Bauman's analysis tends to underplay, however, is the fact that the inhuman distance between the Third and First world is sustained through the literary, aesthetic and philosophical economies in which 'subject' and 'dominant' cultures are represented. If we are properly to understand the relationship between politics, globalization and cultural difference, therefore, we must attend to the events of domination, erasure, silencing and resistance that occur within its shifting economy of representation.

I want to begin this section not with Derrida, but with Edward Said's account of the cultural economics of East and West, Orient and Occident, Christianity and Islam. At the beginning of his book *Orientalism: Western Conceptions of the East*, Said states:

> I have found it useful here to employ Michel Foucault's' notion of a discourse ... to identify Orientalism. My contention is that without examining Orientalism as a discourse one cannot possibly understand the enormously systematic discipline by which European culture was able to manage – and even produce – the orient politically, sociologically, militarily, ideologically, scientifically and imaginatively during the post-Enlightenment period. (Said, 1995, p. 3)

The system of knowledge that is treated by Said therefore, functioned as an instrument of Western European colonialism: as a body of ideas about Oriental geographies, ethnicities, customs and beliefs that facilitated control over the culture, people and resources of the East. The first two chapters of Said's book are about the relationship between orientalist scholarship and the British and French colonial administrations which dominated India, North Africa and the Middle East. For Said, the knowledge that is generated by this scholarship has no empirical referent in Eastern culture or civilization; its standards of verification are internally maintained, and express a disciplinary consensus that evolved simultaneously with the strategic demands of colonialist rule. This consensus is reproduced through an academic tradition whose methods are largely exegetical: the task of the scholar is not to study the present reality of the East with all its complexities and contradictions, but to return to the foundational texts of Oriental civilization and to search out the basic categories (the Arab mind, the Oriental psyche, Islamic superstition) which determine the ontology of the East. The Orientalist project therefore, is shot through with a kind of redemptive zeal; for it portrays the East as a fallen civilization which it is the duty of the West to reintegrate into the purposiveness of universal history (Said, 1995, p. 158).[2]

This reintegration of the Orient, however, begs all of the most urgent questions of colonialism and post-colonialism: questions of race, nation, language, culture and modernity. For in so far as it is the 'timeless, disembodied voice of the [Western] author' who speaks for the Orient, it is he (the colonial voice is always male) who bestows reality on the colonized:

> On the one hand, Orientalism acquired the Orient as literally and as widely as possible; on the other it domesticated this knowledge to the West, filtering it through regulatory codes, classifications, specimen cases, periodical reviews, dictionaries, grammars, commentaries, editions, translations, all of which together founded a simulacrum of the Orient and reproduced it materially in the West, for the West. (Said, 1995, p. 166)

This 'simulation' of the Orient is pervasive in the literary, philosophical and aesthetic culture of Western Europe from the late eighteenth to early twentieth centuries. Indeed, the impressive detail of Said's expositions of Flaubert, Nerval and Chateaubriand, and of Lane, Gibb and T. E. Lawrence, express his concern with the relationship between power and authorial practice. For although we may differentiate their respective works in terms of originality, literary style and aesthetic vision, it remains the case that all of them conceal, disclose and transform essentially Western ideas of the Orient as despotic, superstitious, libidinized, fractious and anti-modern. No matter how well intentioned this 'speaking for' the Orient might be therefore, its least harmful outcome is a kind of benign husbandry in which the Eastern style of being is preserved as an antidote to the functionality and repression of Western modernity.[3] At its worst, this denial of language, independence and reality to the East is presented in explicitly racist terms; that is, as the basis of a violent colonialism designed to keep the 'dark forces' of Islam in check (Said, 1995, pp. 206–7).

At the beginning of the final section of *Orientalism*, 'Orientalism now', Said reiterates the Foucauldian approach that has guided his study:

> My principal operating assumptions were . . . that fields of learning, as much as the works of the most eccentric artist, are constrained and acted upon by society, by cultural traditions, by worldly circumstance, and by stabilizing influences like schools, libraries, and governments; moreover, that both learned and imaginative writing are never free, but limited in their imagery, assumptions and intentions; and finally, that the advances made by a 'science' like Orientalism in its academic form are less objectively true than we often like to think. In short, my study hitherto has tried to describe the *economy* that makes Orientalism a coherent subject matter, even while allowing that as an idea, concept, or image the word *Orient* has a considerable and interesting cultural resonance in the West. (Said, 1995, pp. 201–2)

Several important issues emerge here. First we must understand that Orientalism, in Said's sense of the term, is constituted as a discourse, or body of knowledge, that is produced under the material conditions of Western domination over the East. The condition of the appearance of the Orient within the social, economic and linguistic culture of the West, in other words, is a body of knowledge which derives from the strategic demands of colonial domination. Second, we must recognize that the power/knowledge relation inscribed in the corporate identity of Orientalism expresses an objectifying logic in which non-Western cultures are stripped of their basic living humanity. As we will see, Said identifies a powerful determination within Western Orientalism towards 'large generalizations' (the 'Arab mind' with its tendency to fixate upon a single idea, the 'Arab body' with its excessive sexuality) which condemn the diversity of Eastern civilization to repeat the timeless categories of Orientalist anthropology. Third, this discursive construction of the Orient has profound consequences for the *relationship* between East and West. For in so far as the identity of 'the Arab' appears as a known and unchangeable essence, the capacity for enlightenment and self-recognition which defines European humanity is denied to Arabic societies. Fourth, the institutional structure of Arabic societies (law, policy, state) are conceived as ultimately subservient to the fundamentalist demands of Islam. And so however much the Arab believes himself to be modern, for the Orientalist, he can never 'outdistance the organizing claims upon him of his origins' (Said, 1995, p. 234).

This general explanatory structure requires some elaboration. For Said, the major Orientalist scholars of the late nineteenth and early twentieth centuries continued to elaborate the disciplinary consensus about the difference between the Orient and Occident. The economy of Louis Massignon's writing, for example, is determined through his belief in the veracity of divine revelation. As a Catholic he believed in the mystical revelation of God through the body of Christ and his religious community, and it was this which influenced his account of Islam as a religion cut off from the presence of the divine. Despite the subtlety of his expositions therefore, Massignon's writing presented Islam as fundamentally opposed to accommodation with the other great monotheisms (Judaism and Christianity), and as destined to remain cut off from the spiritual-religious community mankind. The theological framework of Massignon's writing, in other words, 'assigned the Islamic Orient to an essentially ancient time', and in so doing gave it a 'therapeutic' value for what he perceived as the spiritual degeneration of Western modernity (Said, 1995, pp. 270–1).

H. A. R. Gibb's work on the other hand, is far less subtle, and subtly transgressive, of the corporate structures of Orientalism than Massignon's *Opera Minora*. In his *The Religious Attitude and Life of Islam*, Gibb prosecutes an account of the Islamic faith as an encompassing religious unity which binds the social, cultural and economic life of the Orient together. As a unifying force, Islam is conceived as fundamentally premodern, as an unreflective and superstitious faith whose authority derives from its silent and unfathomable antiquity. East and West therefore, are fundamentally opposed; and as the place of secular enlightenment, the West ought not to impose its ideals of political agency and recognition on the traditional authority of Islam. Indeed, for Gibb, it is only in so far as the Orientalist is able to recognize the destructive effects of Western politics on the religious authority of Islam, that it will be possible to maintain peaceful, cooperative relations between East and West. Much more strongly than in Massignon's work, however, the terms of this relationship are dictated by the disciplinary consensus of Orientalism: the Islamic Orient can only remain what it essentially is (tribal, God-fearing, libidinal, superstitious) through the guiding, administrative authority of the professional Orientalist (Said, 1995, p. 282).

Said concludes his book with an account of the latest phase of Orientalism's disciplinary consensus. Since the end of the Second World War and the displacement of the old colonial powers by the cultural and economic hegemony of the US, Orientalist scholarship has become an explicitly instrumental pursuit. The institutional context in which knowledge about the Orient is produced has shifted away from the Classics departments of European universities and moved to the new disciplines of Area Studies and Regional Geography established in the US. What is significant about this shift towards a social scientific approach to the Arab world, is that it corresponds to the growth of American interest in and influence upon the Middle East. Put simply, the knowledge about the social, economic, religious and political life of Arab societies that is produced in Anglo-American universities, has a high practical utility for the economists, foreign policy experts and military commanders who determine the friends and the enemies of the West.

One of the guiding threads of Said's' argument is that Orientalism, in its European colonialist form, has presented the Islamic world as a spiritual-theological monolith incapable of either modernization or self-representation. What Said's account of the latest phase of Orientalism remarks therefore, is the *continuity* between the European tradition of Orientalist scholarship and the orthodoxy established in American Arab and Islamic studies (Said, 1995, pp. 300–1). In its final American phase therefore, Orientalism has become the instrument of truth: a discursive practice which informs policy towards 'the Arab' as an ontological-theological-psychoanalytical type, whose relations with the West are determined by his unchangeable essence. To write about the Arab Oriental world is 'to write with the unquestioning certainty of absolute truth backed by absolute force' (Said, 1995, p. 307). Ultimately, this unequal power of textual production means that the West, or more precisely America, is able to disseminate Orientalist ideology across the putative borders of Orient and Occident. For in so far as the most gifted indigenous students are forced to attend the centres of excellence established in American universities, the received wisdom of Orientalism finds its way into the social, economic and political life of 'the Orient' itself (*ibid.*, p. 323).

Said's reading of authors as diverse as Marx, Flaubert, Disraeli, Renan and Chateaubriand attempts to flesh out historical relationships between 'the author' as he operates within the social, economic and cultural conditions of the present, 'the text' as it is produced as a disciplinary orthodoxy, and 'the Orient' as the signifier of a timeless propensity towards despotism, sexual excess and superstition (Said, 1995, pp. 201–2). However, Said's approach to the disciplinary consensus of Orientalism does not simply reproduce Foucault's genealogical method: it is intended as a Gramscian corrective to what he conceived as his 'curiously passive and sterile view of how and why power is gained, used, and held on to' (Said, 1978, p. 710). The elaboration of the micro structures of power presented in Foucault's genealogies, in other words, distract him from the geopolitical inequalities that exist between economies, cultures and ideologies (*ibid.*, p. 711). To understand the geopolitical function of 'Orient' and 'Occident' therefore, it is essential to recognize that, as signifiers, each is part of a 'positional superiority, which puts the Westerner in a whole series of possible relationships with the Orient without ever losing him the relative upper hand' (Said, 1995, p. 7).

We can infer then that Said's remarks on the nominalism and Eurocentrism of Foucault's genealogies apply with even greater force to deconstruction. For if it is true that Foucault's genealogical accounts of power/knowledge demand to be situated within a Gramscian analysis of hegemony, then we must assume that for Said, the critical practice of deconstruction remains irredeemably foreign to the present geopolitical demands of Marxism. This, of course, returns us to Derrida's reading of Marx, and to the whole question of 'the politics of deconstruction' as it is expounded in his later writing. And so it is to this question, with all of its 'cosmopolitcal' implications, that we must turn.

As Said has correctly pointed out, the principal aim of deconstruction is to disclose the mythology of presence: to bring the enunciation of all its cognates (being, nature, the Idea) back to the textual economy in which they are deployed. However, what Said misses in Derrida's writing, and what is made explicit in his later work on the possibility of the political, is the 'dual responsibility' which we, as Westerners, have inherited. On the one hand we must recognize that we cannot think 'outside' of the metaphysical categories through which our being and identity are organized, while on the other, we must also recognize that metaphysics, conceived as a graphological economy cannot acknowledge the unifying devices which it deploys. Thus, for Derrida, the possibility of political reflection lies between the 'saying' and the 'said' of the logos; between the textual inscription of the law as presence (totality, necessity, identity) and its dispersal into particular forms of legislation, recognition and authority. Ultimately, then, ethical and political reflection is a response to the other as he or she is included in, erased from or secondarized by the ontic necessity of the law; a response whose possibility is always reopened by the differentiation of the logos into the institutional and geopolitical conditions of power.

We are now beginning to get a sense of how deconstruction, far from neglecting the 'contract' between textuality and power, makes this relationship central to its account of ethical and political responsibility. Said, we have seen, argues that Derrida's criticism 'moves *into* the text, Foucault's *in* and *out* of it' (Said, 1978, p. 674); that Foucault's reading method focuses on the relationship between institutional power and textual production rather than simply expounding the internal economy of text, identity and *différance*. This formation of the difference between Foucault and Derrida, however, fails to register the possibility that the movement *in* and *out* of the text described in Foucault's writing, can only take place through the cultural inscription of the logos. The horizon of the present, in other words, is always designated through the metaphysics of identity, the inscription of the law and the question of being: and so we can properly understand the institutional and disciplinary powers that Foucault presents in his genealogies, only by reference to the philosophical categories inscribed in Western culture. Thus, for Derrida, Foucault's construction of the (carceral) relationship of power, knowledge and subjectivity presupposes a particular utilitarian organization of time and being; an organization which threatens to overwhelm the possibility of both ethical and political responsibility.

The suspicion that Foucault's genealogical method might be complicit with the carceral logic it describes, however, is not exclusive to deconstruction. In his essay 'Foucault and the imagination of power', Said remarks that:

> I wouldn't go as far as to say that Foucault rationalized power, or that he legitimized its domination . . ., but I would say that his interest in domination was critical but not finally contestatory, or as oppositional as on the surface it seems to be. (Said, in Couzens-Hoy, 1986, p. 152)

Within a strictly Foucauldian register, in other words, the imagination of power is confined to a productive logic in which the extant form of domination produces new strategies of power, as well as a speculative extension of power to every conceivable fold of culture and subjectivity (*ibid.*, p. 151). Anything beyond this carceral logic (the imagination of an oppositional power, or of 'a range of things that cannot be commanded by a form of power that exists at present') remains 'insurgent and utopian'; for even the visionary imaginings of figures like Nietzsche and de Sade are ultimately absorbed into the productive rationality of the system (*ibid.*). Said's recourse to Gramsci's' notion of hegemony, therefore, should be viewed in the context of Foucault's infinite codification of the power/ knowledge relationship. For in so far as Gramsci conceived the ideology of liberal capitalism as 'the terrain where men become conscious of themselves and their tasks', his analyses focused on the construction of a shifting yet relatively stable consensus between economically dominant and subordinate groups. Implicit in this notion of consensus is a shift away from the idea that capitalism is essentially a coercive system, founded on the ruling class's monopolization of the state and the means of violence. It is the cultural leadership of the bourgeoisie in the sphere of civil society, in other words, that has become crucial to the maintenance of hegemony (Gramsci, 1998, pp. 238–9). Unlike Foucault, however, Gramsci did not equate the ideological productivity of the bourgeoisie with an immediate and inevitable extension of domination; for any exercise of power, in so far as it takes place within the established cultural forms of consensus, instigates a self-conscious response from the subaltern groups upon whom power is exercised. Hegemony, in other words, operates through negotiation and concession, and it is through this educative process that the masses may eventually become the agents of revolutionary change.

Said returns to the concept of hegemony in one of his more recent books. He argues that the 'anglophonic tradition' of writing, with all its continuities, contradictions, tensions and local and national conflicts, is a community bound together under the hegemonic influence of the US. The idea of 'deformation' which Said deploys in *Culture and Imperialism* therefore, refers to the cultural production of this anglophonic community, to the caricatures of Islam, Arabia and Japan through which the West has been able to reproduce the being of its 'others' (Said, 1994, p. 371). The task of mapping these deformations, however, is not, for Said, the Foucauldian one of simply codifying the expanding dominion of power and disciplinarity. Rather, it is closer to Adorno's tracing of a possible community beyond the reifying effects of instrumental reason; a community which responds with compassion for whoever is subject to the ruinous, mechanical caricatures of modern humanity (*ibid.*, p. 371).

For Adorno, 'nothing is innocuous' in modern culture: every technological reproduction or intensification of identity is also an exclusion, a silencing or an erasure of our humanity. The production of the national and ethnic identities which Said expounds in *Orientalism* and *Culture and Imperialism* can be read as part of this Adornian history of barbarism and reification. As we have seen, the canonical British and French expositions of Orient and Occident, Islam and Christianity, have been assimilated into America's cultural and economic domination of the globe. This domination cannot be properly understood within the spatial, temporal and geopolitical parameters of nineteenth- and twentieth-century imperialism; for in so far as the dynamics of hegemony have shifted away from the direct subjugation of the colonized towards the corporate-technological manipulation of culture, the artist and the intellectual must reckon with the hierarchy of dominant and subordinate identities to which this manipulation gives rise. The 'exilic experience' which Said traces in *Culture and Imperialism* then, lies close to the refusal of identity thinking that Adorno sets out in *Negative Dialectics*. For while he accepts that human beings can never escape the totalizing effects of mass culture (reification, objectification, fungibility), he also maintains that it is just these effects which provoke the cosmopolitan testimonies (in art, literature, film and poetry) in which our shared humanity is traced. The 'exile' of the artist or the intellectual, in other words, responds to a global reification of culture, for it is his or her refusal of the absolute privilege of East or West, Christianity or Islam, modernization or postmodernity, that opens the possibility of a reflective political activism (Said, 1994, p. 406).

This vision of power and resistance, of the assertion of a more human reality over against the distorting powers of the world market and mass culture, raises the question of the critical space occupied by Said's' work. Benita Parry has argued that Said's' critique 'never relinquishes the search for signs of colonial and post-colonial self-affirmation', and that his writing is pledged to a future in which 'transnational cross-fertilization will produce new formations' (Sprinker, 1992, pp. 41–2). Parry has also claimed that Said's pursuit of the traces of a common humanity within the corporate, state and military productions of East and West, anchors his critique in a political reality that is missed by the limitless scepticism of deconstruction. What I want to suggest, however, is that the 'reality' of global-technological capitalism has both transformed and transgressed the geopolitical structures (particularly the nation state and civil society) through which Said understands the logic of cultural production and political hegemony. And that perhaps his work, by underplaying the spectralizing effects of new media technologies, is unable to register the political questions that arise from the global dispersion, reintegration and erasure of humanity. We need then, to look at how Derrida approaches the question of cosmopolitan responsibility within the global-technological economy of capitalism.

Globalization and Cosmopolitanism

For Derrida, if we are to understand the concept of Western culture, we must attend to the metaphysical structures (autochthony, ethics, friendship) through which its internal difference has been gathered into a universal 'heading' for all humanity (Derrida, 1992, pp. 27–8). The law to which this historical reproduction conforms is that of supplementarity; for in so far as it is the metaphysical resources of spirit which found the specifically European mediations of culture, subjectivity and law, these resources remain 'excessive' of all their possible configurations of being and collective identity. The concept of spirit, in other words, functions as the 'incomparable condition' of European culture; it is that which determines the inscription of its own universality within the hierarchical structures of ethical life (nation, culture, language, morality). It is this necessity (of spirit's reinscribing itself in the 'substance' of European culture) that is designated in *The Other Heading* by the term 'exemplarity'. For even though Derrida insists that we must respect all of the differences that distinguish Hegel, Husserl, Heidegger and Valéry in their respective accounts of the spiritual unity of Europe, it remains the case that, in general, the resources of spirit are 'linked to the logic of an *exemplarity* that inscribes the universal in the proper body of a singularity' (*ibid.*, p. 72). The gathering of Europe into the place of universal culture and enlightenment therefore, is accomplished through this logic; the logic in which a particular language or culture is presented as the true expression of transformative, emancipatory necessity. For example, when Paul Valéry announces that his 'personal impression' of France is of a people whose 'special quality is to believe and feel that we are universal', he is announcing the exemplarity of France in relation both to the gathering excessiveness of spirit, and to the 'spiritual' totality of an enlightened European culture (*ibid.*, p. 74). The same logic can be said to characterize Hegel's presentation of spirit's relationship to the ethical structures of the Prussian state, and Heidegger's account of the proximity of the German language to the question of Being. Thus, for Derrida, it is spirit 'that marks the day of all our days, of all our gestures, discourses and affects'; for it is that which, in its infinite excessiveness, constantly re-emerges as the 'newness' of every new, enlightened modernity.

It is in *The Other Heading* that Derrida announces the 'axiom' that 'what is proper to a culture is not to be identical with itself'. Thus, when we talk about the 'identity' of a particular culture (in this case the legislative, capitalizing spirit of European humanity), we must recognize that such an identity is never fully present to itself, and that its constitution as the 'subject' of moral, ethical and political activity always depends upon a certain inescapable difference from itself. As Derrida puts it:

> There is no culture or cultural identity without this difference *with itself*. A strange and slightly violent syntax: 'with itself' also means 'at home (with itself)'. In this case, self difference . . ., that which differs and diverges from itself, would also be the *difference (from) with itself*, a difference at once internal and irreducible to the 'at home (with itself)'. In truth, it would gather this centre, relating it to itself, only to the extent that it would open it up to this divergence. (Derrida, 1992, pp. 9–10, original emphasis)

Now, we have seen that the logic of exemplification which 'unites' the great expositors of European identity also involves a certain dispersion which cannot be recuperated in any higher, more universal writing of spirit. And so the categories through which spirit's self-presence is written, reproduce European culture as an essentially conflictual 'saying' which gathers difference into an economy of legislations, forces, coercions and resistances. We can, for example, understand the Nazi designation of 'culture creators' (Aryans), 'culture users' (non-Aryan white Europeans) and 'culture destroyers' (Jews) as an enunciation of 'spirit', which sought to purify the place of its own self-recognition (the German nation state and ultimately the continent of Europe) in the project of absolute, ontological violence. Yet even this genocidal gathering of 'true' humanity into the body of the German *Volk* demands to be understood in terms of the history of spirit; that is, in terms of the disparate and dissonant discourses of race, eugenics, blood and nation that have determined the history of twentieth-century Europe (Derrida, 1990a, p. 109).The ethical stricture that has emerged 'after Auschwitz', in other words, demands that we attend to the religious, philosophical, economic and political forms which 'gather' the realm of culture; forms whose homogenizing power constantly transform the otherness (Islam, the Arab, the Oriental) which founds, and continues to haunt, Western constructions of identity. This reproduction of alterity is essential to Derrida's understanding of international law and cosmopolitan politics. For if it is acknowledged that the capitalizing resources of spirit, as they are empowered and revitalized by the the techno-economic powers of modernity, are neither absolutely realized nor absolutely dissipated by those powers, then our duty towards the others of the European heading must take the form of a reflection which, while respecting 'all that is not placed under the authority [Western] of reason', also remains respectful of the ideals of liberty, equality and justice that inspired the Enlightenment project. As Derrida puts it, our uniquely European responsibility 'dictates respecting differences, idioms, minorities, singularities, but also the universality of formal law, the desire for translation, agreement and univocity, the law of the majority, opposition to racism, nationalism, and xenophobia' (Derrida, 1992, p. 79).

Derrida thematizes the relationship between the 'where' of enlightenment (the place in which the philosophy of spirit inscribes and reinscribes the essence of humanity), and the expansive, colonizing trajectory of European culture through the terms *la capitale* and *le capital*. The first of these terms, the feminine *la capitale*, refers to the problem of constituting a centre, a fixed, determinate core of self-presence, from which the essence of humanity would venture as a universally enlightening, universally liberating force. We have seen that for Kant, this venturing out of the place of enlightenment should take the form of reproducing the conditions of confederal responsibility which are revealed as legislative within the theatre of European identity. Thus, the emergence of republican states from the violence which originally formed the nations of Europe, is linked a priori to the end of conserving the moral culture which had already begun to emerge within those nations. The concept of a legislative centre therefore, is disclosed in Kant's political thought as a 'gathering' of the *sensus communis* (the 'community' of subjective universal feelings which respond to the Idea of freedom) within those states that are already most respectful of the ideals of autonomous humanity and reflective citizenship. For Derrida, however, this account of the signs which mark historical progress (those expressions of pure, disinterested enthusiasm which register the primacy of will and reason in human affairs), could only prefigure the politics of exemplification which becomes fully explicit in the categories of spirit. Such a politics, we have seen, involves the presupposition of a transcategorial essence, whose necessity is the inscription and reinscription of itself within the determinate, hierarchical structures which organize national, cultural and linguistic hegemony. The gathering of the European centre which is accomplished through spirit's capacity for exemplification, in other words, is originally bound up with the demarcation of stable frontiers and boundaries among those nations which comprise the capital (*la capitale*) of enlightened humanity. It is this assumption of the state, or rather states, as the internally differentiated subjects through which progress towards a universal good is to be achieved, which marks a certain proximity of Kant's political thought to the metaphysical resources of spirit. For the reflective gathering through which European cultural identity is to become legislative 'for all other continents', refers to structures and designations (civil society, republican democracy, formal legality) which are conceived as originally amenable to the transmission of subjective culture and the perpetuation of moral progress.

It is here then, that we begin to encounter the difference between traditional discourses of modernity (those which presuppose the logic of exemplification in which particularized forms of language, nation and race are taken into the hierarchical politics of the centre), and Derrida's account of the 'centralizing compulsions' (expressed in culture industries, the growth of new media, the expansion of techno-scientific powers) which do not necessarily go through the mediation of law and state (Derrida, 1992, p. 36). This circumvention of the structures through which the traditional European politics of capitalization and hegemony has been played out, is important in the sense that it obliges us to re-evaluate our relationship to the legislative resources of the Enlightenment. As Westerners responsible to our own cultural and philosophical history, Derrida insists that we can no longer assume that the realm of 'the political' is adequately expressed in the dialectics of citizenship, participation and sovereignty that are inscribed in the concept of the *polis* (the place of political freedom in which the law is simultaneously given and received by a collectively identical subject) (Bennington, 1994, pp. 240–57). Instead, we must attend to a resurgence of the question of the legislative centre, *la capitale*, that has occurred through the loss of spirit's recuperative inscription in the nation state. The question of the capital which 'we Europeans' have inherited therefore, is that of judging how the global forces of dispersion and monopoly have transformed our experience of political freedom and cultural identity. For Derrida, the stricture that has emerged from this experience of living between the spiritual resources of Western culture and the techno-economic expansion of capital, is that of translation; of attempting to phrase the relationship between the other (as he or she is exposed to the latest forms capitalization, spectralization, displacement) and the increasingly fragile demands of Enlightenment culture and metaphysics.

For Derrida, the conditions of ethical and political responsibility are to be found neither in the 'technico-economico-scientific' powers of monopoly, nor in the dispersal of heterogeneous genres, idioms and nationalities which has occurred through the extension of such powers. The condition of this responsibility is 'a certain *experience and experiment of the possibility of the impossible*', in which the concepts and ideas of Enlightenment thought (self and other, subject and object, friend and enemy) are re-marked in their unforeseen relations to the scientific, technical and economic powers of modernity (Derrida, 1994b, p. 7). If there is a political necessity to defend the right of all human beings to philosophical reflection, therefore, this would begin with the necessity of acknowledging the presuppositions that are inscribed in the discourses of science, technology and economy, and attempting to respond to these presuppositions without repeating the exemplarist logic of the philosophy of spirit. As Derrida puts it:

> [A] politics of the right of philosophy for all (men and women) [would] not be only a politics of science and technology, but also a politics of thought which would yield neither to positivism nor to scientism nor to epistemology, and which would discover again, on the scale of new stakes, in its relation to science but also to religions, and also to law and ethics, an experience which would be at once provocation or reciprocal respect but also irreducible autonomy. (*ibid.*)

Thus, when Derrida asserts at the start of 'The right of philosophy', 'I will begin with the question "where?"'', he is attempting to register a basic legitimacy in the foundation of UNESCO – as a cosmopolitcal institution concerned with the possibility of justice and the application of international law – at the centre of European culture. For while such an institution would always be marked by a certain Eurocentrism, this would at least demand that the globalizing powers of science, technology and economy remain accountable to the structures within which freedom, identity and citizenship have traditionally been enacted.

The impossible stricture of responding to the demands of the other (through translation, acts of literature, the gift) while sustaining the necessity of the logos (spirit, the question of being), returns us to the law of hospitality. For in so far as it is the experience of this aporia that opens the possibility of ethical judgement, we can see that the question of hospitality to 'who comes', stands in direct proximity to the legal and political organization of the nation state. Derrida's particular concern with issues such as the enfranchisement of immigrants in France, for example, is a concern both for the fate of the 'revolutionary ideals' of Western democracy (formal equality, legal rights, universal brotherhood), and for the fate of the other as s/he must live in relation to legislative practices to which his/her alterity has no immediate point of access. As he put in an address to the collective '89 for equality': 'The combat against xenophobia and racism *also* goes by this right to vote. So long as it is not gained, injustice will reign, democracy will be limited to that extent, and the riposte to racism will remain abstract and impotent' (Bennington and Derrida, 1993, p. 352). We can begin therefore, to discern more clearly the economics of marginality and centrality which informs Derrida's account of the 'cosmopolitcal' right of philosophy and its 'indissociable' relationship to the movement of effective democratization (Derrida, 1994b, p. 7). For as long as the European centre remains concretely resistant to the others through which it has sustained its internal hierarchies, international law will tend to foreclose upon the unforeseen events of conflict and alterity through which the immigrant, the asylum seeker, the 'guest worker' would be given their chance of justice.

It is to this chance of participating equally in the determination of the structures, categories and judgements of universal justice, that 'cosmopolitcal' institutions like the United Nations or UNESCO ought to be responsible. Their very foundation, for Derrida, presupposes an ethical demand that Enlightenment ideals should remain infinitely – indeed transcendentally – sensitive to the different cultures, idiolects and singularities which the capitalizing history of Europe has expropriated and erased. For Derrida, it is the figure of the friend who has always disclosed this responsibility to who, or what, may come. Throughout *Politics of Friendship*, his exposition concentrates on the ways in which the responsibilities of friendship have been constructed in Western philosophy, and in particular, its limitation to fraternal relationships between virile young men whose famous deeds found and recall the political authority of the nation state. It is this limitation which, for Derrida, organizes the 'becoming political' of friendship: it marks the point in the Western tradition where the law of hospitality (absolute, unconditional openness to who comes) becomes subject to the different modalities of violence by which the nation sustains itself against the foreigner/enemy. The history of friendship which Derrida writes therefore, is the history of an originary appropriation: the *political* appropriation of the hospitality which founds the synchronic presence of the nation, and which continues to haunt its legal, economic and political designations of identity.

The idea of democracy to come, which Derrida traces throughout his expositions of Aristotle, Nietzsche, Heidegger and Schmitt, is closely related to this founding hospitality. As we have seen, the questions of being and truth as they are posed in Western philosophy, proceed from a certain experience of friendship: a pre-contractual, pre-anthropological, pre-ontological friendship which opens the discourse of political community. In a lecture published as 'What is philosophy?', Heidegger proposed that the logocentric pursuit of Being which is characteristic of Western metaphysics is instituted through questions that belong to the fate of an original unity: to the loss of nature (*physis*) as the revealed foundation of human community, of *philia* (Derrida, 1997, p. 242). Derrida discerns two contradictory but inseparable stands in this approach to metaphysics: the first, which he calls 'fraternocentrism', discloses a continuity between the Greek principle of genealogy and the epochal desire of *Dasein* for home and soil; the second, which Derrida has identified as the promise, discloses the condition of this desire in *Dasein*'s original responsibility to the question of Being (Derrida, 1990, pp. 129–36). Heidegger's approach to

Western philosophy therefore, traces a responsibility that is prior to the discourse of metaphysics: a primordial pledge that opens on the excessiveness of Being and which ought to respond to the absolute contingency of the future (Derrida, 1997, p. 244).

Heidegger's notion of 'being with' (*Mitsein*) is never identical with the legal, contractual or technological norms which have come to determine our sense of identity; for in so far as solicitude for the other begins with *Dasein*'s ownmost questioning of Being, the possibility of authentic friendship always precedes/exceeds the presence of our culture. Now for Derrida, this account of the originary demand of the friend both offers and withdraws the reflective obligation of an ethical politics. Heidegger's determination to approach modernity through a critique of the technological erasure of Being, means that the responsibilities of friendship are ultimately called back to the aesthetic sense of community presented in 'The origin of the work of art' (Heidegger, 1996, pp. 243–312). For Derrida, however, if culture is to be the form through which messianic responsibility is to enter the present, and if this responsibility to who comes is not to be overtaken by technological simulacra, we must remain open to the promise in which 'being-with-others', or culture, originates.

This promise is what Derrida calls the law of hospitality. For if it is the case that culture originates in performative relations with others we encounter as proximate and cognitively unknowable, then ethical and political responsibility originates from beyond the ontological designations of culture as blood, birth and fraternity. For Derrida then, the law of hospitality and the ethical demand are opened simultaneously: the former arises with the inscription of friendship within the ontologies of blood and soil, the latter from the responsibility that is always left 'to come' in this inscription. Thus:

> Hospitality is culture itself and not simply one ethic amongst others. Insofar as it has to do with *ethos*, that is, with residence, one's home, the familiar place of dwelling, in as much as it is a manner of being there, the manner in which we relate to ourselves and to others, to others as our own and as foreigners, ethics is hospitality; ethics is so thoroughly co-extensive with the experience of hospitality. (Derrida, 2001, p. 17)

As we will see, the alterity of self and other which is inscribed in their cultural mediation, bears directly upon the possibility of justice, international law and the administration of human rights – what Derrida, following Kant, calls cosmopolitanism. For if, as Derrida claims, it is the law of hospitality which founds the ethical demand of 'being with' (community, culture, society), then we should understand its history as the history of a certain kind of politics: one in which the absolute demand of the other who comes is violently suppressed in philosophical, anthropological and genealogical designations of friendship and enmity (*ibid.*, p. 17). We need then, to look at Derrida's reading of this politics.

Politics of Friendship is an immensely complex reading of what has remained implicit in the Western democratic tradition: the elective obligations that are treated by Aristotle, Kant, Nietzsche, Heidegger and Schmitt (to name only a few) under the heading of friendship. For Derrida, the importance of this 'personal' sphere lies in its becoming political; in the fact that philosophical discourse on the nature of friendship always bears upon the duties and obligations which true friends owe to the nation state and its citizens. The ideal of 'primary friendship' which Aristotle discusses in the *Eudamian Ethics* for example, is marked by the fact that it stands on the side of form, autonomy and independence, and by the fact that it is *he who loves*, rather than the beloved, who is transfigured by the obligations of friendship (*philia*). The horizon of this unsparing devotion is the eulogy: the speech of celebration and remembrance through which the beloved elevates the name of his protector beyond the simple fatality of death (Derrida, 1997, p. 14). For Aristotle, the uniqueness of such friendships is disclosed in their elective nature: a man cannot have a great many true friends because it is only through time that such friendships distinguish themselves from merely pleasurable company (*ibid.*, p. 19). The question which Aristotle's excursus raises therefore, is that of democracy; or more precisely, of the aporia that arises from the elective singularity of true friendship and the designation of those 'others' who, while they remain under the yoke of being, ought not to be treated merely as things (*ibid.*, p. 21).

It is at this point in Derrida's exposition that we encounter what is perhaps Aristotle's most famous remark on the nature of friendship: 'O my friends there is no friend' (Derrida, 1997, p. 27). As we have seen, the distinction which Aristotle makes between the act of friendship and the passivity of being loved is essential to his account of democracy: for only those who are capable of ennobling their lives through absolute sacrifice (ennoblement through the epitaph) are worthy of governing free citizens. Other forms of pleasurable friendship are important because of their promotion of political harmony; yet for Aristotle, these remain derivative forms which belong to the realm of being rather than political action. This aristocratic designation of friendship is important because it discloses a particular distribution of energy (*energia*) within the classical structures of democracy: a distribution in which it is the limited number of 'superior' friendships that sustains the less energetical consent of ordinary citizens. In its very initiation, Aristotle's discourse on friendship registered the impossibility of including the singular, performative responsibility of friendship within the sphere of political being. The latter, as we have seen, is organized through the genealogical narrative of blood and heroic brotherhood, a narrative which gathers the nation and its institutions within the horizon of collective remembrance (the epitaph). What distinguishes true friendship from this genealogical organization of the polis therefore, is its responsibility to who comes from beyond the fraternal inscription of law, right and duty. It is this transgressive responsibility that is announced in Aristotle's exclamation: for in so far as 'O my friends' appeals to a constituency which cannot be designated

209

genealogically, the responsibility of true friendship is to a future (democracy to come) that is kept open by the alterity of 'who comes' (Derrida, 1997, p. 236).

In chapter four of *Politics of Friendship*, Derrida traces the play of spectres that haunt the European tradition of politics. One of the most powerful of these is the ghost of the illustrious ancestor: the fallen brother immortalized in the founding battles of the nation who returns to the present as the determining condition of political friendship (Derrida, 1997, p. 103). Derrida expounds the logic of this political mourning through a reading of a text of Plato, the *Menexenus*. The figure of Aspasia narrates an epitaph which commands the living to answer for the dead, to imitate the virtue and heroism of their deeds (*ibid.*, p. 95). This returning of the dead to the present is fundamental to the constitution of the state, for it is the epitaph which recalls the urgency of transforming equality of birth (fraternity), into an elective system of laws by which the great rule over the many (aristocracy) (*ibid.*, p, 94). Thus, for Derrida, the classical economy of mourning and political recognition, discloses three elements that have remained fundamental in the Western tradition: necessity, fraternity and elective democracy.

The law of hospitality which Derrida traces throughout his political writings is the law of hospitality to the strangeness of the other who comes to disrupt the satisfactions of (my) political identity. These satisfactions, as we have seen, derive from a certain genealogical construction of politics: the structuring of duty and consent around the collective act of mourning. What is characteristic here, and what continues as a basic theme in Western democracy, is the reproduction of blood and birth as the necessary conditions of belonging to the nation, and of responding 'in one's being' to its demands. This construction of belonging has, of course, always been exposed to the worst excesses of political rhetoric, to the historical violence of xenophobia, nationalism and ethnocentrism (Derrida, 1997, p. 99). However, if we are to understand this economy of violence, we must recognize that the remembrance through which the political sphere is founded, is the commemoration of our fathers. For Derrida, the possibility of suppressing the demand of the other *begins* with the masculine confrontation with being that is dramatized in the mythology of nationhood. And so what is hidden in the Greek act of memory is the erasure of the feminine, the suspension of responsibility to 'she who comes' in the fraternal injunction: 'fight for the freedom won by your illustrious fathers' (*ibid.*, p. 101). This, of course, begs the question of democracy; for in so far as fraternal citizenship begins with the erasure of the feminine (female desire, sisterhood), we are immediately referred to the legal, economic and technological foreclosures through which the other retains its messianic demand.

Nietzsche's appearance in Derrida's discourse on friendship marks a vigorous, libidinal registration of this haunting of fraternal democracy by its others. He argued that since Plato and Aristotle, Western culture has precipitated a tragic involution of 'life': a fixation upon irresolvable questions of conscience at the expense of the transfiguring experiences of joy, suffering, pain. In his *Human, All Too Human*, he refers this historical gathering of culture around the metaphysics of identity, subjectivity and equality to the unforeseeable events of suffering and desire which it precipitates (Derrida, 1997, p. 28). Such events, for Nietzsche, are received by those men who live beyond the present economy of desire; the 'philosophers of the future' who intensify the 'perhaps' that is insistent in the ontology of the present. The Greek and Christian metaphysics of friendship therefore, mark a particular kind of 'becoming political' of virtue, morality and obligation: they designate democracy as an 'operative' (proximate, erotic) space whose future is inscribed in the repetitive permutations of desire and possession. The question which Nietzsche poses for the Western tradition therefore, is this: what is the nature, and what is the chance, of a 'higher' friendship which is not determined through the Greco-Christian economics of possessive desire (Derrida, 1997, p. 62).

Three themes are brought together in Nietzsche's interruption of the Western tradition: the messianic demand of the other; the haunting of 'possessive' culture by events of alterity; and the possibility of a higher friendship responsible to who is to come in the future. The 'living fool' whose disruptive unreason Nietzsche exhorts in *Human, All Too Human*, is the figure of humanity made responsible to the dangerous truth of the 'perhaps': he (such fools are always men, always brothers) is responsible to the absolute futurity of what is to come; his vocation is to live in the wicked truth of Nietzsche's inversion of value, and to solicit the arrival of those new philosophers who precipitate the rupture of past, present and future. Now, we know that for Derrida the libidinal economy of Nietzsche's solicitation of the perhaps remains phallocentric; the community of friends responsible to who comes is a fraternal gathering turned away from the 'possessive desires' of the feminine. This foreclosure, however, cannot exclude itself from the economy of events; it is an enactment of authority that provokes, along with every other suppression of difference, the messianic demand for justice. Once the law of hospitality exceeds the masculine, libidinized expression given to it by Nietzsche, therefore, it immediately discloses its cosmopolitical structure. For in so far as it is originally turned to the other in the events of habitation (sharing, the gift, familial relations), its horizon has always been that of translation, of receiving the other without erasing his or her difference.

For Derrida, Nietzsche's rupturing of the desires, satisfactions and consolations of possessive democracy, anticipates both the messianic demand of justice and the spectralization of 'the real' that characterizes our technological modernity. If there is to be a law of hospitality to the other, and if this law is possible between the cultural, philosophical and religious accumulations of 'East' and 'West', then its events must take place within the accelerated time of technological capitalism. Ultimately, then, the difference between Derrida and Said's accounts of hegemony and cosmopolitical responsibility, hinges on the intensification of those cultural simulacra through which Orient and Occident appear as political events. Derrida's claim is that the encounter between East and West has become a geopolitical spectacle that is staged through the simulacra of religious orthodoxy, original territorial rights, and the duties of Enlightenment; and so his critique of international law is focused on the conflicts through which Western culture recuperates its identity against its originary other (Derrida, 1997, p. 89). The Gulf War, for example, was prosecuted on the basis of the 'inalienable right' of Kuwait to exist: a right which, for the Western allies, defined the difference between a modern Islamic state (a 'friend' to the West, a responsible oil exporter) and the evil forces of Islam massed in Sadam's Iraq. Justice for those dangerous spectres (Hamas, Islamic Jehad, al Qaida) who arise in the Orient therefore, depends upon the media-technological conditions which seem to make it impossible: for in so far as their representations always raise the question of my own culture and my own identity, the responsibility of friendship, and so of forgiveness, reconciliation and international law, always remerges within the cultural violence of capitalism.

To conclude, then, I want to look briefly at the ways in which two of the theorists we have examined – Jean-François Lyotard and Jean Baudrillard – have approached the question of cosmopolitan responsibility, and to suggest how Derrida might respond to their arguments. We have seen that, for Derrida, the ethical and political responsibility that comes with 'being European' must find its way experimentally between the claims of 'monopoly' (whether these are expressed in the terms of Marxism, or 'free market' economics, or techno-scientism) and those of 'dispersal' (as they are presented in certain forms of postcolonialist and postmodernist theories of difference). Such a responsibility demands that we attend to the thoughts, concepts and categories of global politics, as forms that remain complicit either with the 'colonizing' values of European culture, or with the 'anti-colonialism' sustained through the registration of supposedly untranslatable singularities of culture, nationality and ethnicity. For Derrida neither of these polarities are adequate to the cosmopolitical demand of the other: for as we will see, their theoretical expression tends to obscure the messianic possibility of democracy to come.

Lyotard's account of the proliferation of expert knowledges that is characteristic of the postmodern condition, is linked to a particular understanding of the question of being. The onset of modernity is characterized as the acceleration of processes of 'shattering and invention': the reality of established moral, ethical, economic and political structures is constantly revolutionized by new forms of knowledge and technical practice (Lyotard, 1991b, p. 77). This labile and contingent temporality has, according to Lyotard, reached the point at which it is no longer credible to insist upon the ontological foundations of the social. For in so far as political discourses which have sought to establish unity on the basis of the race, the nation and the brotherhood have tended to reduce their 'others' to silent and unregistered suffering, we are faced with the (ethical) necessity of phrasing this silence without recourse to the totalizing categories of being. This theme of the radical autonomy of judgement is developed more fully in *The Differend*. In the third of his 'Kant notices', Lyotard attempts to show that Kant's appeal to feelings of agitation as analoga, or signs, of the transcendental unity of Freedom and Nature, gestures towards a reception of difference that remains independent of all established 'genres' of moral, political and economic 'necessity' (Lyotard, 1988, pp. 130–5). The possibility of this reception, in other words, is always co-present with the heterogeneous knowledges that both maintain and disperse the social bond; for it is with the 'unphraseable' feelings of disquiet at the suffering of those who lack any recognition within the dominant discourses of authority, that the ethical moment arises as a performative demand. However, this idea of an affective response whose 'phrasing' (saying, aesthetic expression) would be the event of autonomous judgement is problematic: for its transgression of the structures and mediations of the law, determines a kind of moral sensitivity in which dispersion is valorized in relation to the 'democratic' organization of being.

We should recall here that Derrida's reading of Nietzsche in *Politics of Friendship*, is concerned with his designation of a responsibility to the future that cannot be discharged within the economics of possessive individualism. Those 'free spirits' who are strong enough to live with the transgressive demand of the perhaps are 'friends' whose community is 'without common measure': they live as singularities whose free will always exceeds the ontological resources of bourgeois democracy (Derrida, 1997, p. 37). This Nietzschean dispersal of the messianic demand into an 'inoperative community' of friends, is both necessary and aporetic: for while it discloses the impossibility of organizing democracy around the present economy of desire, it also tends to 'caricature' the complex mediations of difference and alterity accomplished within that economy (*ibid.*, p. 38). There is a sense then in which Lyotard's account of the affective responses through which the metanarratives of law, identity and nationhood are subverted, reproduces this tendency to caricature. For in giving absolute priority to those affections that register the alterity of the other, Lyotard's thought remains complicit with a certain anti-colonialist account of difference, in which the categories of philosophical reason appear simply as totalitarian; as violently expropriative of the cultural, material and linguistic forms which live beyond the European centre (Lyotard, 1988, p. 235). If we refer back to Derrida's notion of absolute hospitality, therefore, it seems that Lyotard's thought does not simply obscure the cosmopolitan demands of our globalized economy; it rather confirms the urgency of the question of being, and its proximity to the messianic demand of friendship to who comes.

Baudrillard's account of simulation, however, raises a different set of issues. The principal claim of his middle and later work has been that the mass media have cut short the processes of mediation and recognition that are assumed in liberal democratic theories of politics. New media technologies do not revitalize the dialogical potential of the public sphere, for once they reach a certain level of saturation, the reflective citizen is overtaken by a constant flow of heterogeneous, escalatory and reversible simulacra. The major consequence of this simulation of reality, according to Baudrillard, has been to abolish any reflexive relationship between the citizen, considered as the addressee of social and political norms, and the representative institutions of liberal democracy (Baudrillard, 1996, p. 214). For in so far as the masses are constantly solicited by the simulacra of sex, beauty, love, morality and suffering, they have become the condition *and the failure* of the social: they both conduct and short-circuit the economy of pure, frictionless simulation through which the social has been hyperrealized. This brings us to the question of 'monopoly' as it is posed in Derrida's writing. As we have seen, the concept of politics that arises from deconstruction concerns the possibility of discharging a dual responsibility: of responding to the demand that the singularity of the other 'who comes' should be allowed a transformative power within the capitalizing structures of Western thought and culture. This possibility, according to Derrida, is the origin of the social; for in so far as culture begins with a fragile and unstable mediation of the other, the law of hospitality is always co-present with the *colonialist* satisfactions of being-at-home-with-oneself. The evil possibility that Baudrillard's account of simulation reveals therefore, is that the law of hospitality (which Derrida conceives as the law beyond the formal organization of legality) has been hyperrealized: that the possibility of its reception in the public sphere has been totally monopolized by the mass media. Indeed, it is just this possibility that Baudrillard explores in his account of 'catastrophe management'. His claim is that the total simulation of the real that has occurred in the 'developed' half of the world, has led to a situation in which the West cannot function without the spectacle of Third World poverty that is presented in the media. Western nations, in other words, need human catastrophes like Bangladesh, or Rwanda, or Kosovo, constantly to re-establish the ethical necessity of their political order. As Baudrillard puts it:

> We [in the West] are the consumers of the ever delightful spectacle of poverty and catastrophe, and of the moving spectacle of our own efforts to alleviate it (which, in fact, merely function to secure the conditions of the reproduction of the catastrophe market). (Baudrillard, 1995b, p. 67)

What this means is that, for Baudrillard, the 'others' who come from beyond the borders of the West have become part of the economy of simulation, and that the messianic demand of their coming (the demand which for Derrida is the very possibility of democracy to come) is lost in the infinite cycle of disaster and 'charitable condescension' (*ibid.*, p. 66).

My final remark, then, returns to the problem of totality and infinity: to the possibility of salvaging the infinite demand of the other (his or her ethical significance) from the monopolistic powers of tele-technological capitalism. In Baudrillard's work, these powers are approached through the concept of the hyperreal: the idea that the mass media have precipitated the dialectics of the social, its moral, ethical, political and aesthetic relationships, into an infinite circulation of signs. Thus, in so far as *every* apprehension of truth, beauty and humanity is given through its simulacrum (Hollywood movies, fashion, TV and video, prosthetic enhancement), the enactment of ethical responsibility is absorbed into the hyperreality of the social. The evil possibility addressed in Baudrillard's work therefore, is that a catastrophe has befallen the West; a catastrophe which, because its nature has been secretly to undermine the dialectical foundations of the real, has fatally ruptured the ethical relations between friendship, philosophy and politics (Baudrillard, 1996, p. 190). For Derrida, on the other hand, this Baudrillardian economy of the hyperreal is precisely what conditions our obligation to the other who comes from beyond the West. The 'spectralizing effects' (of duplication, disintegration, displacement) that he or she suffers in the media, determines the *chance* of an ethical response; of a singular, 'inoperative' experience of alterity that demands justice and asks forgiveness (Derrida, 2001, pp. 55–8). It is through this experience then, that the temporal logic of simulation might perhaps be interrupted; for such moments of unpreparedness before the plight of the other continue to recall the 'old' questions of philosophy (what is the nature of friendship? how should I receive the other into my culture? what is the relationship between justice, autonomy and the law?) to 'the day' of our living present.

Notes

1. In *Postmodern Ethics*, Bauman expresses the outcome of this extraterritorial migration of capital through a model developed by Alf Hornborg (Bauman, 1993, pp. 212–13). Hornborg's argument is that the most developed societies in the global economy are best understood as thermodynamic systems that require more and more energy to sustain their complex technological integration. It is a fundamental law, Hornborg points out, that the most complex thermodynamic systems cannot meet their energy needs from their internal resources, and so the mobility of technological capital is, from the beginning, dedicated to the maintenance of socio-economic systems whose basic tendency is the dissipation of energy and the breakdown of their own internal order. Understood in these terms, the weak and unstable sovereignties that have proliferated in the Third World become the 'grazing fields' of global capital: their own order-giving resources are ravaged by its chaotic intrusions into the fabric of the locality.

2. This conception of 'the Orient' as having already made its contribution to the sum of human enlightenment is obvious both in Kant's 'Idea for a universal history with a cosmopolitan purpose' (Kant, 1991, pp. 41–53) and the 'General determinations' of 'Africa', 'Asia' and 'Europe' set out in Hegel's *Introduction to the Lectures on the Philosophy of World History* (Hegel, 1980, pp. 152–96). For Said, however, it is Marx's account of 'Oriental despotism' which most clearly discloses the extent to which Orientalist representations of the East have determined Western ideals of progress and civilization (1977d, pp. 332–6). For

Marx, it was only through the instrument of British colonial rule, with its importation of modern industries, technologies and bureaucracies, that the feudalistic despotism of India and of Asia in general, could begin to emerge into the transformative dynamics set out in historical materialism. If there was to be a world revolution, in other words, Western colonialism would first have to create a world proletariat, freed from the superstition and dependency that characterized the peoples of the East (Said, 1995, pp. 153–7).

3. See, for example, Lyotard's account of the 'wrong' that always results from this 'speaking for' the other, from the silencing of those narratives, idiolects and phrasings which open the ethical demand of the name (of the plaintiff) and of the event (Lyotard, 1988, p. 12).

Bibliography

Abbinnett, R. (1998a) *Truth and Social Science: From Hegel to Deconstruction*. London: Sage.

Abbinnett, R. (1998b) 'Postmodernity and the ethics of care: situating Bauman's social theory', *Cultural Values*, 2 (1): 87–116.

Abbinnett, R. (1998c) 'Politics and Enlightenment: Kant and Derrida on cosmopolitan responsibility', *Citizenship Studies*, 2 (2): 197–220.

Abbinnett, R. (2000), 'Science, technology and modernity: Beck and Derrida on the politics of risk', *Cultural Values*, 4 (1): 101–26.

Adorno, T. W. (1990) *Negative Dialectics*, trans. E. B. Ashton. London: Routledge.

Adorno, T. W. (1991) *The Culture Industry*. London: Routledge.

Adorno, T. W. (1996) *Minima Moralia*, trans. E. N. F. Jephcott. London: Verso.

Adorno, T. W. (1999) *Aesthetic Theory*, trans. Robert Hullot-Kentor. London: Athlone Press.

Adorno, T. W. and Horkheimer, M. (1986) *Dialectic of Enlightenment*, trans. John Cumming. New York: Continuum.

Adorno. T. W. *et al.* (1977) *Aesthetics and Politics*. London: Verso.

Barnett, S. (ed.) (1998) *Hegel After Derrida*. London: Routledge.

Baudrillard, J. (1980), 'Forgetting Foucault', *Humanities in Society*, (3) 1.

Baudrillard, J. (1983) *In the Shadow of the Silent Majorities*, trans. Paul Foss, John Johnston and Paul Patton. New York: Semiotext(e).

Baudrillard, J. (1993) *Baudrillard Live: Selected Interviews*. London: Routledge.

Baudrillard, J. (1995a) *The Transparency of Evil: Essays in Extreme Phenomena*, trans. James Benedict. London: Verso.

Baudrillard, J. (1995b) *The Illusion of the End*, trans. Chris Turner. Cambridge: Polity Press.

Baudrillard, J. (1996) *Jean Baudrillard: Selected Writings*, ed. Mark Poster. Cambridge: Polity Press.

Baudrillard, J. (1999) *Simulacra and Simulation*, trans. Sheila Faria Glaser. Michigan: University of Michigan Press.

Bauman, Z. (1991) *Modernity and the Holocaust*. Cambridge: Polity Press.

Bauman, Z. (1993) *Postmodern Ethics*. Cambridge: Polity Press.

Bauman, Z. (1998) *Globalization: The Human Consequences*. Cambridge: Polity Press.

Bauman, Z. and Tester, K. (2001) *Conversations With Zygmunt Bauman*. Cambridge: Polity Press.

Beardsworth, R. (1998) 'Thinking technicity', *Cultural Values*, 2 (1): 70–85.

Beardsworth, R. (1996) *Derrida and the Political*. London: Routledge.

Beck, U. (1996a) *Risk Society: Towards a New Modernity*. London: Sage.

Beck, U. (1996b) 'World risk society as cosmopolitan society? Ecological questions in a framework of manufactured uncertainty', *Theory, Culture and Society*, 13 (2): 1–31.

Benjamin, A. (ed.) (1992) *Judging Lyotard*. London: Routledge.

Benjamin, W. (1992) *Illuminations*, trans. H. Zohn. London: Fontana.

Benjamin, W. (1997a) *Walter Benjamin: Selected Writings Volume One: 1913–1926*, eds Marcus Bullock and Michael W. Jennings. Cambridge, MA: Belknap Press of Harvard University Press.

Benjamin, W. (1997b) *One Way Street*, trans. Edmund Jephcott. London: Verso.

Benjamin, A. and Osborn, P. (eds) (2000) *Walter Benjamin's Philosophy: Destruction and Experience*. Manchester: Clinamen Press.

Bennington, G. (1994) *Legislations: The Politics of Deconstruction*. London: Verso.

Bennington, G. (1988) *Lyotard: Writing the Event*. Manchester: University of Manchester Press.

Bennington, G. and Derrida, J. (1993) *Jacques Derrida*, trans. Geoffrey Bennington. Chicago: University of Chicago Press.

Bernesconi, R. and Wood, D. (eds) (1988) *The Provocation of Levinas*. London: Routledge.

Boyne, R. (1990) *Foucault and Derrida: The Other Side of Reason*. London: Unwin Hyman.

Brodersen, M. (1997) *Walter Benjamin: A Biography*, trans. Malcolm R. Green and Ingrida Ligers. London: Verso.

Butler, R. (1999) *Jean Baudrillard: The Defence of the Real*. London: Sage.

Caygill, H. (1998) *Walter Benjamin: The Colour of Experience*. London: Routledge.

Couzens-Hoy, D. (ed.) (1986) *Foucault: A Critical Reader*. Oxford: Blackwell.

Critchley, S. (1999) *The Ethics of Deconstruction: Derrida and Levinas*. Edinburgh: Edinburgh University Press.

Deleuze, G. (1983) *Kant's Critical Philosophy: The Doctrine of the Faculties*, trans. Barbara Haberjam and Hugh Tomlinson. London: Athlone Press.

Derrida, J. (1976) *Of Grammatology*, trans. Gayatri Spivak. Baltimore: Johns Hopkins University Press.

Derrida, J. (1981) *Positions*, trans. Alan Bass. Chicago: University of Chicago Press.

Derrida, J. (1982) *The Margins of Philosophy*, trans. Alan Bass. New York: Harvester Wheatsheaf.

Derrida, J. (1990a) *Of Spirit: Heidegger and the Question*, trans. Geoffrey Bennington and Rachel Bowlby. Chicago: University of Chicago Press.

Derrida, J. (1990b) *Writing and Difference*, trans. Alan Bass. London: Routledge.

Derrida, J. (1992) *The Other Heading: Reflections on Today's Europe*, trans. Pascale-Anne Brault and Micheal B. Nass. Bloomingdale and Indianapolis: Indiana University Press.

Derrida, J. (1994a) *Spectres of Marx: The State of the Debt, the Work of Mourning and the New International*, trans. Peggy Kamuf. London: Routledge.

Derrida, J. (1994b) 'Of the humanities and the philosophical discipline. The right of philosophy from the cosmopolitical point of view (the example of an international institution)', *Surfaces*, 4 (1).

Derrida, J. (1995) *The Gift of Death*, trans. David Wills. Chicago: University of Chicago Press.

Derrida, J. (1997) *Politics of Friendship*, trans. George Collins. London: Verso.

Derrida, J. (2001) *On Cosmopolitanism and Forgiveness*, trans. Mark Dooley and Michael Hughes. London: Routledge.

Derrida, J. and Tilli, M. (eds) (1987) *For Nelson Mandela*. New York: Seaver.

Docherty, T. (1993) *Postmodernism: A Reader*. London: Harvester Press.

Durkheim, E. (1964) *The Division of Labour in Society*, trans. George Simpson. New York: Free Press.

Foster, H. (ed.) (1985) *Postmodern Culture*. London: Pluto Press.

Foucault, M. (1979) *Discipline and Punish: The Birth of the Prison*, trans. Alan Sheridan. New York: Vintage Books.

Foucault, M. (1980) *The History of Sexuality Volume One: An Introduction*, trans. Robert Hurley. New York: Vintage Books.

Foucault, M. (1986) *Power/Knowledge*, ed. Colin Gordon. Brighton: Harvester Press.

Foucalt, M. (1991) *The Foucault Reader*, ed. Paul Rabinow. Harmondsworth: Penguin.

Fukuyama, F. (1989) 'The End of History?', *The National Interest*, 16.

Fukuyama, F. (1992) *The End of History and the Last Man*. New York: Free Press.

Gane, M. (2000) *Jean Baudrillard: In Radical Uncertainty*. London: Pluto Press.

Giddens, A. (1992) *The Transformation of Intimacy: Sexuality, Love and Eroticism in Modern Societies*. Cambridge: Polity Press.

Giddens, A. (1997a) *The Consequences of Modernity*. Cambridge: Polity Press.

Giddens, A. (1997b) *Modernity and Self-Identity: Self and Society in the Late Modern Age*. Cambridge: Polity Press.

Habermas, J. (1994) *The Philosophical Discourse of Modernity*, trans. Frederick Lawrence. Cambridge: Polity Press.

Habermas, J. (1995a) *Justification and Application: Remarks on Discourse Ethics*, trans. Cairan Cronin. Cambridge: Polity Press.

Habermas, J. (1995b) *Postmetaphysical Thinking*, trans. William Mark Hohengarten. Cambridge, Polity Press.

Harraway, D. (1985): 'A manifesto for cyborgs: science, technology and socialist feminism in the 1980s', *Socialist Review*, No. 80 (Durham, NC: Duke University Press).

Harvey, D. (1999) *The Condition of Postmodernity: An Enquiry into the Conditions of Cultural Change*. Oxford: Blackwell.

Hegel, G. W. F. (1967a) *Phenomenology of Mind*, trans. J. B. Baillie. New York: Harper & Row.

Hegel, G. W. F. (1967b) *The Philosophy of Right*, trans. T. M. Knox. Oxford: Oxford University Press.

Hegel, G. W. F. (1979) *System of Ethical Life* and *First Philosophy of Spirit*. Albany, NY: State University of New York Press.

Hegel, G. W. F. (1980) *Lectures on the Philosophy of World History, Introduction: Reason in History*, trans. H. B. Nisbet. Cambridge: Cambridge University Press.

Heidegger, M. (1983) *Being and Time*, trans. John Macquarry and Edward Robinson. London: Blackwell.

Heidegger, M. (1987) *An Introduction to Metaphysics*, trans. Ralph Manheim. New Haven, CT and London: Yale University Press.

Heidegger, M. (1996) *Martin Heidegger: Basic Writings*, ed. David Krell. London: Routledge.

Jameson, F. (1995) *Postmodernism: or The Cultural Logic of Late Capitalism*. London: Verso.

Jameson, F. (1998) *The Cultural Turn: Selected Writings on the Postmodern, 1993–1998*. London: Verso.

Jameson, F. (2000) *Late-Marxism*. London: Verso.

Jay, M. (1984) *Marxism and Totality: The Adventures of a Concept from Lukacs to Habermas*. Berkley, CA: University of California Press.

Kant, I. (1982a) *The Critique of Pure Reason*, trans. Norman Kemp Smith. London: Macmillan.

Kant, I. (1982b) *The Critique of Judgement*, trans. James Creed Meredith. Oxford: Oxford University Press.

Kant, I. (1985) *Foundations of the Metaphysics of Morals*, trans. Lewis White Beck. London: Macmillan.

Kant, I. (1991) *Political Writings*, ed. H. Reiss, trans. H. B. Nisbet. Cambridge: Cambridge University Press.

Kant, I. (1993) *The Critique of Practical Reason*, trans. Lewis White Beck. New York: Macmillan.

Kojève, A. (1969) *Introduction to the Reading of Hegel: Lectures on the Phenomenology of Spirit*, ed. Alan Bloom, trans. James H. Nichols Jr. Ithaca, NY and London: Cornell University Press.

Kristeva, J. (1992) *The Kristeva Reader*, ed. T. Moi. Oxford: Blackwell.

Lash, S. (1993) 'Reflexive modernization: the aesthetic dimension', *Theory, Culture and Society*, 10: 1–23.

Levinas, I. (1981) *Otherwise Than Being or Beyond Essence*, trans. Alphonso Lingis. The Hague: Martinus Nijhoff.

Levinas, I. (1993a) *Outside the Subject*, trans. Michael B. Smith. London: Athlone Press.

Levinas, I. (1993b) *The Levinas Reader*, ed. Sean Hand. Oxford: Blackwell.

Levinas, I. (1994) *Totality and Infinity: An Essay on Exteriority*, trans. Alphonso Lingis. Pittsburgh, PA: Duquesne University Press.

Lupton, D. (1999) *Risk*. London: Routledge.

Lyotard, J.-F. (1988) *The Differend: Phrases in Dispute*, trans. Georges Van Den Abeele. Manchester, Manchester University Press.

Lyotard, J.-F. (1990) *Heidegger and 'the jews'*, trans. Andreas Michael and Mark S. Roberts. Minneapolis, MN: University of Minnesota Press.

Lyotard, J.-F. (1991a) *The Lyotard Reader*, ed. A. Benjamin. Oxford: Blackwell.

Lyotard, J.-F. (1991b) *The Postmodern Condition: A Report on Knowledge*, trans. Geoffrey Bennington and Brian Massumi. Manchester: Manchester University Press.

Lyotard, J.-F. (1993) *Libidinal Economy*, trans. Ian Hamilton-Grant. London: Athlone Press.

Lyotard, J.-F. (1994) *Lessons on the Analytic of the Sublime*, trans. Elizabeth Rottenberg. Stanford, CA: Stanford University Press.

Lyotard, J.-F. (1995) *Toward the Postmodern*, eds Robert Harvey and Mark S. Roberts. Atlantic Highlands, NJ: Humanities Press.

Lyotard, J.-F. and Thébaud J.-L. (1989) *Just Gaming*, trans. Wlad Godzich and Samuel Weber. Minneapolis, MN: University of Minnesota Press.

McLuhan, M. (1964) *Understanding Media*. London: Routledge.

Marcus, M. and Nead, L. (eds) (1998) *The Actuality of Walter Benjamin*. London: Lawrence & Wishart.

Marx, K. (1977a) *Capital, Volume One*, trans. Samuel Moore and Edward Aveling. London: Lawrence & Wishart.

Marx, K. (1977b) *The Economic and Philosophic Manuscripts of 1844*. Moscow: Progress Publishers.

Marx, K. (1977c) *The German Ideology*, ed. C. J. Arthur. London: Lawrence & Wishart.

Marx, K. (1977d) *Karl Marx: Selected Writings*, ed. D. McLellen. Oxford: Oxford University Press.

Marx, K. (1978) *Capital Volume Two*, trans. David Fernbach. Penguin: Harmondsworth.

Nietzsche, F. (1984) *Human, All Too Human*, trans. Marion Faber and Stephen Lehmann. Harmondsworth: Penguin.

Nietzsche, F. (1990) *The Birth of Tragedy* and *The Genealogy of Morals*, trans. Francis Golfing. New York: Doubleday.

Parsons, T. (1968) *The Structure of Social Action*. London: Collier-Macmillan.

Peperzak, A. T. (1995) *Ethics as First Philosophy: The Significance of Emmanuel Levinas for Philosophy, Literature and Religion*. London: Routledge.

Rose, G. (1978) *The Melancholy Science: An Introduction to the Thought of Theodor W. Adorno*. London: Macmillan.

Rose, G. (1981) *Hegel Contra-Sociology*. London: Athlone Press.

Rose, G. (1993) *Judaism and Modernity: Philosophical Essays*. Oxford: Blackwell.

Rundell, J. (1987) *The Origins of Modernity: The Origins of Modern Social Theory from Kant to Hegel to Marx*. Cambridge: Polity Press.

Safranski, R. (1999) *Martin Heidegger: Between Good and Evil*, trans. Ewald Osers. Cambridge, MA: Harvard University Press.

Said, E. W. (1978) 'The problem of textuality: two exemplary positions', *Critical Inquiry*, 4 (4), 673–714.

Said, E. W. (1994) *Culture and Imperialism*. London: Vintage Books.

Said, E. W. (1995) *Orientalism: Western Conceptions of the Orient*. Harmondsworth: Penguin.

Shakespeare, W. (1996) *Hamlet*. Harmondsworth: Penguin.

Sim, S. (1999) *Derrida and the End of History*. Cambridge: Icon Books.

Simmel, G. (1991) 'Money in modern culture', *Theory, Culture and Society*, 8: 17–31.

Simons, J. (1995) *Foucault and the Political*. London: Routledge.

Sprinker, M. (1991) *Edward Said: A Critical Reader*. Oxford: Blackwell.

Sprinker, M. (1999) *Ghostly Demarcations: A Symposium on Jacque Derrida's Specter's of Marx*. London: Verso.

Tester, K. (1994) *Media, Culture and Morality*. London: Routledge.

Tester, K. (1997) *Moral Culture*. London: Sage.

Woolin, R. (ed.) (1998) *The Heidegger Controversy: A Critical Reader*. Cambridge, MA: MIT Press.

Index

For enquiries or renewal at
Quarles LRC
Tel: 01708 455011 – Extension 4009